The Lighter Side of Darkness

Patsy L. Adams

Trilogy Christian Publishers
A Wholly Owned Subsidiary of Trinity Broadcasting Network
2442 Michelle Drive
Tustin, CA 92780

For information, address Trilogy Christian Publishing
Rights Department, 2442 Michelle Drive, Tustin, Ca 92780.
Trilogy Christian Publishing/ TBN and colophon are trademarks of Trinity Broadcasting Network.

For information about special discounts for bulk purchases, please contact Trilogy Christian Publishing.

Manufactured in the United States of America

10 9 8 7 6 5 4 3 2 1

Library of Congress Cataloging-in-Publication Data is available.

ISBN 978-1-64088-363-5 (Print Book)
ISBN 978-1-64088-364-2 (ebook)

DEDICATION

The Lighter Side of Darkness is first dedicated to my Lord and Savior, Jesus Christ, who planted the vision of this opus in my heart.

To my son, Jymm, my agent, who, after having read *The Lighter Side of Darkness*, encouraged me to move forward with my dream. Jymm has played an integral part in bringing this book to publication.

To my grandchildren, Jordan, Sierra, Izaiah (Z), Korey, Dazmin, Leila, and Jackson, whose wonderful personalities breathed life into the characters.

Last, but not least, to my amazing husband, James, who is now in glory, but who stood by me while I locked myself in my office for hours at a time to complete this work.

I love you all.

INTRODUCTION

Torn between their existing paradise, where light shines day and night, where flowers bloom with vivid hues that never fade, and where the power of love abounds, and conflicted by the allure of an alleged greater life in an unknown land, Janu and Ariana embark on a journey that brings them face to face with an evil they never knew existed, thereby placing the family they cherish in danger of being completely destroyed.

Against all odds, and the overwhelming forces working against them, Janu and Ariana struggle to return to the paradise they regrettably abandoned.

Their journey is one of everyday human existence filled with temptation, tragedy, triumph and the strength of family and faith. *The Lighter Side of Darkness* is a story of redemption and the power of love, confirming that no matter what, we can all go home again.

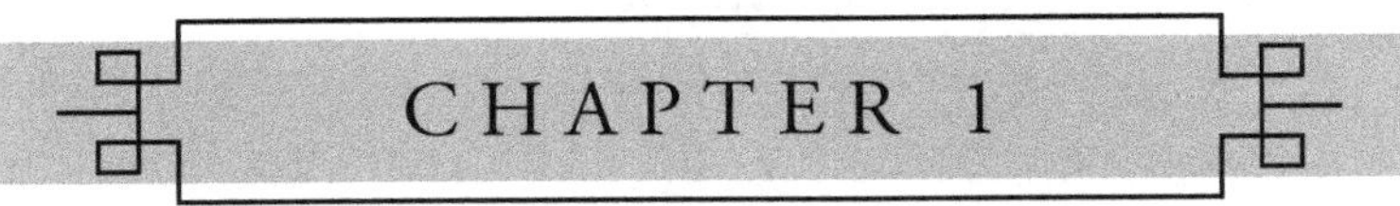

The Decision

He needed sleep badly, but it escaped him. Trembling, Janu was grateful the cold sweats had interrupted the horrific nightmare he was having—something he'd never experienced before. His sleep had always been restful and his dreams pleasant, but not tonight.

He listened to his wife's steady breathing and wondered how she could sleep so soundly considering what they were about to do.

His senses were at their peak as the *ticktock* of the bedside clock seemed louder than usual. Even the old owl's hooting seemed magnified as he made his presence known in the nearby tree.

Ariana's flower arrangement smelled twice as pungent as when she first picked the bouquet six weeks ago, and he wondered if this amazing phenomenon existed on the other side of the river.

He tried to still his mind and not focus on tomorrow, but his thoughts were out of control. Anxiety finally won the battle and forced him out of bed.

He gently moved Ariana's arm and eased from under the covers. Pacing up and down the floor for what seemed like hours, he questioned his decision. When he glanced at the clock, he saw that only ten minutes had passed.

He was drowning in a sea of guilt, knowing Ariana was not alone in her quest to discover what was beyond their homeland. He reasoned that since many of their friends had walked away from everything that they knew…life *must* be better on the other side.

Janu moved quietly to the window and pulled back the heavy drapes. Uriel, the King of Fa'i, was away on a journey, but his ever-present radiance still shone throughout the land.

Janu marveled at his manicured landscape and the flowers that never faded. They simply transformed themselves once a month—a phenomenon that still fascinated him.

The beautiful scarlet roses with their perfect blooms were surrounded by yellow mums and blue and purple irises, and the magnificent stone in his curved driveway glistened from the evening dew. The white picket fence he had labored to build with his own hands still made his chest rise with pride.

But the mystical waters flowing down from King Uriel's home was what Janu loved most. The stream gathered in the ponds of every home in Fa'i, on its way to the River of Life.

Although Janu could always depend on the soothing sounds of this mystifying stream to unnerve him, tonight was the exception. The crystal waters with its power to heal, restore, and relax seemed to whisper his name as it gently cascaded over the rocks and pebbles, making an already-anxious Janu even more uneasy.

Suddenly, the peace of all that was familiar was waging war with an uncontrolled desire to know the unfamiliar, and Janu again wondered... *Should he, or shouldn't he?*

It all began two weeks ago when Janu was waiting on his front porch for Ariana to return from her rejuvenation swim in the River of Life.

He spotted her coming down the road and chuckled, amazed that after all these years she still made his heart race. *She's still the most beautiful woman I've ever seen*, he thought.

Her shoulder-length curls bounced with every stride, and her light brown eyes twinkled as she drew near. She reached the top step, looked up at Janu, and smiled. She stood on tiptoes and surprisingly kissed her six-foot-tall husband lightly on the lips.

"We have a good life," she whispered. "But have you ever longed for more?"

"What *specifically* are you asking?" Janu replied, somewhat disturbed by the inquiry.

"What has Uriel *really* told us about life across the river?" she asked. "All he'll ever say is it's for our own good that we never cross over. Well, I think we have a right to live as *we* see fit, and I want to know what's on the other side."

They had never discussed life on the other side, and this conversation was making Janu very uneasy. "Where did all this nonsense come from?" he asked calmly. "We have a wonderful life in Fa'i. Uriel's been like a father, supplying our needs and satisfying our desires. What more could we ask for?"

"I love you, *and* Uriel, *and* my life here," Ariana replied. "But what if there's more? I often wonder why our friends left home and never returned. If life is so bad on the other side, they would've come home by now."

"I'm certain Uriel understands our temptation to know what's across the river," Janu replied. "But he *must* have a good reason for commanding us to stay on this side."

"We have *everything*," he continued. "We've inherited land we didn't harvest, houses we didn't build, and we even swim in a river that renews our youth. No place on *earth* could be more beautiful than Fa'i. And you want to throw it all away because of one command you can't live with anymore?"

"What do *you* know about any other place?" Ariana challenged. "You've never *been* any other place."

Janu replied almost in a whisper, "I'll admit there are times when I swim too close to the forbidden boundary trying to discover what's on the other side. But I've never imagined crossing over."

Several days had passed, but Janu couldn't rid his mind of their conversation. He was sitting quietly in his study one evening, when Ariana hugged him from behind and purred in his ear.

"I *have* to know what's across the river," she stated firmly. "Look, Uriel's away and who knows when he'll return. We can go and be back before we're even missed," she continued, trying hard to mask her frustration from his lack of support.

"There must be a reason beyond our understanding why we shouldn't cross the boundary," Janu replied.

"Honey, I've *always* respected your wishes," Ariana stated sharply. But I *am* going to find out why our friends have never returned home. I was hoping you'd come with me, but I *can* go alone."

After several days of Ariana's much sulking, and knowing deep down he *wanted* to be persuaded, Janu finally agreed.

"All right," he said, pretending frustration. "If Uriel's not back within forty-eight hours, we'll cross the river. But we can't tell anyone, not even our families."

"We won't be gone long," she said cheerfully, and kissed him on the cheek.

Two days had passed, and Uriel had not yet returned. Unbeknownst to anyone, Janu and Ariana were leaving in the morning for the other side of the river.

Tonight, however, Janu was physically and emotionally drained. He stared into his fish tank and dropped in a little extra food to soothe his conscience. As the fish scurried to the top with opened mouths, he wondered who would feed them in his absence.

"We won't be gone long," he whispered. "This should hold you until we return."

He could only hope his prediction was true as he crawled back into bed, stunned by the dread that suddenly engulfed him.

Before dawn the next morning, the couple was standing at the river's edge. Janu was wishing someone, anyone, would come and put a stop to their madness.

They waded toward the forbidden boundary, gazing across the river like children in pursuit of hidden treasure, unaware that Uriel had returned and was watching from afar.

The King stood helpless, watching his friends journeying toward an awful fate. But they had a free will, and he could no more stop them from making the biggest mistake of their lives than he could stop the horror he felt at their choice. His heart was broken. He wept.

As dawn appeared over the horizon, the passion Janu had initially felt disappeared. Doubt and fear, uncommon emotions to him, seemed to be winning the battle over his original hope and enthusiasm.

He knew they were doing wrong, but his overwhelming desire to know the forbidden propelled him forward. Still, he continued looking back, hoping someone would suddenly appear and call them back to shore.

Finally, the burden of guilt was too heavy, and he told Ariana that he felt naked and ashamed, something he'd never felt before.

She felt the same way, but she was not about to admit it. Purposely avoiding his eyes, she replied, "We'll be fine. It's a new experience with unfamiliar feelings, but they'll pass."

She forced a smile and continued, "We'll see what the mystery is about, visit with our friends Jacque and Elisabeth, and then come home. I miss them and I know you do, too."

As they swam away from all they'd ever known, their beautiful home, with its lush greenery and blue-green waterfalls cascading over majestic mountains, was now in the distance. Fa'i, the City of Eternal Light, was fast becoming a speck on the horizon.

As the two ventured closer to their destination, they came to a bend in the river and swam to the edge of the mountain to rest. They could see the beautiful riverbed in the warm crystal waters, but the magnificent fish that customarily rushed to meet them were nowhere to be found.

"We better keep going," Janu said with concern evident in his voice.

They reached the forbidden boundary, hesitated, then crossed over. Immediately, Janu knew they were no longer in the River of Life.

The waters were now dark and murky. And they could see the line of demarcation, as if it had been drawn by a huge black marker.

The rapid change in temperature caught them by surprise, and the once-warm waters were now freezing. Their bodies shook like leaves in a strong wind, and, as if skinned alive, their blood waxed cold in their veins.

The previously calm river began to rage, and the uncertain waters roared like a lioness guarding her cubs. The wind howled like a wounded animal, and the sound was deafening. They knew they were in trouble.

Janu signaled to Ariana to turn back, but they were impeded by an unseen fortress. They swam frantically back and forth making futile attempts to find an opening, until they realized they were banished, locked out…

They stared at their beloved Fa'i through the invisible stronghold, wondering how they would ever get home again. For the first time in their lives, they understood fear.

The air was pungent with an overpowering acidic stench, and they labored for every breath. The raging waters became an eddy, and terror gripped their hearts like a vise as they struggled to stay above the angry current.

As they reached for each other, a thick dark cloud wrapped itself around them like a shroud, and they disappeared into the blackness.

Their entire lives had existed in Uriel's presence, whose radiance lit the nation of Fa'i day and night. So, it was understandable that they were terrified of this unknown phenomenon called darkness. Suddenly, they were being propelled through the waters by an unseen force.

The once-icy waters began to boil and foam, and the unforgiveable torrent rose to an incredible height. Suddenly, the walls collapsed into the shape of two hands and scooped the couple up like weightless nothings, dropping them repeatedly on the riverbed. Being tossed around like rag dolls, they soon became sick to their stomachs. They tried not to swallow the bitter liquid, but the undercurrent was brutal and unforgiving.

"We'll never survive this," Janu lamented, as tears streamed down Ariana's muddy cheeks.

Just when they thought things couldn't get any worse, something hideous took a chunk out of Ariana's leg and she let out a bloodcurdling scream. Immediately, the surrounding waters became a dark crimson, and she battled to stay conscious.

At that moment, something slimy crept up Janu's legs. It encircled him from the waist down, entangled him like a fly in a spider's web, and dragged him to the bottom.

He had no idea such evil existed, as he peered into the eyes of horrific underwater creatures with both human and demonic features.

He freed himself from the colossal green thing, and he had wrestled his way to the top again when a snaky creature baring shark-like teeth swam swiftly toward him.

Ariana, hurt and bleeding, punched the creature with her fists and sent him scurrying before she disappeared underwater. Janu quickly dove down and pulled her to the top again. Their arms were pathetically outstretched toward one another as they bounced around like rubber balls in the angry current, coughing and gasping for air.

Ariana knew this was her doing and cried, "Save yourself."

Janu shook his head.

Suddenly, the waters merged in the middle separating them. Monstrous talons rose from beneath and grabbed Ariana around her waist, tossing her downstream. Janu watched helplessly as his wife disappeared in the angry undertow.

Suddenly, he was struck hard in his back by a large tree stump. He flung himself wildly at the passing log and held on for dear life.

As he traveled downstream in pursuit of his wife, he thought of the pain their decision would inflict upon Uriel and their families, and he sobbed like a baby. He wanted to die...then he thought of Ariana.

Meanwhile, Ariana was exhausted, disoriented, and finding it more difficult to stay afloat. As the raging current carried her weakened body farther downstream, she thought of her family and friends and the beautiful home she had left behind. Suddenly, a wave of nausea reminded her of her unborn child, and she wept. Trying to ease her conscience for not telling Janu about the baby, she reasoned that he couldn't grieve over something he didn't know existed. She believed the child was a girl and destined for great things and had already named her Sierra, meaning *"high places"*.Now she wondered if the child would even live.

Ariana's limbs were numb from trying to stay afloat, but it was no longer just about her. She willed her aching body to move, and just when she felt she couldn't go on, the waters ceased raging. The movement of the tide, however, made her vomit, but the nausea was better than being tossed around out of control. Having little fight left, she turned on her back and allowed the current to carry her, hoping the turbulence in her gut would cease.

Out of nowhere, a flat piece of driftwood brushed against her weary, aching body. It was large enough to give her the support she needed while providing her worn-out limbs with a much-needed rest. She lay halfway on the mini raft and hung on.

Meanwhile, Janu's entire body was in pain. His eyes burned, and his mouth was filled with gravel from the bitter waters. He was once again plunged into blackness so inky he couldn't see his hand in front of his face. And he shook uncontrollably from the inconceivable evil encircling him.

He was weak and could barely hold on to the bulky tree stump, but he was alive *and* frightened for Ariana. Although she was a strong swimmer, he wasn't sure she could survive in these unpredictable waters. He had to find her.

He gingerly lifted his head and spotted the riverbank, but he had no energy left to push against the current. Desperately clinging to his life raft, he allowed the runaway tree to take him where it destined him to go.

Just as he realized that his nightmare the previous night had been an omen, he slipped from reality and was suddenly back in the River of Life. The pristine waters resembled polished glass, and the light shimmering from the liquid resembled millions of tiny diamonds.

As he quenched his thirst, the sweetness of the water floated over his tongue like a soft cloud and dripped down his dry, parched throat. Yet this was not real. He was hallucinating. Several minutes had passed before he was aware of his current state, and a tremendous sadness engulfed him. He would never again experience the wonders of his beloved Fa'i.

It was only this morning he and Ariana had left home. But it felt like weeks, maybe months, since he'd been adrift. No one had to tell him he and Ariana had made the worst decision of their lives and this was the consequence of their choice.

Suddenly, he understood why his friends had never returned to Fa'i; they *couldn't.* A fierce foreboding consumed him, and he realized his life would never be the same again.

Meanwhile, downstream, Ariana was experiencing darkness and a presence so evil she was horrified, an emotion she was becoming familiar with *beyond the boundaries*. Having known only peace and tranquility, she longed for home.

She finally reached the shore. As she lay in the wet dirt, she wept uncontrollably, knowing *she* had orchestrated this lunacy.

CHAPTER 2

The Whisperer

It had all begun two weeks ago while Ariana was relaxing by the River of Life. A cluster of swaying reeds grabbed her attention, which was unusual, as there was no breeze to speak of.

"Ariana," a mysterious voice whispered.

She thought it might be Janu playing games again and crawled toward the rustling. She slowly parted the tall grasses, but she saw no one.

"Who's there?" she asked, but no one responded.

On subsequent occasions when she sat at the river, she would hear the *Voice* whisper her name, but she never once mentioned the bizarre happenings to Janu.

One day, the *Voice* asked her if she missed her friends Jacque and Elisabeth, and she was taken aback.

"I'll answer you," she said, "if you tell me who you are."

"I'm Dovev, the Whisperer."

"Yes, I miss my friends very much," she replied.

"They miss you too," Dovev hissed. "They would love to see you…and Janu, of course."

"How do you know our names?" Ariana asked.

"Your friends told me all about you."

"When are they coming home?" she asked.

"They're not," he replied, "but they'd like you to come and visit them."

"I couldn't do *that*," Ariana replied. "Uriel would be very unhappy."

"Allow me to reveal to you what your King doesn't want you to know," Dovev whispered.

"How…how can you do that?" she stammered. "Are you a magician?"

"I have special powers," Dovev replied.

"Well, I guess it can't hurt to look," Ariana replied, curious about life on the other side. "But make it quick, I'm due home any moment."

As if a curtain had been drawn, Ariana was looking across the River of Life at a beautiful city resembling Fa'i. The colors were vivid and bright, and she gasped with pleasure at people dressed in stunning fashions, laughing and having a good time. Children were playing everywhere, and carousels were spinning some around as they screamed with delight. Tall, magnificent buildings loomed large in the background.

Suddenly, her best friends, Jacque and Elisabeth, appeared onshore waving frantically. Ariana waved back. She missed them so much her heart ached. Looking closer, she noticed Elisabeth was pregnant. "Congratulations," she shouted.

"Come on over," Jacque replied.

At that moment, a seed of deception was planted in Ariana's soul, and an itch she couldn't scratch had to be satisfied.

Now, two weeks later, and with her face pressed in the wet dirt, she wondered why her friends would lure them to this evil place. Pregnant and alone, and not knowing if Janu was dead or alive, she was terrified.

She stood up but fell quickly to the ground. She examined the deep gash in her leg and could see clear to the bone. The skin surrounding the wound had turned three shades of purple, and yellow pus was seeping from the holes where the creature's fangs had penetrated her skin. The lesion was disgusting and beginning to smell.

Grimacing, she took some water from the river and washed the wound. Hoping to delay any infection from rapidly spreading through her body, she ripped one end of her tattered shirt and tied it tightly around her leg.

She was hungry and had to find food, but she wasn't sure how to do that. Everything she had ever needed or wanted Uriel had provided. She had never had to survive; she just lived.

Meanwhile, Janu's head felt like it would burst from the movement of the tide. When the waves subsided, he slowly lifted his head and spotted the shoreline again.

He reached the water's edge and pulled himself and the miniature tree ashore before falling asleep on the cool earth.

He awoke suddenly. His belly was on fire as he heaved up the river's bitter waters, too weak to move out of his own vomit.

Meanwhile, Ariana painfully raised herself from the damp ground and peered as far as she could into the distance.

There were no happy children, no carousels or magnificent architecture. Only a thick gray mist swallowed up the entire atmosphere, further confirming that she had been cruelly deceived.

As the night she didn't understand quickly approached, the temperature suddenly dropped. She had to find a place to rest and keep warm until morning; things she had never had to previously worry about. She had taken her home, Fa'i, with its perfect temperature and perpetual light, for granted, and an overwhelming sadness enveloped her. She suddenly recalled walking with Uriel and Janu in the cool of the day, as Uriel had tried to define darkness.

"But you'll never have to experience it, or be afraid, or even have to worry about hunger or a place to lay your heads, *if* you remain in Fa'i," he had warned. But as they had never considered leaving home, they didn't take his words seriously.

"Life is choice-driven," he had told them in his soothing voice that always made them feel safe. "If you choose unwisely, you'll reap the negative consequences established and attached to your unwise choices. So, choose prudently. And if there ever comes a time when you're not sure what choice to make, ask me," he had gently coached. He hugged them long and hard and slowly walked away.

"He *knew* we were going to cross the river before *we* did," Ariana sobbed.

Back at the river's edge, every bone, muscle, and tissue in Janu's body was on fire. He cried out in agony as he forced himself up off the ground, blood seeping out of his cuts and bruises. He had to find shelter before the darkness was complete and the cold night air set in.

He discovered a dry place farther inland and set up camp for the night. At first sight of light, he would search for Ariana.

She, meanwhile, was overwhelmed by the darkness. With no one there to comfort her except her unborn child, she felt abandoned for the first time in her life. Having never been hungry before, her growling stomach surprised her. She envisioned the sweet purple grapes in Fa'i grapes so large it took several people to pull them down from their vines, and she licked her dry, parched lips. Trying not to let these new feelings of loneliness, hunger, and fear get the best of her, she gathered leaves from the ground, tore bark from the huge trees, and fashioned a crude bed and cover to keep her and Sierra warm.

"Don't worry," she told her unborn child, "I'll take care of you."

She discovered several eucalyptus leaves, and with another scrap from her tattered shirt, secured them to her wounded leg. She tried meditating on the home she had left behind and her warm, comfortable bed, but her hunger and thirst overwhelmed her. Mercifully, she fell asleep.

Ariana was experiencing her first nightmare, or was she awake? She couldn't tell. She unconsciously fended off creatures more horrifying than the ones in the river, as she felt her face and body being gnawed.

Waking in a cold sweat, Ariana saw nothing; it was still dark. She fought hard not to return to the horror she had just left. Fortunately, when she awoke again, it was morning. She examined her body and discovered bite marks everywhere. It wasn't a nightmare, after all. Ariana knew she couldn't endure another night alone and screamed for Janu.

Meanwhile, he slowly opened his eyes to the hazy morning and quickly jumped to his feet. The sudden movement made his head spin, and he gingerly lowered himself back to the ground. The growl of his stomach was something he'd never heard before, and he realized for the first time in his life he was hungry. But, first, he had to find Ariana.

Janu ran his hands over his aching body and discovered bites and scratches that weren't previously there. Without warning, lamentable sounds of torment echoed throughout the canyon, and the hairs on his neck stood at attention.

He forced himself to his feet again and headed farther inland. Janu noticed several sets of footprints in the dirt and hoped one set belonged to Ariana.

He started out with a fast walk that became a trot. Making his way through the strange maze, his thick, curly mane became entangled in a low-hanging branch thick with purple berries. He carefully untangled his tresses from the limb and freed the berries from their vines. He ate until he was full, thanked the berry tree, and continued his pursuit. But satisfying his appetite for food made his need for water more pronounced. If he didn't find a stream soon, he'd die a slow, agonizing death, full stomach and all.

Janu labored to hear the sound of running water as the temperature rose and the heat became unbearable. He slowly ran his tongue over his cracked, parched, and bleeding lips, imagining how empty life would be without Ariana. Suddenly, he was knocked to the ground. Blood seeped into his eyes and a terrifying screech pierced the quiet morning, but he saw nothing and no one.

Growing weaker by the minute, Janu continued on the road until it forked; he chose the path veering left. He struggled up the steep slope, grateful for the cooler air at the top.

Janu stumbled into a barren meadow, appearing as if it had been set afire. He eyed the lifeless vegetation and called out to Ariana. The response was bloodcurdling shrieks from a host of black creatures perched high in the leafless trees.

Then he heard the sound of running water in the distance. Scarcely able to move his aching body, he slowly put one foot in front of the other. He came to the edge of a cliff; at the bottom of the narrow ravine was a brook. It was a beautiful sight. Creatures were bathing and quenching their thirst in it, but Janu didn't care. The only thing that could keep him from that stream was death itself.

He tried running his tongue over his swollen and bleeding lips again. But his saliva had dried up and his thick tongue stuck to the roof of his mouth.

Creeping vines hung lazily down the side of the moss-covered cliff. Once Janu determined the vines could hold his weight, he began his slow descent, which was every bit as difficult as he presumed. Halfway down, he grabbed a large shrub jutting oddly out from the cliff. The branches were covered with small crimson-colored berries that had a peculiar taste.

Janu ate quite a few. He was unaware that the glycoprotein in the berries would cause the fruit to taste sweet on his tongue but turn sour in his stomach, and when eaten in large quantities, it could be poisonous.

He was continuing his descent, when unexpectedly his stomach began to gripe. His back arched, then, as if someone was yanking out his guts, he lunged forward. His vision became impaired, and he couldn't tell how close he was to the bottom. He was fighting to stay conscious when something hit him hard in his back. A chorus of creatures screamed wildly as he felt their foul breath on his face. He vomited before plummeting down the side of the cliff at a sickening speed.

Meanwhile, the heat of the morning awoke Ariana. She slowly removed the eucalyptus leaves from her leg and noticed the wound had slightly improved. Scowling, she pulled herself up from the ground and limped down a narrow pathway. Ariana heard running water as she approached a cliff. Clutching the moss-covered vines, she slipped over the side, cautiously avoiding the jagged rocks.

Ariana rested on a ledge, then reached for the next clump of vines, but there were none. She would have to jump several feet to the valley floor. Ariana stretched out her arms to break her fall, then toppled hard to the ground. She lay there for what seemed like hours trying to recover, hoping she hadn't harmed the baby. She stood and was immediately knocked down again by an invisible ogre. The creature brushed her cheek with its wings, and his foul smell made her gag.

Grabbing her shirttail, the beast dragged her along the valley floor. She could feel her flesh tear as she toppled over rocks and stones. When the creature finally released her, she crawled toward the sound of water like an animal stalking its prey. Her voice echoed throughout the gorge as she called Janu's name.

Ariana came upon a stream in a large clearing. It was surrounded by eerie-looking trees, dead flowers, and strange-looking creatures whose sickening smells made her retch. She spotted Janu's tattered shirt off in the distance and slowly limped toward him. She screamed and yelled, scaring away the buzzards, crows, and other horrible creatures that were encircling him for their morning repast. Disregarding the pain in her leg, she fell down beside him. He was lying face down, and he was so still, she wondered if the creatures had already satisfied their appetites.

Ariana nudged Janu, then gently eased him onto his back. She gasped, as her husband was hardly recognizable. Janu's entire body was bloated, and his tangled hair was matted with all kinds of debris. His skin resembled animal hide, and his color was a sickening purple. The putrefying smell reeking from Janu's cuts and bruises, and his odor, made Ariana dry-heave. Janu barely had a pulse, and his chest moved up and down ever so slightly. Ariana gently lifted his head and stroked his face, speaking Janu's name softly until he opened his eyes.

He tried to communicate how happy he was to see her, but he was too weak. Instead, he coughed and gagged on his swollen tongue. Ariana thought if she could get him to the water, bathe his wounds, and get him to drink, he might survive. She searched wildly for a conveyor to help her get him to the stream but found none.

"You have to help me," she said, as she pulled him from behind. He tried to assist her by digging his heels into the dirt, but it was no use. She was tired, hungry, thirsty, and terribly afraid. Her arms ached and her legs felt like heavy boulders, but she got him to the water. Her wounded leg was a constant reminder of her rebellion, and she cried out in anguish, not so much from the pain, but from the realization that this was all her doing.

With her last ounce of strength, she rolled Janu over and over until she rolled him into the stream, then she quickly fell in beside him. She scooped the cool liquid into his mouth as he coughed and gagged, then she bathed his wounds. They both drank until their thirst was quenched. She somehow maneuvered Janu out of the water, where he vomited up the poison berries. The bluish tint of his skin began to fade, and his breathing was no longer labored.

The couple lay on the cool earth holding hands, neither able to move or speak. The towering mist was beginning to lift, and Ariana could see clearly.

Looming large before them were blood red mountains. A huge bust of a man donning a crown was carved atop the peak. Its red, beady eyes seemed to follow Ariana's every move, and she wondered what kind of a place this could be.

After a much-needed rest, she trudged along the foot of the mountain, racing to beat the darkness that was quickly chasing the light away. She gathered dry twigs, branches, leaves, and bark from the large trees to keep them warm. They snuggled closely together under the scratchy makeshift blanket, grateful to have found each other.

"First thing tomorrow," Janu whispered in a raspy voice, "we'll find our way back home and beg Uriel's forgiveness."

That sounded great, but Ariana knew neither of them could endure that horrifying river again. They fell asleep as the coolness of the night settled in.

Morning came, and a beam of grayish light crashed through a crevice in the mountain and awakened Janu. He wasn't sure he had even slept because he was still exhausted. His mouth was dry as the desert, and the pain in his empty stomach was agonizing. He thought if he could make it back to the stream for more water, he might have enough strength to look for food. Instead, he fell asleep again.

A heavy weight on his chest woke him, and he tried to sit up. But a large man wearing a tan uniform held him down with his boot.

The man was accompanied by four other men carrying weapons the likes of which Janu had never seen before. The man in charge smiled as if he was very pleased with himself. Yet Janu knew the man was not there to help them. The subordinates laughed wickedly as Ariana instinctively wrapped her arms around her stomach.

"Welcome," the man said. "We've been expecting you."

CHAPTER 3

Sierra

It was a miserable Friday evening. Sierra stared out the window at the pouring rain, wondering if her life would still be this dull and uneventful after her seventeenth birthday, a week from tomorrow. She tried many times to dismiss her desire for something more than the norm, but her craving had become as much a part of her as her own skin. Unaware that she would soon long for her uncomplicated existence, she watched the wind amuse itself with a newspaper, wondering if she, too, was destined to travel aimlessly through life.

Suddenly, the rising and falling of the *Weekly* once again ignited in her a sense of being tossed about in deep water. It was an eerie experience she didn't remember having before, and one that had caused her to dread the river her entire life.

Her early forebodings had prompted her dad to teach her to swim before she could walk. "*Being able to stay alive in the river will one day pay off,*" he'd remind her. But the river outings had only caused her to wake up in a cold sweat, struggling to breathe, as if she were underwater.

The sudden clap of thunder brought her back to the present, and she gasped as the lightning's brilliance pierced the darkness, staging a breathtaking display across the heavens. But the lightning in its splendor was no match for the dazzling brightness that perpetually shined across the river. Sierra couldn't imagine living with light that bright day and night. *How would you know what time of day it was, or when to go to bed?* she wondered. *Well,* she thought, *that's something we'll never have to worry about here in Keres. The best we can do is a dull misty gray.*

She had asked her dad why the light across the river never shined in Keres. She was told that *Keres* means "Place of Evil Spirits" and that the light across the river wouldn't shine where there was evil. Never having seen or met an evil spirit before, she had simply smiled in disbelief.

The helpless periodical was presently traveling up and down the street without direction when the telepad chimed. Sierra pressed the visual button, glanced at the screen, and muted the sound.

"Aren't you going to answer that, Sierra?" Ariana called from the kitchen.

"It's Monica, Mom. I'll call her back later."

Monica was Jacque and Elisabeth's daughter. Her parents were Janu and Ariana's best friends in Fa'i, and they, too, had been deceived into crossing the river. Monica was like a daughter to Janu and Ariana, and a sister to Sierra. She, like Sierra, had also been born in Keres.

Sierra laughed at her best friend's animated gestures, something Monica often did while speaking. But Sierra's smile suddenly faded as she thought of Monica's mom and her mysterious disappearance, and the lack of support from her father, who was always working and leaving her alone to fend for herself. *I must tell her how proud I am of how she's coping*, Sierra thought.

"Your dad phoned," Ariana said, interrupting Sierra's thoughts. "He'll be late and would like us to hold dinner."

"I can wait," Sierra replied. "But that son of yours is always hungry. We might have to feed him Champ's doggie bones to hold him over." She laughed at her own wit. "Why is Dad late?" she asked.

"He's stopping by the gallery to make sure everything is ready for the exhibit," Ariana replied. "You know his love for detail."

To Sierra, this delay was unnerving. Her parents promised to reveal something at dinner that would change their lives forever.

She continued preparing the dinner table, remembering the night her dad brought the large, round monstrosity home. He had needed three friends to help him get it into the house.

He had announced with pride that he had it made especially for the family. Now, they could face each other while dining, making conversation easier.

Before setting the new table in place, however, Janu's oldest friend, Jacob, had reached down to remove the worn-out rug that lay beneath the old table.

"Let that alone," Janu had snapped. Then he said softly, "We'll lay the new rug on top of the old one to give the table more stability."

No one but Janu knew what lay beneath those rugs, and the importance the table would play in the near future. Ariana immediately fell in love with the mahogany piece, treating it as if it was a prized heirloom.

Sierra finished setting the table, filled a large round multifaceted crystal bowl with water, and placed it in the center of the table. She trimmed the roses picked earlier and carefully placed them in the bowl, smiling as they danced around each other. The light from the chandelier caused the bowl to sparkle like a huge diamond. She sniffed the odorless flowers, knowing they would be dust by the end of the meal. But for now, the table looked stunning.

Ariana was finishing dinner when Izaiah came barreling down the stairs.

"I'm hungry," he said. "What's to eat?"

"You're always hungry, Z," Sierra replied, using the nickname she'd given him when she was a little girl. "And must you make so much noise?"

"You're not my mother, Sierra. And I'm not a little boy anymore," he loudly proclaimed. "So, stop bossing me around and telling me what to do. I have *one* mother, and that's quite enough, thank you."

"Lower your tone, Izaiah, and get washed up," Ariana scolded. "Your dad's running late, but he'll be here any minute." Normally, Izaiah was a mild-mannered child, but he had recently morphed into someone Ariana no longer recognized.

Meanwhile, as Janu was leaving his office, his mobile chimed. He had planned to stop by Ariana's gallery, and the delay was annoying.

"Hello," he said curtly.

"*I can help you, if you'll let me*," the stranger whispered.

Convinced the caller had dialed the wrong number, Janu hung up the phone and pressed the elevator button to go down. His mobile rang again.

"Hello," he answered cautiously.

"*I can help you, Janu, but it's imperative we meet tonight.*"

Stunned that the stranger knew his name, Janu stumbled back to his office trembling. He thought he had prepared for every contingency. But the thought of being discovered by the Establishment, which was the governing body of Keres and which wouldn't take kindly to his intentions, hit him like a ton of bricks. They were known for their cruelty toward anyone who opposed their way of life. He had to be careful. The hour was fast approaching for him to escape Keres and take his family back to Fa'i. And although terrified, he felt compelled to meet this mystery man to determine what, if anything, he knew. The lives of his family depended on it.

"You know *my* name," Janu said, trying to keep his voice steady. "What's *yours*?"

"*Malakh*," the stranger replied.

Janu hesitated. "I'll meet you at the Light Art Gallery at seven o'clock," he said. "Do you know where it is?"

"*I'll find it*," Malakh replied.

What better place for the rendezvous than Ariana's Gallery? Janu thought. *I personally designed it and know every nook, cranny, and escape route...if needed.*

Janu couldn't be too careful. He wanted to ensure he'd be meeting with the man he was speaking to. He established a code between him and Malakh before ending their phone conversation.

Janu hung up and tried to stop shaking. He'd been exploring ways to escape Keres since he first arrived, but he had been challenged with one obstacle after another. He thought of alerting Ariana about the stranger, then changed his mind. No need to alarm her unnecessarily. He left the building and stood on the top step for about two minutes, watching for strange cars that might be lurking about.

Pulling his coat collar up around his ears and his hat down on his head, he started for the parking structure, listening intently for footsteps.

He picked up his pace as thunder shattered the quiet night. Lightning lit up the sky, and it started to rain again. By the time he reached the parking garage, he was soaked. He glanced over his shoulder, checked his watch, and peered into the back seat before unlocking his vehicle. Assured he didn't have any unwanted passengers, he drove out of the parking lot and headed for the gallery.

As he drove down Grove Street, rain blanketed his windshield. The wipers couldn't wipe fast enough, and Janu could barely see in front of him. The wind howled like a wounded animal, and he wondered if the elements were warning him of impending danger. Although the meeting was for seven o'clock, Janu wanted to be one-up on this stranger. He reached

McGinnis Street at six forty-five, dimmed his lights, and drove slowly toward the gallery. Not wanting to be lured into a trap, he continued around the block, hoping to spot any unforeseen enemies.

At six fifty-six, he parked down the street and turned off his lights. He sat staring at the gallery sitting on a grass-covered slope surrounded by tall trees and a circular driveway. It was a magnificent structure by day, but it loomed dark and foreboding at night.

Five past seven and the stranger hadn't shown. Janu sat nervously chewing flavorless gum, peering into his rearview mirror. If Malakh didn't arrive by seven fifteen, Janu was leaving.

Headlights finally appeared at the end of the street. The dark utility vehicle cruised slowly past Janu and stopped in front of the gallery. Janu could barely see the license plate for the deluge, but the car didn't appear to belong to the Establishment.

Malakh sat for two minutes before getting out. His wide-brimmed, black leather hat pulled firmly down on his head prevented his face from being drenched. His long black leather coat was tied securely at the waist, and he had on black leather boots. He stood with one foot on the running board and peered at his watch.

When Janu felt certain the stranger had come alone, he got out of his car. His heart was beating like a drum as he approached the man.

Janu muttered, "The light is so bright." And Malakh responded, "I can hardly see the night." Janu relaxed slightly.

He led the way up the gallery steps, constantly looking over his shoulder. He unlocked the door and turned on the light. He invited Malakh in with a hand gesture and led him down the corridor to the conference room.

"Have a seat," Janu told the stranger, as he dimmed the lights.

"Thanks," Malakh said. "It's been a long, hard day."

Both men were like boxers in the ring, one waiting for the other to throw the first punch. Finally, Janu asked, "So, what is it you want to help me with?"

"Your plan," Malakh said forthrightly.

Janu stopped breathing. He wanted to run, but he took a deep breath instead. "And what plan is that?" he mumbled, taking a weak stab at naiveté.

"The one you've been working on for years," Malakh replied.

The light in the dimly lit room cast an eerie shadow on the stranger, and the taste of fear was like bile spewed up from Janu's guts. The only time had he been this afraid was in the Acheron River of Woe.

"Who says I've been *working* on *anything*?" a terrified Janu asked.

"It takes one man with a plan to recognize another," Malakh replied, "and we may be able to help each other." He sat back in the chair and crossed his long legs.

"Who else is aware of this so-called plan?" Janu asked, trying hard to conceal his nerves.

"No one that I know of," Malakh replied. "See, like you, I'm also employed by the Central Control Agency, or the CCA, or, as you call it, the Control the Citizens Agency."

"How do you know where I work?" Janu whispered, eyeing the man closely.

"I'm responsible to know everything I can about our citizens, including what they're up to. I keep a big '*E*' on the associates—get it? *E* for *Establishment*." Malakh thought it was funny, but Janu was not laughing.

"I've been ordered to keep an eye on you, Ariana, Sierra, and Izaiah," the stranger continued.

The hair on the back of Janu's neck stood up. "You've been spying on my family?" he asked.

Malakh ignored the question. "How much do you know about the CCA's operations?" he asked instead.

"It's an Establishment-controlled agency that conducts and monitors the affairs of the nation, including the private activities of its citizens," Janu answered with disdain.

"*Tsk, tsk*," Malakh said. "You could be arrested for such contempt." He leaned forward in his chair and rubbed his rough beard. "I know about every plot and plan in our little nation…even yours. That's why you need me."

"And you want to help me…why?"

Malakh leaned in closer. "You have knowledge of a place that most people in this nation have never heard of."

"What…what makes you say that?" Janu stuttered.

"You've been working after hours on an escape plan, but you've been sloppy, and I've been covering for you."

"I…I don't know what you're talking about."

"We can dance around the maypole all night," Malakh said, "or you can let me help you."

"I don't even know you," Janu replied. "And, if you know so much about my plan, why haven't you reported me?"

"I think the citizens have a right to know what you know," Malakh replied.

"How do I know this is not a setup?" Janu asked.

"Because I could've exposed you long ago," Malakh replied.

"If it's money you're after, I don't have any," Janu announced with as much loathing as he could muster.

"I don't need your money," Malakh replied. "But if you want to succeed, you need to trust me. I know better than you what will happen if your plan is exposed."

"Listen," he continued, "I'm privy to all incoming and outgoing communication, as well as every activity conducted at the agency. Including those activities performed after hours." He stared at Janu. Then Malakh flashed his identification, and a terrified Janu sat speechless.

"I know the plans and strategies of the Establishment before they're implemented, which could be useful to you." He paused for effect. "Nothing is even shredded without my authorization," he continued without arrogance.

"I also know the characteristics of every person living in this nation, including what they eat for breakfast, but most importantly, whether or not they're loyal to the prince.

"I hunt down rebels and uncover acts of treason against the Establishment and report them. However, what's most important to you is that I'm the first to be aware of actions even remotely suspicious, which led me to you. Besides Prince Diablo and a chosen few, I'm the eyes and ears of this nation, and I can be your eyes and ears, if you'll let me."

Pretending indifference, but well aware of the danger he could be in, Janu replied, "I've been at the agency for seventeen years, and I've never seen you before."

"My position can be compromised, and my life put in danger," Malakh replied. "So, at times I work incognito, and with minimal classified staff."

"Why are you telling me these things?"

"Because I also have a plan and I believe we can help each other. And if you want your plan to work, you'll have to trust me."

"Are you incognito now?" Janu asked, hoping for Malakh's sake that the big, black ugly mole over his right eye was part of his disguise.

"No," Malakh replied.

Janu was no fool. His escape plans had thus far failed. But with the power and authority of this weird-looking creature assisting him, he just might be able to achieve his goal.

"You know more about me than most people," Malakh said. "And since I know a few things about you, I trust we will keep each other's confidences. If you don't accept my offer, I'll walk away and never mention you or this meeting to anyone. You have my word."

Malakh stood and extended his hand, but Janu hesitated. He was still reeling from this bizarre encounter and wasn't sure exactly what he'd be agreeing to.

He stared into Malakh's eyes for about ten seconds, slowly raised himself, then shook the stranger's hand.

"One condition," Janu said. "My family must be kept safe."

"Agreed," Malakh replied. "We'll meet in a few days and discuss how best to accomplish your goal. Now I must leave." He whispered in Janu's ear, "Someone's watching over you."

Suddenly, there was a bang at the door. "Open up."

Janu turned to hide Malakh in the storage room, but he had disappeared.

"Open up," the Enforcer shouted again. Janu cautiously opened the door. "Kind of late for you to be conducting business," the uniformed man said, peering over Janu's shoulder.

"I'm locking up now," Janu replied, trying to block the man's entrance without appearing suspicious.

"See to it," the Enforcer replied gruffly.

Janu's hands were shaking as he bolted the door and searched for Malakh, but he was nowhere to be found. He left the gallery wondering how the stranger had simply vanished.

The rain had ceased, but the night was still moist and strangely quiet. Unaware of the creatures lurking in the trees, Janu assumed the cold chill was from his clammy clothes. As he headed home, the wind unexpectedly let out an eerie, mournful wail.

CHAPTER 4

The Stranger

Janu drove home with Malakh foremost on his mind. The stranger possessed an unnerving presence and no doubt was a force to be reckoned with. Still, he was no closer to finding out what the stranger knew than before their meeting.

Malakh stood about six feet, five inches tall, with dark curls that hung down to his shoulders. His dark eyes were like deep pools of liquid seemingly peering into Janu's soul. Janu had tried to demonstrate his lack of fear by maintaining eye contact, but the big black mole above Malakh's right eye, with a strand of hair peeping out of it, had become the focal point of his attention, and he wondered if the hideous thing obstructed the stranger's vision. Malakh's large frame was solid and muscular, and Janu could still feel his powerful handshake, which he had tried to emulate by squeezing back just as hard.

Janu thought he'd been covert in his after-hours research of how to escape Keres. Yet this stranger seemed to know all about his plan to flee this evil nation.

He drove into his driveway, turned off the engine, and sat staring at the warm glow inside his home. His family was his life, and their well-being was all that mattered.

The porch light revealed the flower bed Ariana had recently filled with the best flowers she could find. She tried duplicating what they had abandoned in Fa'i, but it was a sad imitation. Without the proper light and environment, flowers in Keres barely bloomed and within hours would turn to dust. How he missed his breathtaking garden in Fa'i.

"I *cannot* fail," he muttered, tears spilling from his eyes.

He wiped his face, left his vehicle, and walked through the door of his modest home. The aromas from the kitchen filled his nostrils, and he was again reminded of what was important. Removing his damp overcoat and hat, he kissed Ariana on the cheek. As he expressed his appreciation for her efforts in trying to feed the family nutritious meals in this crazy environment, he wondered if Ariana could tell what was really on his mind.

"Dad, what took you so long?" Sierra said, running in and kissing him on the cheek. "Z's been threatening to eat my flower display."

Janu laughed for the first time that day. How he loved his family.

"It couldn't be helped, Precious. I'll get out of these damp clothes so we can eat."

"Don't forget the revelation, Daddy."

"Not tonight, sweetheart, I'm exhausted. I just want to eat and go to bed."

This was not the time to tell his children what he had kept from them their whole lives; not until he found out exactly what Malakh knew.

Sierra was disappointed, having gone to so much trouble to make the dinner table special. "It's okay," she said sadly.

"Be patient," Ariana told her. "Your dad will tell you when the time is right."

Ariana watched her husband climb the back stairs, seemingly carrying the entire nation of Keres on his slumped shoulders.

He stepped into the shower and sighed as the hot water cascaded over his weary body. Later, not having much appetite at dinner, he excused himself. Although exhausted, he tossed and turned all night, dreaming he was being chased by Malakh's obnoxious mole.

The next morning, he told Ariana about his bizarre encounter with the stranger. "Why would he want to help us when he'd be putting his own life in danger?" he asked.

"Be careful," Ariana replied. "He sounds too good to be true. Find out all you can about him before committing yourself."

Janu's extensive research revealed that Malakh was all he had claimed to be. There was nothing untoward about the odd man, and Janu needed him like he needed air to breathe. Still he felt uneasy. He watched Malakh like a hawk, even followed him on several occasions. But, as if Malakh knew Janu was tailing him, he managed to elude him each time.

A week later, Malakh revealed Janu's plan to him. "How do you know all this?" Janu asked, trying to mask his dread. Malakh ignored him and began mapping out his strategy for Janu's plan. Janu was impressed, but he didn't let on. He had to admit Malakh was a tremendous resource, but he kept wondering what was in it for him.

As if Malakh had read his mind, he said, "My friend, with what you're about to do, no one, not even me, should be above suspicion. Families and friends are betraying one another to prove their loyalty to Prince Diablo. By the way," he said, "there can't be any association between you, me, and this plan, or we're all dead."

For months, the two men worked tirelessly in Malakh's secret cottage planning the Great Escape. Because of Malakh's clandestine work for the nation, he often worked away from his office in a cabin in the woods.

Janu couldn't believe his eyes the first time he saw the hideaway. It appeared to be an abandoned run-down shack surrounded by a swamp. The windows were covered with mud and grime to keep suspicious eyes from peering in. The brick walls were intentionally covered with close-grained birch wood, and papers and trash were strewn about the place. But when he stepped inside the cottage, it was neat as a pin. A red potbellied stove sat in the corner of a large living space. His host reached behind an oversized hutch, pulled out a remote control, and pressed a series of buttons. The side wall began to revolve, and Janu thought he'd been lured into a trap. But when the rotation was complete, a light inside the vault revealed sophisticated technological equipment.

"Wow," Janu said. "This resembles the system we have at the agency."

"I designed that too," Malakh said humbly.

Janu entered the vault, and cameras positioned at every angle began to quietly rotate.

"I've connected the security system to my residence," Malakh stated. "If this alarm is ever activated, I can push a button from anywhere in my home, and every file and piece of equipment will be immediately destroyed.

"That's clever," Janu remarked.

"We're dealing with very clever minds, and we must stay ahead of the competition."

"How long have you been putting this together?" Janu asked.

"As long as you've been planning your escape," Malakh replied.

"But how would you know when I began planning my escape?" Janu asked, feeling uneasy about his host again.

Malakh didn't reply. Janu shook off his apprehension once again and remarked, "This must've set you back a pretty penny." Malakh ignored him.

The men worked past midnight, locked up the shack tighter than a fortress, and headed home, ever watchful for Enforcers. Three weeks later, Malakh announced to Janu that Phase One of his plan was complete.

"Since our homes, vehicles, and even the cameras on the streets have Organisms," Malakh said, "there's no safe place to talk with your children. So, I've created a program allowing you to temporarily shut down the Organism in your home without alerting the Establishment."

Janu was overwhelmed and confessed to Ariana that he never could have achieved this without Malakh. She, however, did not share his enthusiasm.

"This is very dangerous," she said. "How do we know we can trust him? He could record our entire conversation with the children and turn it in to the Establishment. You know what happened to Elisabeth."

"If Malakh betrays us, he also betrays himself," Janu replied.

Janu hugged his wife and retreated to his study, closing the door behind him. He eased his tired body into his recliner and recalled that rainy night when he and Malakh had tried to outsmart each other, Malakh getting the better of him.

Since then, the two men had worked tirelessly, and Janu was mentally and physically exhausted, and understandably worried about how his dangerous revelation could affect his children. As he dozed off, he thought, *This disclosure could be the beginning of something great, or the end of something never quite started.*

CHAPTER 5

The Organism

Ariana, meanwhile, was shaking like a leaf in a rainstorm. She knew Janu was working hard on their exodus, but by this time tomorrow, they could all be in prison…or worse. She *wanted* to be positive, but she felt like throwing up instead.

From Janu's accounts to Ariana, Malakh seemed creepy but exceptionally intelligent and, so far, he had kept his word. But Ariana was still apprehensive.

Sierra, meanwhile, was humming her favorite tune as she finished preparing the dinner table. She entered the kitchen and noticed her mother's shaking hands.

"It's time for dinner," Ariana said. "Please get your dad."

Ariana had waited seventeen years for this moment, but excitement and fear battled for first place in her emotions. At eight o'clock tonight, Janu would unplug their Organism, for which the penalty was imprisonment or death. She paced the floor like a caged lion. The well-being of her family depended on trusting this stranger. And if he betrayed them, there would be nothing they could do and no place to hide.

It didn't help that the big red Law Book on the shelf was a constant reminder. "*If the Establishment, or its subsidiaries or assignees, [to include family members] believes insubordination or revolution is being perpetrated by any citizen, the Establishment has the right to monitor said person(s), albeit in a private residence, with or without permission of said person(s) in order to obtain evidence to prosecute said perpetrator(s) to the fullest extent of the Law.*"

Sierra knocked lightly on Janu's office door and walked in.

"Wake up, sleepyhead," she whispered. "It's time to eat."

Sierra took her seat just as Izaiah dashed into the dining room. As usual, they tried to outtalk each other as they piled food on their plates. Janu, normally part of the conversation, picked at his food.

"Did you have a hard day, Dad?" Sierra asked as she shoveled mashed potatoes into her mouth.

Janu slowly put down his fork. "I told you children one day you would know the truth," he whispered, "and that day has come."

Sierra's fork stopped midair.

"We need your undivided attention," Ariana added. "And we need you to keep an open mind."

"Izaiah, would you please stop eating for one minute," Janu said. "This is important."

"If it's about that revelation business," Izaiah replied with a mouth full of food, "you guys have been talking about that forever."

Janu gave his son a stern look. "All right," Izaiah said. "I'm listening."

Suddenly, the Organism's speakers began to crackle. The revelation would once again have to wait, as they were in for another dreadful "sermon" from Prince Diablo.

But this time, Janu welcomed the interruption. Now he wouldn't have to wonder whether a message would try and come through while the Organism was disabled, thereby alerting the Establishment.

While eerie music played in the background, Diablo, the potentate of Keres, cleared his throat.

"Do we have to listen to his rhetoric tonight?" Sierra asked.

"Unfortunately, we do," Janu whispered.

"*Good evening, fellow citizens and loyal patriots of the Cause,*" the monarch began softly. "*Pardon the interruption, but I have exciting news.*

"*Plans for the Great Commission have been finalized, and I expect everyone's loyalty and patience during its implementation.*

"*As you are aware, I've been working diligently to bring about a new way of life for all Keresians. Yet, there are some who oppose my endeavor to provide us with this better life.*

"*Be on notice,*" the potentate exclaimed. "*I will ferret out all subversives, and they will be arrested and tried for treason.*" Breathing heavily, he stated intensely, "*You and your entire families.*"

Near the completion of his speech, he was ranting like a madman about the injustices and disloyalties he had to endure from his own people.

The sermon lasted exactly seventeen minutes, after which he wished everyone a pleasant evening and a peaceful night's rest.

Ariana and Janu laughed. "He's mad," Ariana stated.

"*Sicko,*" Sierra added. "We have to listen to this nonsense in our classrooms, on the streets…even at the malls."

But Izaiah appeared to be captivated. "Be quiet," he whispered. "They could be listening."

Sierra eyed her brother. "It's an invasion of our privacy, and I'm tired of it," she said. "How anyone can feel good after hearing that garbage is beyond me."

"If the citizens knew the truth, and the evil force behind these lectures, they would resist," Janu said. "That's what enables your mother and me to withstand this propaganda."

"What truth?" Sierra asked.

Janu moved closer to his children. "You can't repeat one word of what you're about to hear," he whispered.

"You're scaring me," Sierra said.

"I'll be right back," he stated.

Janu closed the door to his study and sat down at his desk. Malakh, pretending to work late, was waiting for Janu's signal. With trembling hands, Janu phoned Malakh's burner mobile.

"Are you ready?" Janu asked.

"Yes," Malakh replied, "and I have good news. No Enforcer raids are scheduled for your neighborhood tonight. Are you ready?"

"It's now or never," Janu replied.

"Once we disconnect this call," Malakh said, "I will hit the scratch button on the mainframe connected to your Organism. From that moment you have exactly thirty minutes before the system reboots itself. Did you disconnect the memory board?"

"I almost forgot," Janu said.

He found the portal in the back of the Organism and removed the panel.

"It's done," he reported.

"Now, quickly talk to your children," Malakh instructed.

Janu returned to the table.

"Can we talk freely?" Ariana asked.

"We have thirty minutes," Janu replied.

"What's happening?" Izaiah asked.

Janu took a deep breath. "We're forbidden by law, under penalty of imprisonment—even death—to speak of what we're about to share. But you knowing the truth far outweighs the consequences. I hope for all our sakes we haven't waited too long."

Suddenly, anxiety replaced the excitement Sierra had previously felt.

Janu began, "Before Sierra was born, your mom and I were lured away from our home in Fa'i and forced to live in Keres against our wills."

"Lured away from your home?" Sierra asked. "You're not making sense."

"Hold your questions," Ariana stated. "We have a lot to say and little time in which to say it."

"Across the river," Janu continued, "is an enchanted nation called Fa'i, The Realm of Endless Light. Your mom and I were born and raised there, and we're planning to return with you children."

Ignoring the disbelief on their faces, Ariana interjected, "The perpetual light you've been staring at since you were a little girl, Sierra, comes from Uriel, the King; he *is* the light. His radiance illuminates the entire nation day and night. There's never any darkness or shadows in Fa'i because Uriel's brightness dispels them."

"How can light come from a person?" Izaiah chuckled.

"It defies human explanation," Ariana replied. "But our king emanates light because he *is* light. His name means God is My Light, and he's magnificent, radiant, transparent, breathtaking, and all-consuming. He's all that's good and perfect...the direct opposite of Prince Diablo."

"The environment is perfect," Janu added. "Uriel's brilliance controls the temperature and the atmosphere, not like here." Janu ignored Izaiah's snickers. "And his estate is a wonder to behold—"

"It sits atop a hill," Ariana interrupted, lifting her head for effect. "And an extraordinary rainbow of magnificent colors surrounds the estate, an assurance of Uriel's love and protection."

When Ariana began to tear up, Janu added, "Twelve large towers reaching into the heavens sit atop the estate. And each of the twelve gates surrounding the palace is one gigantic pearl."

"Two huge lions adorn the front portico of the estate like fierce sentinels," Ariana exclaimed. "They're made of priceless stone and stare through ruby eyes. Cherubim carved from onyx, beryl, and other precious stones are placed strategically inside and outside the splendid home."

"You never need an appointment to see him," Janu added, "because he's able to make himself available to everyone simultaneously."

"In his presence," Ariana resumed, "you're bathed in a warm glow of love and peace. Everyone is treated with respect, and no one person has more than any other, eliminating jealousy and greed. And he will find humor in whatever your situation."

Sierra and Izaiah, with eyes wide and mouths agape, didn't know what to make of their parents' eccentric behavior. Janu and Ariana were so caught up in bringing Fa'i to life, they were tripping over each other's words.

Ariana, noticing her children's expressions, realized that had she not lived in Fa'i, she, too, would think her and Janu crazy.

"The palace is a place of beauty, stretching the length and breadth of the land," Janu exclaimed. "It's surrounded by an enormous, flawless garden that is home to the most beautiful flowers you'll ever see."

"And they never fade," Ariana stated passionately. "Not like here in Keres."

"Are there any animals there?" Sierra asked, wondering why she was contributing to this nonsense.

"Yes," Janu replied, "a magnificent species of birds and animals. Peacocks spread wide their plumes, displaying rich colors of deep purple, royal blue, and green, while others have feathers patterned with muted magenta and yellow. They strut through the garden like royalty with their crowns flaunting the same radiant colors as their tail feathers. They're beautiful…and they know it."

"The rolling hills and meadows are covered with a blanket of the most marvelous blue-green grass," Ariana said. "And although the grass is always green and perfectly manicured, you'll never find a sprinkler or lawn mower in all the land."

Sierra sat dumbfounded, watching her mother display a sense of pride she'd never seen before. Her dad's head was elevated, too, as he recalled a place and time of long ago. Their eyes literally sparkled.

"Some of the fruit trees have a variety of fruit hanging at the same time from their branches," Ariana said. "It's a mystery I'll never understand. And the fruit is sweeter than the honey on any honeycomb." She paused for a moment, then laughed.

"What's so funny?" Sierra asked, feeling sorry for her delusional parents.

"I was recalling the many hours your dad and I wasted trying to catch the fruit in its metamorphous state. But we never could, because it's divinely transformed."

"Here's another mystery," Janu said. "The fruit is ripe and ready to eat the moment it appears on the trees and it stays fresh until picked. It doesn't rot and fall to the ground like the fruit here."

"Something you children have never experienced," Ariana added sadly.

They need help, Sierra thought.

"Izaiah, as much as you love fruit, you would have a field day," Janu added. "The grapes and strawberries are so large it takes two or three people to remove them from their vines, and they're plentiful and free to all."

"I don't believe a word," Izaiah said, visibly shaken. "You're making this up. And why are we just now hearing about this? Keres is our home, so stop talking like this."

"Don't speak to Mom and Dad like that," Sierra said, also greatly disturbed by this revelation.

"Children," Janu said, "let's not waste time arguing. Reserve judgment for now and listen. I know it sounds insane, but Fa'i is real, it's our home, and we're going back."

"You're never tired there after a hard day's work, or exhausted like we are now," Ariana explained. "You simply swim in the River of Life and you're revitalized. And there's no aging or dying in Fa'i because the waters perpetually renew your youth."

"There are no mobile phones, vehicles, or computers in our world," Janu added. "We learned to use those devices in Keres because of necessity, but in Fa'i, they're not needed. It's a simpler way of life you'll only understand when you get there."

Although Sierra couldn't imagine life without her mobile phone, she could, with her vivid imagination and love for beauty, see herself running through the blue-green meadows, smelling and picking the beautiful flowers and tasting the delicious fruit. And although she was not fond of water, she felt she might be able to swim in the River of Life. *Sounds like a wonderful place*, she thought, *if it exists.*

"Why are you talking about this if it could put our lives in danger?" Izaiah asked. "And if this Fa'i is so cool, why did you leave?"

"One day when we have more time, I'll tell you," Janu replied sadly. "Until then, you can't breathe a word of this to anyone, not even your friends. It could put them and their families in danger."

"You have our word," Sierra said, giving Izaiah a stern look.

"I think that's enough for tonight," Janu said. "Clear the table. It'll be bedtime soon."

"It's Friday night," Izaiah complained.

"Then read a book or something," Janu snapped.

Suddenly, he glanced at his watch. He had exceeded the allotted time by four minutes. *Why didn't Malakh warn me?*

He was racing to his study to reconnect the panel when someone pounded on the door.

"Enforcers, open up."

"Just a minute," Janu shouted.

"Open up…NOW!" the officer barked.

"Sierra, wait one minute, then open the door," Janu whispered.

"If I don't open it now, they'll kick it in," she replied.

He reconnected the panel just as an Enforcer entered his study.

"We were alerted that your Organism has been disconnected for four minutes," the Enforcer said, laying hands on the machine to see if it was warm or cold. "Is there a problem here, Mr. Calder?"

"You know how children are," Janu replied. "It was probably disconnected by mistake." He knew the Enforcer wasn't buying his story, but it was the best he could do in a pinch.

"This is a felony," the Enforcer said, "and I should arrest you."

"Sir, it won't happen again," Janu replied.

"See that it doesn't, Mr. Calder. We're watching you."

The Enforcers left, and Janu immediately called Malakh. "The Enforcers showed up at my door," he said.

"I know, but it wasn't safe for me to warn you," Malakh replied. "Watch your back. I'll be in touch."

Janu hung up. "I'll be watching you," he mumbled.

Meanwhile, Sierra had so many questions her head was throbbing. This was not the revelation she had expected. She gazed at Ariana, whose eyes were red and swollen from crying, and wondered what was next. Izaiah wanted to sneak out, find his buddies, and be around normal people. But it was late, and he, too, had a headache. He went out on the back porch to try and make sense of what he'd heard. This was the only home he knew. If another nation did exist across the river, surely he would've heard about it before now.

I wish they hadn't told us that stuff, he thought. *I don't plan on spending the rest of my life in prison or on death row.*

After doing the dishes, Sierra went straight to her bedroom and locked the door. Deep down, she knew her parents were telling the truth; they had never lied to them before. And just watching their pain as they relived those memories assured her of Fa'i's existence.

How tragic, she thought, *to have lived in a paradise they love, now forced to live in a land they despise.* She felt sorry for them as she belly-flopped on her bed. But as Z had questioned, why would they leave such an idyllic place?

She rolled onto her back and placed her hands behind her head. *I've seen that light my whole life*, she thought, *but never imagined it came from a being. Now I understand why mother would stare across the river with tears streaming down her face when she thought no one was watching.*

If only Uriel would shine his light in Keres, she thought, *maybe the flowers wouldn't fade so rapidly, the fruit would ripen, and we wouldn't have to labor so hard to make the food edible. I might like to meet this king*, she thought. She drifted off to sleep, dreaming of blue-green meadows.

Meanwhile, Izaiah was pacing up and down outside Sierra's bedroom. Finally, he tapped lightly on her door, but there was no answer. He tried the door, but it was locked. He listened for movement, but he heard none. He knocked again then retreated to his bedroom, thinking, *She's probably as confused as I am.*

CHAPTER 6

Jackson

Izaiah was glad it was Saturday. He had tossed and turned most of the night and was exhausted. He rang Jackson's home and General Armon answered.

"Hello, is Jackson home?"

"He's at Valiance Diner," the general replied.

"Thank you," Izaiah said and hung up.

He knew he should talk to Sierra first. She had warned him about revealing family secrets to her boyfriend, Jackson, but he needed answers.

Jackson was the big brother Izaiah had never had, and the son of General Armon, Prince Diablo's chief Enforcer. Izaiah thought, *If anybody would know if another nation exists, Jackson surely would.*

Sierra opened her eyes to another gray morning and realized she'd slept in her clothes. She had a date to meet Jackson later at Sports Junction, but she was not looking forward to it. She had grown weary of his love for himself. True, he was good-looking, tops in his class, and a tremendous athlete, but he was also arrogant and conceited. Before stepping into the shower, she pulled back her curtains, hoping last night had been a sick dream. But even through the haze, the light shone bright in the distance.

Meanwhile, Izaiah was listening at Sierra's door. He needed to find Jackson before her date with him. He heard her shower running, grabbed his helmet from the hall shelf, and dashed down the steps.

Leaving without breakfast was a first for him. "Be back later," he told his parents, and took off on his motorbike for Valiance Diner.

Sierra, meanwhile, heard Izaiah pull out of the garage on his bike, and wondered where he was headed so early in the morning. She suddenly felt sick. She quickly threw on a pair of jeans and a T-shirt and bolted down the steps.

"Where's he going?" she asked her parents.

"We don't know," Ariana replied. "He ran out of the house without breakfast. Good morning to you, too."

The knot in Sierra's stomach tightened as she realized her decision to ignore Z last night could come back to haunt them.

"We might have a problem," she said.

"What do you mean?" Janu asked.

"Z's been confiding in Jackson about family matters. I didn't say anything before because I didn't want to get him in trouble. But if he's looking for answers, he might confide in Jackson about your revelation."

"I don't believe he would do such a thing after the stern warning we gave him last night," Ariana said.

"Well, I'm glad you're confident," Janu replied. "But that boy's behavior has been radical, to say the least, and I'm worried he just might do something stupid." Sierra didn't let on just how sold out Z was to the Establishment, and to Jackson. But she had to stop him from betraying their family secret, or they would all be imprisoned...or worse.

Sierra grabbed her keys. "I'll be back," she said, then quickly headed for Valiance Diner, hoping to find Jackson before Z did.

Janu recalled when he first saw Jackson. It was at Ariana's Art Expo last year. He thought he had spotted General Armon. But when he looked closer, he realized the man was too young. Still, the resemblance was eerie and unsettling.

He must be the general's son, Janu thought. *But what's he doing here?*

Janu was not the least bit pleased when Jackson later called asking his permission to date Sierra.

"Aren't you the general's son?" he had asked.

"Yes sir, I am."

"Why do you want to date my daughter?"

"I met her at the Expo, and frankly, I'm impressed with her intelligence and how she carries herself," Jackson had replied. "She's not like other girls."

Janu didn't care how impressed Jackson was with Sierra. He did not want his daughter dating the general's son.

"I'll speak with Sierra and her mother and get back to you," Janu replied curtly.

"At least he had the decency to call and ask," Ariana grumpily remarked after hearing the news.

In the beginning Jackson seemed polite and mannerly, unlike his father, whom Janu and Ariana despised. Then one day Malakh warned Janu that Jackson was a plant by the general to gather information about his family's activities.

Janu was furious. "The next time he darkens my door, I'll throw him out on his rear," he had ranted.

"Keep your enemies close," Malakh had calmly advised.

"He's too close," Janu had replied, "always in and out of our home."

"If you play your cards right," Malakh advised, "the boy might unwittingly reveal something that may aid you in your exodus. Don't let your emotions get in the way of your ultimate goal."

Ariana was not happy using their daughter this way, but she had reluctantly agreed. They watched Jackson like a dog watching a bone, hoping he'd reveal anything that would help them escape Keres. Presently, Ariana was wishing they had let the children ask questions last night. "I don't feel good leaving them with so many uncertainties," she told Janu.

"But there wasn't time," he replied. "We'll take them to a safe place soon where they can ask all the questions they want."

"There is no safe place," she replied. "But as frightened as I am, I'm glad they finally know the truth." She nestled in Janu's arms, clutching him tightly.

He chuckled. "It's been so long since we discussed our home, we sounded insane even to me. I can imagine how we sounded to the children."

"They think we're nuts." Ariana giggled. "Especially Izaiah. He makes me so mad sometimes with that logic and reason nonsense. These misguided teachings have literally ruined the population, who have no faith for anything they can't see or understand."

"They're not taught faith," Janu stated simply. "But whether our children believe Fa'i exists or not, we're all going there."

He squeezed her gently, then retreated to his study. He closed the door, then plopped down in his chair. How would he tell his daughter she'd been a pawn, not only in Jackson's hands, but in his, as well? Mentally exhausted, he leaned back in his recliner.

Meanwhile, Ariana retreated to her loft to work on a painting for her upcoming exhibit. She hoped it would take her mind off what they were about to do.

"I wasn't this afraid when I left Fa'i," she mumbled.

Sierra, meanwhile, was hoping to find Jackson before Z did; she knew that her family's lives depended on it. She took every shortcut she knew and tried reaching Z on his mobile, but he didn't answer.

Izaiah, meanwhile, was inquiring of Jackson's whereabouts from the proprietor of Valiance Diner.

"He and his friends just left," Mr. Dagger replied. "They're headed for Sports Junction."

Izaiah's stomach suddenly growled. And although he felt he was racing against time, he still ordered home fries, three eggs, four pieces of bacon, wheat toast, and a large glass of chocolate milk, with a side of apple pie. He gulped down his breakfast and then rushed from the diner, almost knocking down an incoming patron.

Simultaneously, Sierra turned the corner of Mission Avenue and came to a screeching halt. In the middle of the street was a large delivery truck trying to back into a narrow driveway.

"Move it," she yelled to the driver, who replied with a "finger sign".

She tried backing up, but the car behind was too close. Finally, the truck backed far enough into the driveway, and she inched by, honking as she sped past.

Izaiah found Jackson at Sports Junction talking with the manager.

"Hey, big guy," Jackson said. "Where's your sister? We had a date."

"She'll be along, I guess," Izaiah replied. "You got a minute? I need to talk."

"As soon as I burn these guys on the track," Jackson replied with his usual arrogance. Izaiah took a seat on the bench and waited nervously.

Sierra, meanwhile, rushed into Valiance Diner. "Hey, Sierra," Mr. Dagger chuckled, "your little brother, who's not so little anymore, just tried to eat me out of business."

"How long ago did he leave?" she asked hurriedly.

"Not long."

"Thanks, Mr. Dagger."

Meanwhile, Jackson had finished his three laps around the track, outmaneuvering every other driver as usual. He stepped out of the race car, took off his helmet and gloves, and wiped his brow.

"Izaiah, are you and your posse in some kind of trouble?" he asked.

"No," Izaiah replied.

"So, what's troubling you?"

Sierra, meanwhile, was speeding through the streets like a maniac. As she neared Sports Junction, an Enforcer in the distance was drawing closer to her.

She tried not to appear obvious as she applied the brakes to slow the vehicle. He pulled alongside her and gave her the evil eye, trying to communicate his dislike for teenage drivers, then sped away.

"Whew," Sierra mumbled.

In the meantime, Izaiah didn't know where to begin. He felt foolish and ashamed. But he had to know the truth or bust.

"I'm waiting," Jackson said.

"Before I tell you, you have to swear not to mention a single word to anybody, especially Sierra."

Jackson lit up inside, but swore he'd never tell a soul. The twinkle in his eyes went unnoticed by Izaiah.

"Well, last night at dinner, my parents told me and Sierra that…"

"Hey, Jackson," Sierra said, panting. "Sorry I kept you waiting."

She squeezed Izaiah's arm as hard as she could. "Z, you must've been in a hurry. Mom said you left the house without breakfast." She and Jackson laughed at that oddity. "Well, get on home. Dad has your chores lined up."

Izaiah knew Sierra was on to him. The look on her face told him she knew exactly what he was up to.

"Wait," Jackson said. "What did your parents tell you?"

"It can wait," Izaiah replied, hurrying out of the Junction.

Jackson had seen the frightened look on Sierra's face when she thought Izaiah had said too much. Now he was certain the general's suspicions were warranted; this family was up to something.

"What was that all about?" Sierra asked, as if she didn't know.

"The big guy was telling me something about your parents when you interrupted him. Are they okay?" he asked, feigning concern. Sierra didn't answer.

Janu, meanwhile, was glad Ariana was occupied with her art; he needed time to think. He reclined in his chair and eventually fell into a deep sleep, reliving his and Ariana's capture.

He slowly turned the knob of a door that had been locked for seventeen years and stepped inside. The room was dark, but he had a panoramic view of himself and Ariana being forcibly dragged from the gorge.

The scene changed and Ariana was on the valley floor in labor. General Armon was in a far corner sneering hideously, foam spewing from his twisted mouth. Janu watched as the doors of an isolated dungeon clanged shut, locking him inside. The stench of sickness and death filled his nostrils, and he involuntarily trembled in his sleep.

He flinched as a long needle was shoved into his arm, then watched the drugs course through his veins as if his body was transparent.

He tried to shout "*Enough*", but his tongue was stuck to the roof of his mouth and he was so thirsty. He wasn't allowed a moment's rest, and his loyalty was tested nonstop as Enforcers tried to break his spirit. They screamed continually for him to renounce Uriel as he quivered under the heavy lashes that tore the flesh on his back. Considerable hours of deprogramming and brainwashing had left him naked and exhausted on the cell floor. Beads of sweat presently dotted his forehead as he battled the all-too-real Enforcers in his sleep.

Suddenly, he was standing before a huge red door. He was shoved into a very bright room where many ugly faces loomed large above him. An Enforcer left the room in slow motion and returned with a recorder. A tape screamed loud, outrageous propaganda about Uriel. Painful attempts were made to strip him of his dignity as demonic beings cursed him and his beloved Fa'i. Their nasty words bore into his soul, and he felt exposed and ashamed.

After what seemed like days, a dark being entered the room and commanded Janu to recant his loyalty to his king. The ordeal was hideous, and Janu knew he couldn't endure much more. He spotted Ariana in a large chair with her feet six inches from the floor. Still in labor, she was crying and holding her belly.

Enforcers surrounded her, threatening her with death, but she would not renounce Uriel. How proud he was that she was strong, even in her weakest state. He tried to reach her to protect and comfort her, but he couldn't move.

In the next vision, he was pumping iron in a dark basement trying to restore his mental and physical strength, when suddenly he was seated and bending over a large opened book.

A map of Keres' underground construction and waterways lay before him, and he quickly scanned the pages and began planning their escape.

The couple was then thrust before a huge podium, where a faceless man in a black robe began badgering them. They feigned submission to Diablo and his Establishment by reciting what the man wanted to hear. Finally, the faceless judge lifted his gavel and pronounced them free to go.

In a moment, Janu and Ariana were standing outside the Deprogramming Camp with only the tattered clothes they had arrived in. A piece of paper with an address was thrust into Janu's hand and enough money for a cab. The cabbie took them down a long, eerie corridor before stopping in front of a dismal, filthy, and degrading house in which they had been assigned to live. Janu turned slowly and wiped away Ariana's tears. Even in his sleep, his heart raced, and his hands shook.

Janu awakened from his "daymare" shaken and breathing hard, wondering how he and Ariana had ever survived that ordeal. Doubtless, that was the second worst time of their lives.

CHAPTER 7

Jordan

It was a brisk Monday afternoon. Sierra had thought all weekend about how she could help her parents return to their beautiful home.

She drove to the river, remembering the days when her father had taught her and Izaiah to swim before they could barely walk.

"You'll need this ability one day," Janu had told them.

"Why?" Sierra cried, as her father dragged her kicking and screaming into the water.

"One day you'll understand," he simply replied.

Izaiah, however, had been a natural, taking to the river like a fish. But when Janu would lower Sierra into the water, she was immediately shrouded with a sense of foreboding, followed by horrific night-mares. It was as though she was reliving some dreadful event that she had no knowledge of ever experiencing. Finally, after much encouragement from Janu, she became an excellent swimmer. Presently, however, she had no clue that in the near future that skill would be her salvation.

She parked her vehicle and got out. A thick vapor hovered over the water. But then she saw it: the light that could never be extinguished, even by a thick haze. She continued along the river's edge, wishfully hoping to catch a glimpse of Uriel himself. Farther down the bank, she climbed onto a ledge jutting out from the mountainside, looking for the unusual rainbow her mother had described. Suddenly, a tall young man appeared. "Hi, Sierra," he shouted from afar.

The young man moved toward her like a gazelle. His dark wavy hair hanging just above his shoulders bounced with every stride. Sierra thought to herself, *Boy, is he handsome.*

"Do I know you?" she asked as he neared.

"I'm in your Reason and Logic class."

"I've never seen you before," she said.

"Maybe you haven't been looking hard enough," the young man replied with a smile. "Anyway, I sit in the back of the class and leave as soon as the bell rings."

"What's your name and number?" she asked.

"My name is Jordan, and my number is 777," he said, kicking the sand with his foot.

"And where do you live?" she asked.

"Not too far from here, with my uncle."

She wanted to ask about his parents, but she didn't dare. The sound of his voice was comforting, and he seemed more mature than the boys she knew.

"What's your number?" Jordan asked.

"Uh, 620," Sierra stuttered, as she stared into dark, piercing eyes that seemed to bare her soul.

"Do you know what your name means?" Jordan asked.

"No," she replied.

"High ground," Jordan answered. "You're destined for high places and great things."

"How do you know that?" Sierra asked. "You just met me."

"I study names and their meanings, and I researched yours at the beginning of the semester. Names are important. They often deliver a message about the person they belong to."

Sierra chuckled. "And where do you get your information?" she quipped.

"I have my sources," he replied. "I can show you sometime, if you're interested."

"I have a little brother named Izaiah," she remarked. "I'd like to know what his name means besides 'pain in the neck'."

Jordan chuckled.

"I have been told by my professors that I have a great destiny," Sierra continued, tearing her eyes away from his.

"And I believe them," Jordan replied softly.

"And how would you know?" Sierra asked, wondering who this person was who thought he knew her so well.

"I've watched you in class," he replied. "You're very intelligent."

She didn't know why she was blushing, but this stranger was making her feel awkward and clumsy. She wanted to bite her nails, but Jordan would notice her shaking hands.

"Well, I'd better head on home," Sierra said. "My mom will be expecting me." *There's something about those eyes*, she thought.

"Maybe we can walk along the river again sometime," Jordan said.

"Maybe," she replied, surprised at her awkwardness.

Get a grip, she told herself. *He's just another boy.*

"Look," Jordan pursued, "I'm a pretty good student too."

I bet you are, she thought.

"If you ever want to study together, let me know."

"I'll think about it," she said and hurried to her car. She was heady with excitement, and she didn't dare turn around in case he was watching her. If she had, she would have seen that he was, with a mile-wide grin on his face.

The next morning in class, Sierra turned around and saw that Jordan was smiling at her. She quickly faced front again, wondering how she could have ever missed him.

She asked around school and discovered he was a senior who was popular with his peers. During breaks and after school, he sometimes "held court" around the statue in front of the Academy.

He either analyzed a viewpoint mentioned in class or dissected a point of contention; he was constantly punching holes in the materials studied and the theories discussed, and astounding his listeners with his wisdom.

He didn't possess expensive "toys" like some of the other students. Instead, he drove an old clunker and loved nature, which greatly impressed Sierra. Consequently, she was disappointed when a week passed and he hadn't spoken to her. One day she was strolling out of her last class when he gently took her by the arm and whispered, "Meet me at the river."

The thought of being with him again by the river thrilled her in ways she had never felt before. She tried to remain calm as she drove to where they had previously met. She smiled at him as she climbed out of her car. He took her by the hand and led her to the river's edge, where she stopped short.

"Don't be afraid," he said. "You're safe."

Suddenly, she was unexplainably at peace. Until then, her parents had been the only ones she had trusted that close to the river. He led her to a large rock, where they removed their shoes. Sierra leaned back on her elbows and allowed the warm water's gentle flow to soothe her tired feet.

"Can I ask you a question?" she said.

"Anything," he replied.

"Why are you just now taking Logic and Reason, the major course that has to be passed before we can even think about graduating? And how did you get away with it for so long?"

"I thought you said *a* question," he teased. "First, I already know logic and reason, and second, I don't believe it's fundamental to my life. However, I was informed that if I hoped to graduate on time, this was my last opportunity to take the course. So, I sit in the back of the classroom and leave promptly after the bell."

"What do you believe?" she asked, wondering how this mild-mannered young man had the courage to rebel against the Establishment and get away with it.

"That's a complex question that would take longer than we have today for me to answer. But," he said, looking deep into her eyes, "one day you'll know the truth."

"You sound like my dad."

"Do I, now?"

They talked, and she discovered they had much in common—unlike Jackson, with whom she had very little in common. In fact, she wasn't sure how she felt about Jackson anymore. Jordan made her feel important, not like it was a privilege for her to be with him.

Jordan, aware of Ariana's art gallery, invited Sierra to his home to view his own collection. She thought about the implications of going to the home of a boy she barely knew, but she decided she could trust him. Once she got to his home, she saw the most unusual paintings hanging on his walls.

As she viewed the art, an unusually bright light in the background of each painting seemed to come to life, and she thought, *How odd.*

Jordan then sat down at his baby grand piano and began playing like no one she had ever heard before. The unusual concertos reached into the depths of her soul. She had to leave, but she promised to bring her violin the next time she visited so they could play together. She wanted him to experience her musical talent as well. She enjoyed their friendship, but she kept it quiet. Jackson was possessive, and his friends could be cruel to anyone not belonging to their inner circle.

Jordan enjoyed her company as well, and her sense of humor often made him double over with laughter. Finally, he persuaded her to study with him. It was Wednesday evening, and they were at the library cramming for their Logic and Reason exam. Sierra had to admit that not only was her new secret acquaintance fun to be with, but he was tremendously helpful with her studies.

Out of nowhere, he whispered, "One day, I'd like to meet your family."

No way, she thought. *Z would blab to Jackson, and I'm in no mood to deal with his jealous and controlling behavior. He's been trying to change me since our first date.*

"Well, I'm no man's trophy," she blurted out.

"I just want to meet your family," Jordan replied, staring at her curiously.

"I'm…I'm sorry, Jordan, I wasn't talking to you. Let me ask my parents first."

"No pressure," he replied. His voice dropped to a whisper. "Sierra, do you know that the teachings of Logic and Reason are not necessarily truth?"

He had her attention. "But why would our professors teach us a lie?" she asked naively.

"They wouldn't know the truth if it bit them in the face," he replied with conviction. "Anyway, how can they teach us what they don't know?"

He had to be careful and selective about the information he was about to reveal. He didn't want to endanger her or her family.

"Can you keep a secret?" he asked.

"Of course," she replied.

"This nation has been under the false assumption that Diablo is some kind of god, or savior, if you will," he whispered. "But he's not who he appears to be, and one day soon he'll be exposed for who he really is."

"Again, you sound like my dad," Sierra replied. "But quite frankly, I don't know what to believe anymore. Seems all that I've ever valued has been a lie. Anyway, isn't truth relative?"

"The real truth is so astounding," he replied, "that when you finally discover it, it will change your life forever."

"I do feel change coming," she replied, "but I'm not sure I'm ready for it. My life seems to be spiraling in a direction I don't understand, and I feel helpless to do anything about it."

He paused. "You said I sounded like your father. What has he told you?"

"It isn't important," she responded.

She had been tempted to disclose her parents' revelation. But if it sounded weird to her, she could only imagine what it would sound like to a stranger. She was fond of Jordan, and she didn't want to chase him away with the impression that her parents were insane.

CHAPTER 8

The Showdown

It was ten o'clock Friday morning, and the Gathering at Future Prep Academy was about to begin. The professors were scurrying to their places on the platform of the huge auditorium. Jordan hated these assemblies, but attendance at a Gathering was mandatory in every learning institution throughout Keres. Once a month, students in all twelve districts gathered for random debriefing by their professors. The parents were told that it was the Establishment's way of determining whether the students were academically astute. But in reality, the authorities wanted to ensure that the students remained loyal to the propaganda they're being fed.

Professor Darius, the assigned emcee for this semester, was standing behind the podium shuffling papers in platform shoes. He was a short man who was quite often made fun of by the students and his peers. His five-foot-three-inch frame was covered in layers of fat and dressed in a snug navy-blue pin-striped suit.

He wore thick black glasses, and his head bent so low trying to read the agenda that he appeared asleep. The students swore he was blind as a bat, and several upperclassmen tested that theory by placing a dead rat in his lunch box to see if he would recognize it. Jordan was asked to participate, but he refused to take part in such a repulsive display of so-called fun.

The prank caused quite a stir, and Professor Darius demanded the perpetrators be expelled, which meant they would not graduate. After their parents begged and pleaded with the Establishment, the boys were let off with a slap on the wrist, and the privilege of sweeping their community streets with tiny brooms for the remainder of the semester.

Jordan watched as chattering students scrambled to take their seats before the late bell rang. Suddenly, the usual music announcing an unexpected visit from Prince Diablo blared through the loudspeakers. He often appeared impromptu at Gatherings, causing much upheaval and terror in the hearts and minds of the students…and the faculty.

The air seemed to be sucked out of the room as the ring-clad finger slowly pulled back the heavy purple drapes. The prince was dressed in black, and a long scarlet cape hung on his lean but muscular six-foot frame. A small bejeweled crown sat atop his head, and he was trailed by an entourage of staff all stumbling over each other to keep the cape from dragging the floor. The prince all but twirled onto the platform. Jordan quickly covered his mouth to keep from laughing out loud. The entire spectacle was nauseating, and Jordan wanted to puke.

The prince finally made his way to the podium and pushed Professor Darius aside, causing him to trip over the long cape. The students burst out laughing. Diablo rubbed his pointed goatee with his right hand, while extending his left. He waited as each professor left their seat and knelt to kiss his large ruby ring. Numerous gold chains hung around his neck, and one in particular dangled his image. Jordan thought, *Maybe one day he'll get entangled in all those chains and hang himself.*

An unholy hush came over the auditorium as Diablo raised his gavel. He held it in midair for what seemed like eternity, then slammed it down so hard the entire assembly nearly jumped out of their seats. Professor Darius ran behind the curtain and dragged out the prince's special high chair and placed it behind the podium. All the professors resembled bumbling cartoon characters as they clumsily fussed over the prince, trying to make him comfortable in a chair that was way too small for a cape that was way too long.

Jordan chuckled and commented to his neighbor, "You'd think by now they'd get a bigger chair or that the Prince would get a shorter cape."

Tired of their fussing, Diablo waved them away. He sat for several minutes staring out of lifeless eyes at his captive and fearful audience. Jordan actually saw terror on the faces of the students, each wondering if today they would be called to the mike. But Jordan wasn't afraid of the prince and savored these opportunities to see him in person. He wanted to stand up and expose Diablo's real reason for the Gatherings, which had nothing to do with academics, but everything to do with exercising control over the students and faculty with fear and intimidation.

"Failure in any subject is unacceptable," Diablo bellowed, "especially Logic and Reason. It's for the sake of the Great Commission that you excel in these two courses."

Jordan felt sorry for the students who were visibly shaken. They knew nothing about a Great Commission, yet they were terrified. Some probably needed to relieve themselves, if they had not already done so.

After a lengthy, spine-chilling oration, Diablo further creeped out the trembling spectators by leaning back in his chair and closing his eyes. In a loud voice, he reminded them of his discerning powers, and that he planned to flush out every rebel, putting an end to the disloyalty the students had no idea existed.

Diablo searched the crowd for Jordan, then stared him down with utter contempt. Jordan knew today he would be the sacrificial lamb. He was warned last week that his rebellious behavior in Logic and Reason would be reported to the Establishment. No longer able to listen to the nonsense they were teaching, Jordan had raised questions for which Professor Nolita had no answers, making her look foolish.

She now stood and pranced across the stage, her stiletto heels making a terrible clacking sound on the hard wood floor. Her red-framed reading glasses hung on her long nose, and her hair was tied in its usual bun. Her expensive gray suit was way too short and way too tight.

"She must've raided her daughter's closet for that one," Jordan mumbled.

She handed the prince a folder and *click-clack*ed her way back to her seat. Diablo opened the file and took a few minutes to read the contents. Then he called on two students, who made their way to the mike at the front of the aisle nearest them. Their faces were washed in perspiration as they stammered and stuttered through a lengthy oral examination of Logic and Reason.

"Sir Jordan," the Prince shouted, "would *you* please step to the mike?"

Jordan slowly stood. He knew Diablo had purposely called the other students prior to calling him to give the impression that he was not singling him out, but Jordan knew better. The prince, having heard about Jordan's intelligence, was going to enjoy taunting this young smart-aleck. *The boy will have to be broken,* he thought.

"Jordan. That is your name?" Diablo asked.

You know it's my name, Jordan thought. *I'm a constant topic of conversation at your little round table.*

"How do you apply my concepts of logic and reason to your everyday life?" the Prince asked.

"I don't," Jordan replied curtly, staring at Diablo, whose eyes suddenly turned fiery red. Jordan wondered if anyone else noticed.

"What do you mean, you don't? How else is there to live? Neither you nor anyone else in this room can make it in my world without applying my logic and reason to your everyday lives. And that is the truth."

"I don't believe that is the truth, sir. You teach that there are no absolutes, but I live by absolutes every day and I'm okay."

"Well, how do you make choices, Jordan?"

"By the truth I know," he replied.

"And what truth is that, son? Certainly not absolutes. How can one set of absolutes benefit everyone when everyone's needs are different?"

"By everyone practicing standards and applying absolutes that are good for all mankind," Jordan replied.

"Nonsense," Diablo replied. "How is that possible?"

"By treating everyone the way you would want to be treated," Jordan replied. "Not by everyone deciding for themselves what is right or wrong or being kind only when it suits their own selfish desires. We should be people of integrity, helping family and friends when they're in need, even when it's not convenient...or when we're not appreciated."

"Everyone doesn't deserve to be treated the same," Diablo retorted.

Jordan ignored the Prince's ridiculous comeback. "I know you're an avid sports enthusiast," Jordan continued. "What if the rules were not understood and applied by all members on a playing team playing the same sport. There would be chaos on the field. Wouldn't you agree?"

Diablo glared at Jordan through bloodshot eyes, then cleared his throat.

"What if when I came to a stoplight and decided it meant 'go' for me because I was in a hurry?" Jordan continued. "I could cause irreparable harm to myself or someone else. Wouldn't you agree that applying absolutes in traffic keeps motorists and pedestrians safe?"

"So," he continued, "if absolutes are necessary in the two situations I've just cited, then it would stand to reason they would be necessary in every area of our lives as a guide to how we treat ourselves and each other. I believe—"

"We're not interested in what you believe," Diablo snapped. "This nation will never be governed by absolutes, but by the logic and reason I have established. I think too much of my people to demand that every individual follow the same set of standards and principles."

"Then why are we punished if we don't do things exactly as you command," Jordan asked, "or we don't think the way you demand us to think, or believe what you have instructed us to believe, whether we believe the commands are right or not? Your logic and reason have gone as far as spying on us in our own homes…sir. And we are imprisoned, or worse, if we dare to disagree with you. Wouldn't you say that your logic and reason are absolutes?"

There was a loud murmur in the room.

"Quiet," the Prince shouted, banging his gavel on the podium. He took out his handkerchief and wiped his brow. This was not going according to plan, and he was becoming weary of this young man. He tried changing the subject.

"Let's see how you're faring in calculus," Diablo stammered, hoping a difficult problem would embarrass Jordan.

"I'll answer your next question, Prince, if you'll answer mine," Jordan replied. Without waiting for permission, he charged ahead.

"Sir, this question has bothered me for some time. And if I'm right, and I think I am, it has puzzled many of the students and faculty in this room, as well as the entire nation of Keres."

This rebel has the nerve to challenge me, Diablo thought. "I'll answer any question you pose," he said arrogantly, as if he knew all there was to know about everything.

"You say you have great wisdom and know all things," Jordan stated.

The Prince looked around at his faculty and chuckled. "Go ahead, ask whatever you like," he replied arrogantly, pride dripping from his every word. "The students can benefit from my wisdom."

Jordan moved closer to the mike. "Sir, can you tell us who or what generates the bright light that shines across the river day and night?"

Sierra sat straight up in her chair, as a low murmur coursed throughout the assembly.

"Why," Jordan continued, "is this land covered with a mist that never dissipates? Why does the air we breathe reek with pollution and toxins? We're all under the impression that in addition to knowing all things, you can do all things. If this is true, then even as I speak, make this horrible mist go away and cause light to shine in Keres."

A loud buzz rose throughout the auditorium. Diablo was furiously banging his gavel on the podium to quiet the students. But Jordan continued talking above the din.

"Sir," he shouted into the mike, "I don't know about the others, but I would love to have just a little light every now and then."

The prince was desperately wiping sweat and banging his gavel.

Lowering his voice for effect, Jordan stated with feigned compassion, "Aren't you weary of this continuous haze? Tell us, where is the light for the nation of Keres?"

The room was so quiet you could hear a pin drop. The professors were stunned and sat with mouths agape. Never in the history of the learning institutions of Keres had the Prince been challenged in such a manner—or rendered speechless by anyone.

Suddenly a young man feeding on Jordan's courage shouted from the back of the auditorium, "Give us your answer, Prince." Sierra then yelled from across the aisle, "Where's our light?" Another student joined in: "Lift the mist." Then another and another, until pandemonium erupted. The entire faculty was in shock.

"It seems you're unable to answer my questions," Jordan stated. "However, I'll answer yours anyway. Fire away."

The Prince, caught completely off guard, stammered like a frightened child. "Young man, I can do all things, and don't you forget it. Do you not know who I am?"

Jordan knew exactly who he was, but now was not the time to expose him to the public. Instead, he stood waiting for the calculus question that never came. He turned to go back to his seat, then slowly returned to the mike.

"Sir, I understand the throne in your palace is constantly shrinking," he stated with false compassion. "Maybe my calculus expertise could redesign it so it would maintain its original size and construction. I can work wonders with wood."

The students, in pain from their futile attempts to hide their snickers, laughed until tears ran down their cheeks. The Prince was shocked and furious. No one was to know about his debacle of a throne. How dare this young snot embarrass him in front of his inferiors? He banged his gavel so hard it shattered, causing the students to howl even louder.

"THAT WILL BE ENOUGH!" Diablo screamed, as little beads of foam gathered at the corners of his mouth.

"Young man, my throne is perfectly fine. One more remark like that and you'll be in detention for eternity. Do you understand me, mister?" His crown sat askew his head as he growled, "Take your seat *now.*"

"Yes, sir," Jordan replied.

On his way back, he winked at Sierra, who smiled and quickly lowered her head.

The Prince was completely and utterly humiliated. He couldn't believe he had been taken down by a student. He fixed a stare on Jordan that could've melted concrete. *Now I'm certain this rogue is an enemy of the Establishment*, he thought. Diablo felt a migraine beginning and had to flee the building before his true self was revealed. There would be no explaining his repulsive transformation.

Almost running from the auditorium with his cape flying behind him, he rushed into the hallway and headed for the secret passageway. Tabor, his aide, was in hot pursuit, but the Prince was too far ahead. Tabor could only watch as the secret door closed in his face. The aide exited the building by the rear door, found the Prince trembling in the back lot, and hurried him into his limousine.

CHAPTER 9

The Throne

"Tabor, did you hear how that student disrespected me in front of the entire Gathering?" Diablo whined.

"Calm yourself," Tabor insisted. "You'll rupture a blood vessel."

"There's something familiar about him," Diablo continued, "but I can't put my finger on it. Find out who he is and why he wasn't afraid to publicly humiliate me. Nobody makes a fool of me."

"Yes, sir," Tabor replied. "When should I start?"

"YESTERDAY, YOU IDIOT!" the Prince shouted, putting his aching head between his legs to ward off the nausea.

When they arrived at his estate, the Prince fled to his throne room and locked the door. He didn't want Tabor or anyone else to know how vulnerable he was during these attacks. Grabbing his stomach, he fell to his knees, foam spewing from his mouth. His bulging, bloodshot eyes revolved to the back of his head, and he lay on the floor in a heap. Rolling back and forth, he growled like a beast as demonic creatures filled the room.

Morpheus, the creature in charge, stood four feet, eleven inches tall. His oversized, protruding eyes almost touched his extremely large ears, and his birdlike body was covered in dark brown feathers. And he reeked horribly. He touched the Prince's head with his long talon, and Diablo's torment subsided.

"I've been humiliated beyond measure," the Prince whimpered as Morpheus helped him to his throne. "You were there. I couldn't tell them the truth about the light. I would have been a laughingstock."

"Patience, Master," Morpheus stated in a low, croaky voice. "Your time is not yet. Soon, all will know your true identity, and then you'll be able to unleash your powers for your purposes."

"My throne was my private affair," Diablo whined as he struggled to get comfortable on the hard surface. "No one except my cabinet knew about this fiasco." He pulled the creature's disgusting face close to his. "Take care of things out there, Morpheus. Do you understand?"

"Yes, Master."

"And find someone capable of building me a throne worthy of who I am," he screeched.

Diablo was unaware that his shrinking throne was common knowledge, and that almost everyone in Keres was laughing behind his back. The original throne had been designed by the best master craftsmen in Keres. It was made from the finest cedar and smoothed and polished to perfection.

Its high back was ostentatiously carved and inlaid with the most expensive precious and semi-precious stones in the land. It was a beauty to behold.

The seat cushion measured ten inches high, was filled with down, and was covered with the finest red velvet material. The edges of the cushion were trimmed with double piping of costly gold threads.

Three crowns extended upward from the back of the throne and were encrusted with rubies and onyx. The left and right crowns were twelve inches high, and the crown in the middle, sixteen, adding additional height to the already massive chair.

The arms of the throne were covered in the same red velvet as the seat, and the feet of the chair resembled lions' paws. It was spectacular.

The Prince had spared no expense when it came to his throne. It had to be as magnificent as Uriel's, his eternal nemesis.

Yet no one, not even his guards or the builders themselves, could explain why one day the massive chair was barely large enough for a child.

This once remarkable throne now consisted of two small gray slabs of concrete, one for the Prince's bottom, the other for his back. Having no armrests on which to lean, his arms dangled at his sides like a monkey. It was a pitiful sight.

In addition, the three crowns on the back of the chair, symbolizing the Prince as all-powerful, were reduced to three small dunce caps. He looked hideous on his counterfeit throne, but no one dared say so.

The finest and most expensive builders and designers in the land were summoned time and again to "get it right, or else," but to no avail. Try as they may, the throne reverted back to the childlike seat.

Believing it was a conspiracy to make him look foolish, the Prince imprisoned the craftsmen, replaced the guards, and stationed new sentinels outside the throne room day and night, hoping to catch the perpetrators.

Presently, Tabor was banging on the door. "Are you all right, my prince?" he shouted. The creatures in the room instantly disappeared.

"Go away," Diablo bellowed.

The pain was getting worse. He reached into his pocket and pulled out a jewel-encrusted pillbox and swallowed a small black tablet. He knew his migraines were a curse from Uriel that began after his exile to Keres. Whenever he became aggravated or frustrated, they began at the base of his neck and slowly ascended to his brain, often preceding his horrific transformation. Leaning on one knee, and with sweat running down his face, he cursed Uriel. "Once I return to Fa'i," he whispered, "I'll be free of this damnable affliction."

His secretary, Miranda, was knocking on the door. "What do you want?" Diablo shouted, annoyed at being disturbed once again.

"The chief general is here to see you. He says it's urgent."

"Show him in," Diablo said, glad his migraine was diminishing. "How's the family?" he asked when the general entered, feigning interest.

"Very well, thank you. And how are you?" the general asked, noticing the Prince's washed-out and disheveled appearance as he bowed to kiss his ring.

"Couldn't be better. Now, what can I do for you?" He wanted the general to state his business and leave before his migraine intensified again.

"Last Friday evening, an Organism in Ward Seven was disconnected. All Organisms in that district are now being tested at the Agency to determine if it was a mechanical failure or a lone citizen's tampering. Once the inspections are completed, you'll receive my full report."

"Do you know whose home it was?"

"Janu Calder's, sir. And if his Organism was purposely disconnected, the entire family will be punished to the fullest extent of the law."

The general despised Janu and Ariana. He knew they'd feigned their loyalty to Diablo years ago in order to be released from the Deprogramming Camp. And ever since, he'd been looking for an opportunity to imprison them once and for all.

"Thank you, General. By the way, have you considered that if it was citizen tampering, someone inside the CCA had to have aided them?" The Prince waved his hand, indicating the meeting was over.

"It's always a pleasure to serve you," the general stated. His heels made a disturbing noise on the highly polished floor as he left the room, intensifying Diablo's pain.

"Idiot," Diablo screamed when the door closed. "Wait until the investigation is complete, *then* give me a report. That man will be the ruin of me."

Diablo sat back on his tiny throne, hoping the medicine would soon take effect. But having nowhere to rest his arms, he screamed, "Miranda, find someone to fix my throne…NOW."

It was Saturday evening, and as Izaiah gulped down the last bite of his ham and cheese sandwich, he glanced at the clock for the third time. If he didn't hurry, he would miss his induction into the PsyOps' secret society. He had received a call yesterday morning that Grand Master Nuri would pick him up at seven tonight, and he didn't want to be late.

It was three weeks ago, the day after Izaiah's fifteenth birthday, when Jackson had invited him to dinner at Spartica's Bistro, where, for one price, Izaiah could eat all he wanted without sending Jackson to the poorhouse.

"So, what did you want to talk to me about?" Izaiah had asked after the busboy filled their water glasses.

"I have something important to tell you," Jackson had said, "and I think you'll be pleased. I've presented your name for membership into an elite secret society."

"What is the society's purpose?"

"The basic requirements for membership are to believe and obey every law of the Establishment without question, with a willingness to fight for Diablo's Cause. In addition, you must have a high IQ and good academic grades, which you possess. The Society offers many benefits, but you must be endorsed by a member in good standing. Now that you're fifteen, the general and I would like to sponsor you."

Izaiah was so honored he missed that Jackson never revealed the organization's purpose. Jackson's true motive, however, was to obtain Izaiah's allegiance to PsyOps, obligating him to "tell all" about his parents.

"Who are the PsyOps?" Izaiah asked.

"They're men, women, boys, and girls, ages fifteen and older, from every background and walk of life."

"Girls can join too?" Izaiah asked, not sure he wanted to be part of anything involving a bunch of giggling females.

"Girls have just as much to contribute to the association as boys do," Jackson replied.

"Is Sierra a member?" Izaiah asked.

"No, and you mustn't say anything to her about this."

"So, what do I have to do to join?" Izaiah asked, satisfied now that his sister would not be looking over his shoulder.

"Fill out this application, and if you pass probation, you'll be ceremonially inducted. You'll meet your brothers and sisters in the faith and be given a new name. Meanwhile, the society will be watching you closely."

"For what?" Izaiah had asked.

"Just stay out of trouble," Jackson warned. "One more thing is required."

"What's that?" Izaiah asked.

"You must never reveal your membership to your family or friends. We don't want them involved in matters they wouldn't understand. This is your life to live as you see fit. Can you handle that?"

"Yes," Izaiah replied, pleased that Jackson considered him mature enough to make his own decisions.

By the time dinner was served, Jackson had described an important and mysterious organization Izaiah couldn't wait to be part of.

Subsequently, he endured and passed probation. And although tonight was to be the proudest night of his young life, he couldn't share it with anyone.

Unbeknownst to Janu and Ariana, their son would soon be inducted into a very powerful, dangerous, and demonic organization.

Izaiah was now nervous and excited as he stepped into the shower. He had hoped the hot water cascading over his body would calm his nerves, but it didn't.

He frantically searched for the right outfit to wear, but his room looked like a tornado had hit. Still he was no closer to making a decision.

He would've called Jackson regarding the proper attire, but he'd been dodging him. His mentor had been pressing for more information about his parents, and he was not yet ready to give him any information.

Suddenly, fear gripped him like a vise as he put on his navy-blue blazer. *What if Jackson already knows about my parents' plan to escape Keres and he asks me to confirm it?* Izaiah worried. His fears were warranted. Once a PsyOp, he'd be required to report all acts of rebellion and treason by anyone, including family or friends, or be considered a traitor himself.

A horn blew, and he ran down the steps two at a time. He yelled goodbye to his parents and dashed out the front door.

"Wow," he remarked when he spotted the black stretch limousine waiting for him several doors away from his home.

Jonas, the chauffeur, was about six foot four, and from what Izaiah could tell, around two hundred and fifty pounds of muscle. He wore a black tuxedo with a white shirt and black bowtie, and he stood like a statue holding the car door open. A black derby donned his head, and his boots were spit-shined. He helped Izaiah into the back seat, where Grand Master Nuri was waiting.

The Grand Master introduced himself. "Don't be offended," he said as they pulled away from the curb, "but I must blindfold you until we reach our destination." Izaiah was already nervous and being blindfolded didn't help. Jonas made numerous turns and U-turns on purpose, and after what seemed like hours, Izaiah was told to remove the scarf.

In front of them was a gothic-looking house covered in creeping ivy. It stood three stories high, and it appeared sinister as it towered into the night sky. The lights covering the dome roof stood out against the darkness. With wide eyes, Izaiah observed several odd-looking creatures perched atop the steeples. Suddenly, they began screeching. No one but Izaiah seemed concerned.

Jonas pressed several numbers on the keypad in front of the entrance and the wrought-iron gate opened at a snail's pace. He drove to the side of the building, then assisted Grand Master Nuri and Izaiah from the limo.

"Grand Master," Izaiah said, "I thought I saw some odd-looking creatures on top of the house."

"They're special sentinels that bring good luck," Master Nuri replied. "You'll be seeing more of them in the future, then they won't seem so odd."

Master Nuri swiped his key card at the door, and then placed his left palm on the scanner. The huge black door opened, and Izaiah was ushered into a large vestibule and told to wait.

He crammed his sweaty palms into his pants pockets and wondered if Jackson and the general would be there to witness his induction.

Grand Master Nuri returned and handed Izaiah a red tie, which he then helped him put on. He ushered him into the main hall, where he was met by a pretty young girl about his age dressed in white. The young hostess took Izaiah by the arm, and, as if gliding on glass, slowly ushered him across the highly polished black granite floor to a table in the center of the room. She positioned him behind a black placard on which his name was written in gold calligraphy. He was impressed and felt important.

The five boys and six girls at his table had various looks on their faces. Some appeared smug and self-righteous, pretending they belonged, while others looked terrified. Some, like Izaiah, were in awe of their surroundings and were checking out the magnificence of the room, the likes of which they had never seen before. *Sierra loves pretty things*, Izaiah thought. *If only she could see this place.*

He was struck with wonder at the ornate interior, whose walls were covered with gold lame fabric. And the red cushion on which he sat was so thick Izaiah thought his bottom might get lost in it.

The snow-white tablecloths and napkins symbolizing Diablo's purity were starched and pressed to perfection. A large black urn was filled with blood red roses, supposedly symbolizing the blood the Prince had shed for his people. It sat in the middle of the table emitting a strange, intoxicating aroma.

The busboys were mirror images of Jonas in their attire, and the pretty waitresses wore red satin dresses with white lace-trimmed aprons starched so stiff they could probably stand by themselves. Izaiah's hostess removed the beautiful red charger plate from beneath the mother of pearl dinnerware, unfolded the napkin, and placed it in his lap. Clearly, he was in unfamiliar territory as he continued surveying the room. The many outstanding elements were almost too much to absorb. In addition to the magnificent crystal chandeliers hanging from the ceiling, lighted wall sconces in the shape of skulls were placed strategically throughout the room, each emitting a disturbing ambiance.

A large oval mosaic was inlaid in the middle of the floor, and the glow from the fireplaces situated at both ends of the room cast a brilliant glimmer on the stonework. Huge banners with life-sized portraits of Prince Diablo and the Masters hung from the dome ceiling, the varying heights indicating rank and level of importance. *What a strange but magnificent room,* Izaiah thought.

The grand auditorium with its many balconies seemingly suspended in midair encircled the entire circumference of the room, and all fifteen hundred seats were quickly filled. The Grand Masters were clad in black velvet robes trimmed in purple satin, while the lower-ranked Masters wore royal blue robes trimmed in gold satin. Tassels dangled on the left sides of their matching berets, and their right forefingers were adorned with large rings inlaid with diamonds.

While the well-dressed crowd buzzed with excited anticipation, most of the inductees at Izaiah's table had sweaty palms and nervous twitches. Next to each plate was a small black and red booklet describing the nation's history and Diablo's feats and accomplishments, including the many sacrifices he had made for the people of Keres…mostly lies.

To try to ease the tension, Izaiah introduced himself, but no one responded. His hostess appeared from nowhere.

"Sir," she whispered, "inductees are not allowed to speak until given permission to do so."

"Sorry," Izaiah whispered.

Grand Master Nuri and the general were seated on the first tier of the east balcony eyeing Izaiah. There was much hustle and bustle, as hundreds of young boys and girls moved in synch to serve dinner to every attendee. Older boys wearing white jackets with black towels draped over their arms poured water into alabaster goblets trimmed in solid gold. The base of the ornate chalice was shaped like a small pedestal and was so heavy Izaiah held it with both hands to keep from spilling the contents. He had never witnessed such opulence.

Waitresses came behind the busboys and placed soup and salads in front of the inductees. Izaiah, who normally hated salad, was starving and admitted it looked appetizing.

The first-course dishes were collected with a flurry, and things became even more of a blur. Waiters appeared from everywhere with large platters of steak, rabbit, chicken, baked potatoes, and caramelized carrots. Supplementary waiters filled additional goblets with cranberry juice, during which a tray of assorted breads, rolls, and butter appeared. And so it went, until everyone in the room was served. It was a feast for a king.

Izaiah was about to attack his food with a vengeance when someone he couldn't see in the balcony cried out, "Raise your glasses to the prince of princes," the crier shouted, "and soon to be king of kings. May your kingdom reign forever, and may you live throughout eternity."

"Hear, hear," the assembly roared.

While they were yet dining, Grand Master Nomed, the emcee for the night, stepped to the mike. "Fellow Masters, members, and new recruits, Prince Diablo is from everlasting to everlasting. Long live the Prince."

Pandemonium broke out as the assembly stood and sang "Hail to the Prince", a song that neither inductee knew. Izaiah could not have cared less; his stomach was growling.

Once the bedlam ceased and everyone took their seats again, Grand Master Nomed continued, "Brothers and sisters, tonight we will induct twelve new recruits into our elite society. They have successfully passed their probationary period and come highly recommended by outstanding members of our privileged community." Everyone applauded.

"At the conclusion of our meal, the induction ceremonies will begin, after which these recruits will be members of our beloved PsyOp society." The applause was deafening.

Just as Izaiah was about to eat the last piece of his steak, he noticed Jackson watching him from across the room. He gave a half-hearted wave, and Jackson responded in kind.

The dishes were quickly cleared, and Grand Master Nomed revisited the mike again. He called the meeting to order and asked Master Stonemack to join him at the podium.

"Tonight is very important for these young recruits," Master Stonemack declared in a deep voice. "It is a night they will never forget. They will witness and experience things they never thought imaginable—things only we, the chosen, are privy to. We continually seek young men and women with their genius and leadership abilities to play a strategic role in our privileged world."

Izaiah wondered if he was talking about him.

"They've been under close scrutiny," Master Stonemack continued, "and have been found worthy for the important tasks that lie ahead. Each recruit will be introduced by first name only, as family names have no significance in our sacred culture. And, as you know, they will soon be given new names shared only within the society."

The applause was thunderous.

Grand Master Nuri handed the recruits' personal profiles to Master Stonemack, who asked each recruit to stand. He described their talents, abilities, academic IQs, athleticism, and most importantly, the deeds they had performed proving them worthy of membership.

"When I call your name," he continued, "take your place on the floor around the perimeter of the inner circle."

"Abraham," he shouted, "come forth. Nigel, come forth. Benoit, come forth." When Izaiah's name was called, he could barely move. He was sure everyone could hear his knees knocking as they waited for him to take his place beside the others. Finally, he was standing with his peers.

When the last recruit was summoned, the Grand Masters converged onto the main floor and formed a circle behind them. Then the Masters, except for Master Stonemack, came down and stood behind the Grand Masters, followed by the Senior Council. The remaining members congregated behind the Senior Council until the entire first floor was packed.

Master Stonemack shouted, "Recruits, we are a special breed elected by our god. And when being a

PsyOp becomes part of your soul, you'll understand why we live and would die for our creed."

In the center of the inner circle was a large, brilliant medallion comprised of purple, gold, and black granite, and inlaid with precious stones. If Izaiah had been in the balcony, he would have noticed the stones formed the letter "D" for Diablo. A three-foot wrought-iron fence overlaid with gold encircled the medallion to keep members away.

Master Stonemack asked for a moment of silence in reverence to Prince Diablo. Then once again, everyone sang "Hail to the Prince". It was quite a ceremony, and Izaiah was proud to be a part.

Suddenly, the already-low lights were dimmed further, and strange music began to play. Everyone except the recruits began to sway to the slow, rhythmic beat. Not wanting to appear obvious, Izaiah began to move slightly. He peered across the room and saw that Jackson was swaying, chanting, and staring straight at him with a faraway look in his eyes.

Someone from the back of the crowd shouted, "Diablo is eternal. His kingdom is from everlasting to everlasting. There will be no end to his dominion. He will rule and reign forever, for he is lord."

The assembly began chanting the mantra nonstop. It was like nothing Izaiah had experienced before, and suddenly he felt uncomfortable. He remembered his parents' revelation about the king across the river, that his kingdom was eternal. Not that he believed any of that nonsense, but still he found that he couldn't chant the mantra. He finally lowered his head and gave the appearance of unity by mouthing something senseless.

Master Stonemack ordered the members to join hands as a sign of solidarity to Diablo and his Great Commission.

"Victory for our prince," he continually shouted.

Suddenly, the tempo increased, and the crowd gyrated faster. Grand Master Nuri put his hand on Izaiah's shoulder, and suddenly he, too, was moving to the rhythm. The music lowered, and someone put a mobile mike in Grand Master Nuri's hand. "Fellow PsyOps," he said, "the time is fast approaching when we will secure victory for the prince of this world." He hesitated for effect.

"I promise," he continued, "your efforts will not be in vain and your labor of love will not go unrewarded." He took a deep breath. "Now, close your eyes and envision our prince reigning victoriously in our new world."

Izaiah had no idea what the Grand Master was talking about, as he closed one eye but kept the other slightly ajar.

"Diablo, Diablo, Diablo," the PsyOps chanted in a low, rhythmic tone. When they had worked themselves into an emotional frenzy, the floor began to quake, and Izaiah opened both eyes wide. The center of the circle revolved, and the medallion uncoiled. Seemingly rising from the bowels of the earth, Prince Diablo's head ascended to midair.

Izaiah didn't know where the rest of his body was, but the high-tech trickery was fascinating…if indeed that's what it was.

Diablo's eyes were flaming red, and the winged creatures outside howled as if they were being skinned alive. The ruckus was unnerving as smoke billowed everywhere. Diablo's head hanging suspended above the assembly made quite a spectacle.

The entire congregation went mad, and the noise was deafening. Some even wept as they chanted, "Long live the prince. He is lord."

Diablo's skull was in flames, and Izaiah waited for its ashes to fall to the floor, but they never did. Instead, a voice like a rushing river began to speak from the head.

"Welcome, fellow PsyOps and comrades for the Great Commission. This is an important time in our history. The day is fast approaching when we will march against our enemies, pursue and overtake them, and recover what rightfully belongs to us."

Izaiah was dumbstruck.

"We have enemies who want us to fail," the Prince hissed. "Tonight, I need your pledge of allegiance that you will keep a watchful eye and a listening ear for anyone who would oppose us, even your friends and families, your neighbors, coworkers, and schoolmates. No one is exempt.

"Success can only be realized if we unite," he insisted. "Remain strong in your commitment to me," he whispered, "and I will never leave you nor forsake you. You've been chosen, called by my name, and I have sanctified you and set you apart for such a time as this."

"What we will accomplish in the very near future will not be easy," he declared. "But if you put your faith and trust in me, and obey all that I command, victory…will…be…ours."

The assembly sent up a roar that shook the foundation as they watched the head descend back into the abyss. Everyone stood staring into the hole hoping the Prince would reappear. But Izaiah wanted to run. He decided, however, to at least pretend he was as excited as everyone else, but he was truly terrified.

Finally, when Grand Master Nomed realized the head would not reappear, he asked everyone to return to their seats.

There was much excitement as everyone found their places and tried to calm down. But Izaiah, still stunned, kept gazing at the medallion in the floor, hoping the talking cranium would not reappear.

Grand Master Nomed spoke to the recruits in an awestruck voice. “You have just witnessed a sacred phenomenon that cannot be shared with anyone. Do you understand?”

“Yes,” the stunned recruits replied.

“Each of you will be given a life coach who will guide you in our way of life. Your covenant with your mentor can never be broken. Finally, you will be given an assignment that will ultimately test your loyalty to our society. Once you have completed your task successfully, you will receive your new names, and rewards and benefits most only dream of.” He raised his glass and shouted, “Once a PsyOp, always a PsyOp.”

The meeting adjourned at ten o’clock, but Izaiah didn’t stick around for the meet and greet; he left quickly to avoid Jackson. He knew that because of his big mouth, he would be obligated to report his parents’ plan of escape.

While waiting for Jonas to bring the limo around, he suddenly felt a hand on his shoulder. “You’re not avoiding me, are you?” Jackson asked.

“Of…of course not,” Izaiah stammered.

“You’ve been a hard man to catch lately,” Jackson stated.

“I’m cramming for exams,” Izaiah replied.

“We must talk,” Jackson stated.

“Is next Friday good?” Izaiah offered.

"The Diner, tomorrow at six," Jackson replied brusquely, "and don't be late. Since I will be your life coach, I'll expect complete honesty from you."

Maybe it was the bizarre evening, but this was a side of Jackson Izaiah hadn't seen before, and he felt uneasy. He knew what his mentor wanted, but he needed more time. Before tomorrow's rendezvous, he would have to devise a believable story about his parents.

CHAPTER 10

Eavesdropping

The next morning, Ariana dragged Janu out onto their bedroom balcony to talk privately.

"We're running out of time, Janu. Can we disconnect the Organism again to speak with the children about returning to Fa'i?"

"They're listening and watching our every move since the first disconnection," he replied. "Plus, I don't trust Izaiah right now. He hasn't spoken to us since we first mentioned Fa'i."

"By the way," he continued, "Malakh has agreed to coach us until we're sure of our assignments. Only then will we move forward with our plan. It won't be easy, but it'll be worth it when we're back in Fa'i. I'm also telling Sierra the truth about Jackson today, and my purpose for allowing her to date him."

Meanwhile, Sierra was on her way downstairs when she saw her parents whispering on their balcony. She didn't mean to eavesdrop. But as she entered their bedroom, she heard her name mentioned and hid behind the armoire.

"Your little girl is stronger than you think, and stronger than she thinks," Ariana said. "Any baby that survived in my womb what she did is tough as nails."

"I hope you're right," Janu replied.

"Mom, Dad," Sierra called.

"We're out here," Ariana shouted.

Sierra wondered if this was the best time to tell her parents about Jordan.

"Good morning, sweetheart," Janu said. His daughter was twice as beautiful on the inside as she was on the outside, unlike most teenage Keresians who seemed to lack values and respect.

"Have a minute?" she asked.

"Of course," Ariana replied. "But before you begin, we know that you and your brother have a million questions about the revelation."

Sierra chuckled. "You bet, but that's not what I want to talk to you about."

"Then what is it?" Ariana asked.

"I met a boy I like a lot, and I want to invite him for dinner," she replied in one breath.

"What about Jackson?" Janu asked, trying to mask his joy.

"Jackson's selfish," Sierra replied. "He's possessive and mostly talks about himself, when he's not quizzing me about you and Mom. And I don't trust him."

"My new friend is Jordan," she continued. "He's fun to be with, a good study partner, and a great musician."

"Who knew?" Janu said, smiling.

"I know you'll like him," she said. "But there's one problem. You know how Z feels about Jackson, and how strange he's been acting lately."

"I found him at Sports Junction the morning after your revelation talking to Jackson. And when he saw me, he clammed up. I believe he was going to tell our secret, but I think I stopped him in time."

"He trusts that guy way too much," Janu said.

"I don't want him blabbing to Jackson about Jordan before I do," Sierra said.

"He's planning a sleepover at Korey and Dazmin's next Friday," Ariana said. "Maybe we can have Jordan over then."

"Thank you," Sierra replied. She hugged her parents hard, tears welling up in her eyes. "I would die if I lost either of you. Promise you won't do anything stupid," she whispered in their ears.

Thankfully, she couldn't see the worried looks on their faces. Returning their family to Fa'i meant putting the two people they loved the most in harm's way.

"Sierra, I have something to tell you," Janu whispered. "I would never intentionally hurt you, and whatever I've done or will do is for the good of this family. You are my princess, and I hope you can forgive me for what I'm about to say."

"You're scaring me," Sierra replied.

Janu cleared his throat. "Right after you agreed to date Jackson, I was informed that he was infiltrating our family through his relationship with you to find out what we were up to and report it to the general."

"How does the general know we're up to anything?" Sierra asked, taking Jackson's betrayal better than her parents had imagined. "I wasn't aware we were that important to him," Sierra said.

"We've always been anti-Establishment," Janu continued, "and the general's afraid we might escape and warn Uriel about Diablo's Great Commission."

"Do you know what the Great Commission is?" Sierra asked.

"Yes, but it's best if you don't. When I discovered Jackson's intentions, I was furious," Janu continued. "Your mother wanted me to tell you, but I didn't want you involved. I thought if he came to trust you, he might unknowingly reveal something that could help us with our cause."

"What is our cause?" Sierra asked, as if she didn't already know.

"Returning to Fa'i," Janu remarked.

"And how do you plan on doing that without getting us all thrown in prison…or worse?" Sierra calmly asked.

"I have inside help, someone I've grown to trust."

Sierra tried to appear calm. "But how do you know he's trustworthy, Dad? He could be playing you like Jackson played me."

"I personally vetted him," Janu replied. "He made it possible for me to disable our Organism so we could share our revelation with you and your brother."

Sierra was trembling. "No disrespect, Dad, but this is utter madness. Is your cause worth putting the whole family at risk? Mom, what do you think of this inside man…what's his name?"

"I trust your dad's judgment," Ariana replied, "and his name is Malakh. We're going home, Sierra, by any means possible."

Sierra hesitated. "Well, it's evident you're serious, so how can I help? And Dad, I never liked Jackson that much anyway. He was just somebody to hang out with. But thanks. Now I feel less guilty about dumping him."

"That's my girl," Janu replied. He then revealed their plan of escape and their individual assignments.

"What about Z?" Sierra asked, fearing her brother had no intention of cooperating.

"I'll handle him," Janu responded.

"Meanwhile, I'll try to find out from Jackson when this Great Commission will be launched," Sierra said. "Maybe we can be out of here before then."

"I don't know, Precious," Janu replied. "We're dealing with an evil force, and I wouldn't forgive myself if anything happened to you."

"You said I was strong, so let me do my part. And I'd love to meet your King."

Janu had waited so long for this moment. He couldn't speak lest he sob like a baby. But only half the battle was won; Izaiah was not yet on board.

When Sierra left, Janu admitted he was concerned he hadn't heard from Malakh since disconnecting the Organism.

"I know it's not safe to contact him at work," Ariana said, "but maybe you can reach him at home."

"Our wires could be tapped, and our homes bugged," Janu replied. "And Malakh must remain undercover if our plan is to succeed. But this waiting is making me crazy."

Meanwhile, the general had assigned additional Enforcers to track Janu's every move. He also hoped the ongoing investigation would reveal intentional Organism tampering; then he could imprison the whole family.

"Never send a boy to do a man's job," he griped on his way down to supper one night. "Jackson, invite your girlfriend to dinner Friday night, seven o'clock sharp," the general commanded.

Sierra was in her bedroom staring at the light across the river when her mobile chimed. Expecting Jordan's call, she dove for the device.

"Hi," Jackson said.

"Hi yourself," Sierra replied.

"You sound disappointed," he remarked.

"Just tired, I guess. What's up?"

"I haven't seen much of you lately and was wondering if you'd come to dinner Friday night at my house."

She hated lying, but this might be the opportunity she needed.

"I'd love to," she replied.

"I talked our cook into preparing something special," Jackson declared.

"What is it?" Sierra asked.

Having just made up the "something special", he answered, "It's a surprise. Would you mind driving yourself? I have an errand to run before dinner."

"What time should I be there?" she asked.

"Is seven okay?"

"Seven's good," Sierra replied. She inputted the address into her mobile and said goodnight.

With a plan in mind, she rang Monica.

"Hey, you," she said.

"Hey, yourself," Monica replied turning on the vision screen.

"I desperately need your help," Sierra stated. "But you have to swear on our sisterhood that you won't breathe a word of what I'm going to share, not even to your dad."

"Can you be a little more mysterious?" Monica quipped.

"Meet me at the river tomorrow after school," Sierra instructed, "and don't tell anybody where you're going."

She's certainly been acting strange lately, Monica thought as she disconnected. *She's even canceled several trips to the mall this week. What's next?*

Monica was suddenly drawn to the light across the river, convinced her mom, who had been taken from them over a year ago, was reaching out to her from the light. She had tried numerous times to discuss Elisabeth with her dad, but he always quickly changed the subject, leaving her feeling lonely and abandoned. When the pain was too heavy, she would sometimes lie on her parents' bed, where she could still smell her mother's sweet aroma.

The next day, as Monica left her last period Trig class, she spotted Sierra heading for the exit, laughing with a dreamy stranger.

"So that's what's been going on behind my back," she mumbled. Hurt that Sierra hadn't confided in her about her new relationship, she tore out of the parking structure, met up with Sierra at the river, and climbed into her car.

"I saw you and your new boyfriend after class today," Monica said with all the sarcasm she could emit. "Care to explain?"

"What new boyfriend?" Sierra asked.

"Don't play dumb with me, Sierra. I saw you leaving Prep with dreamy eyes today."

"He's just a friend I like a lot," Sierra said.

"Where was I while you were 'falling in like' with this creature?" Monica asked, her arms flailing in every direction.

The girls had decided not to use the word "love" where a boy was concerned. A lot of their friends were compromising their standards in the name of love, and by the next week, they would be in "love" with somebody else.

"Well…what's his name?" Monica prodded.

"Jordan," Sierra replied. "I met him at the river."

"You were falling all over him laughing," Monica countered. "Seems like more than a friend to me."

"He's in my Logic and Reason class," Sierra replied, "but I never noticed him before. He says he noticed me because I was different from the other girls."

"What a crock," Monica teased. "Does he have a brother? I'll settle for a second cousin, as cute as he is."

"Sorry, he's an only child," Sierra teased.

"What are you going to do about Jackson?" Monica asked. "He thinks you're his property."

"I'm going to tell him," Sierra replied. "Maybe you can help me."

"No way," Monica replied. "I'm not getting in the middle of this mess. The fallout could be dangerous. But you should tell him before someone else does. Do your parents know about Jordan?" she asked.

"Yes. He's coming to dinner to meet them."

"Meeting the parents. Must be serious," Monica quipped.

"Not really. But he's super intelligent and has the best sense of humor."

"I saw that at Prep today," Monica reiterated. "Seriously, Sierra, be careful. Jackson can be really mean at times."

"You know what's funny, Monica? Mom and Dad are happier than I am about the breakup. Go figure."

"And when do I get to meet Prince Charming?"

"Soon, I promise. Enough about Jordan," Sierra said. "There's something important I need to tell you."

"I'm listening."

"You're my best friend in the whole world, and I couldn't love you more if we were joined at the hip," Sierra began.

Monica had needed all the love she could get since her mother's disappearance. Teary-eyed, she said, "Thanks, I needed that. Not to mention I know all your dirty little secrets. Now, stop stalling, my stomach is growling."

"This will sound unbelievable…downright crazy," Sierra said, "but hear me out."

"Get on with it. You can trust me with your life."

"I just might have to," Sierra mumbled.

"Now you're scaring me," Monica replied.

"Monica, you know the bright light we've been fascinated with since childhood?"

"I'm drawn to it every night before I go to sleep," Monica replied. "I feel the light is Mom watching over me."

"I know who the light is," Sierra said.

"Who the light is?" Monica questioned.

Sierra portrayed Fa'i, the City of Eternal Light, to Monica. She described the blue-green meadows, the birds and animals, the king in his splendor, and the palace in which he lives. Lastly, she revealed the restoration powers of the River of Life, which keep the inhabitants from growing old.

"And, Monica, guess where the light comes from?"

Monica was speechless.

"From King Uriel himself," Sierra announced. "He is the light. Day and night, he lights the entire kingdom with his brilliance. There's never any darkness or haze in Fa'i like we have here in Keres. Oh, and another thing. My parents originated from there, and they're taking us back to meet their king."

When Sierra finally came up for air, Monica's mouth was agape.

"Oookay," she finally said. "I've saved some money, and I'll see that you and your mom and dad get the help you need. And I take back every negative thing I've said about you lately." She reached out to hug her friend.

"Stop that," Sierra said. "Z and I reacted the same way when we heard it."

"You mean Izaiah is involved in this madness too? Well, he'll get treatment, as well. I'll talk to my dad when I get home."

"You'll do no such thing. You'll put my family's life in danger. Swear you won't mention a word, or I'll drag you to the river and drown you."

"Okay. Okay," Monica replied. "But you can't stop me from worrying."

"Worry on your own time. I need you this Friday night. I've been invited to Jackson's for dinner and I have a plan. Are you up for a little covert operation?"

"I'm always up for a little excitement," Monica replied, rubbing her hands together.

"Dad plans to escape Keres," Sierra said. "And if you keep your mouth shut, the Establishment won't know about it until we're long gone."

Amazed and fearful, Monica agreed. Sierra filled her in on the details of her plan and warned her of the possible dangers.

"This is better than the movies," Monica stated.

"Only difference is that this could be a real life-or-death drama," Sierra remarked. "One slipup and we could be arrested or put to death. We must take into account every contingency, so we're not caught."

"My dad has a late-night meeting tonight," Monica stated. "We can finalize the details on my back porch so we're not overheard by the Establishment."

"Good," Sierra replied. "And, Monica, if you breathe a word of this to anyone, we'll die. And I mean that literally."

Monica drove home envisioning lights and kings and palaces… *OH MY.*

CHAPTER 11

The Dinner

It was Friday night, and Sierra's mission was foremost in her mind. She purposefully donned a black pinstriped pantsuit, turtleneck sweater, and boots.

She looked sophisticated with her brown eyes highlighted, her full lips enhanced with a bit of lipstick, and her curly hair pulled atop her head. She glanced in the mirror and headed downstairs.

Janu and Ariana weren't happy about the invitation. And had they known their daughter's true motive, they would have forbidden her to go. This was not a game, and the general was no one to be played with. But, they reasoned, if anyone could convince the general they weren't up to something, Sierra could.

"I'm leaving," she announced. "I'll be home around ten."

"Be careful, sweetheart," Janu stated. "Only eat from the dishes they eat from."

"Dad..."

"I mean it. Let the others eat first. And only drink bottled water. They should have it, they're all health nuts."

She kissed and hugged her parents as if she might not see them again and headed for the door.

"Don't trust the general," Janu continued, "and watch his every move. He's an evil man. Your mother and I know firsthand."

"May I go now?" Sierra asked.

"And don't do anything stupid," Janu added.

That she couldn't promise. Her plan tonight had stupid written all over it.

Meanwhile, Monica donned her bomber jacket and weather boots, then placed the essentials she would need in her backpack. She was surveying her bedroom as if she might not see it again, when she was unexpectedly drawn to the light.

"I know I've done some dumb things," she said to the radiance, "but this has *got* to be the dumbest." She flung her backpack over her shoulder and left the room.

The night was eerie as the wind howled and a light rain began to fall. Sierra slowly turned onto Karrob Circle and pulled in front of the general's large and impressive home. She pressed the buzzer on the huge gate, and it slid back slowly on its track. She parked in the circular driveway, exited her vehicle, walked nervously up the steps to the large portico, and rang the bell.

Several odd-looking creatures were perched on the streetlamp and the rooftop. She wanted to leave, but too much was at stake. The creatures let out a chorus of ear-piercing wails, and Sierra was sure the knocking of her knees could be heard behind the large double doors.

"Good evening, miss," the tall, gray-haired man said as he opened the door.

"Goo…good evening, my name is Si…Sierra," she stammered.

"I know," he said. "I'm pleased to meet you. Come in. I'll take your coat, then escort you to the parlor."

Sierra had never seen such opulence. The foyer was rotund in shape, and her reflection glowed in the brown and cream granite floors. The walls were covered with creamy sateen fabric, and breathtaking art and tapestries hung from them. The large, oval-shaped yellow and burgundy throw rug appeared hand-painted. The light from the crystal chandelier hanging in the center of the room bounced off the water in the fountain directly beneath. Artifacts were displayed on gilded pedestals, or were they solid gold? Sierra couldn't tell. Everything appeared so luxurious.

"Right this way, miss."

"What's your name?" Sierra asked.

"Barnard, miss."

The sound of her footsteps echoed throughout the large corridor as she followed the slow-walking man. Jackson and the general stood as she entered the parlor. She wiped her sweaty palms on her jacket and reminded herself of why she was there.

Jackson's mother, Moselle, was sitting on the window seat looking somewhat preoccupied. She nodded, but she did not get up. Sierra was glad the general didn't extend his hand because hers were wet with perspiration.

"Come in and have a seat," he said.

He looked handsome in his black dinner jacket, and he truly resembled Jackson, except for his perfectly trimmed moustache.

"Good to see you again, General," Sierra said calmly. "How have you been?"

"Wonderful," he replied. "Glad you could come. I told my wife we previously met at Jackson's Letter Day celebration, and she wanted to meet you, too."

Sierra smiled, but she knew exactly why she had been summoned.

"I've been dying to meet you, too, Mrs. Armon," Sierra said, using a poor choice of words. "Your home is marvelous. Did you decorate it yourself, or hire a professional?"

"Most of the ideas were mine," she replied in a low, sultry voice, "but someone else made them a reality. And please, call me Moselle."

"I'd love to tour your fabulous home before dinner," Sierra said.

"And I'd love to escort you," she replied. "I understand your mother owns an art gallery."

"She does," Sierra said. "And she's kind enough to let me display some of my work."

"My son purchased two of her paintings and one of your sculptures," Moselle said. "They're in our library. What's the name of the gallery?"

"The Light," Sierra replied.

The general flinched, and Sierra knew she was doing the right thing, no matter the danger.

"I'd like to attend the next exhibit," Moselle said, ignoring her husband's lack of interest. "Maybe the general will accompany me."

"I'll see that you receive an invite to next month's showing," Sierra replied. "I'm sure my parents would love to meet you both."

The only interest the general had in Sierra's parents was in putting them behind bars. This time for good.

"What's your mother's name?" Moselle asked.

"Ariana. It means Chosen One."

Sierra couldn't appear too anxious, but she was ready to end the small talk and tour the home.

Meanwhile, Monica was parked across the street surveying the huge house that was surrounded by a wall, thick shrubbery, and immense trees.

She turned on her music and inserted her earplugs. Then she noticed something odd in the nearby tree and whipped out her binocs. Perched on the streetlamp were two identical ogres.

"What kind of foolishness?" she mumbled.

Back inside the estate, Jackson's aloof demeanor confirmed to Sierra that this was his father's doing, and that he was a puppet yet again. She also noticed that Moselle was not as timid and frail as Jackson had portrayed her to be. This tall, slender woman's brown, almond-shaped eyes seemed to follow Sierra's every move, and the shape of her full lips gave her a pouty mouth.

"Are you hungry?" Mrs. Armon asked.

"I'd rather see the house first, if you don't mind," Sierra replied.

"Then have some hors d'oeuvres," Moselle offered. "You can eat them while we tour and get acquainted. Our pets won't mind if you drop a few crumbs here and there. You boys will excuse us, won't you?"

The gentlemen stood as the ladies left the room. Moselle took Sierra by the elbow, and her hand was cold as ice. Sierra wondered if she was alive or the walking dead. As her host led her down a corridor, a horrifying sound pierced the silence.

She turned to go back, but Moselle held her steady. *What kind of pet sounds like that?* Sierra wondered as sweat ran down her back.

Outside, Monica was screaming hysterically as an ogre suddenly landed on her windshield. She wanted to bolt, but she couldn't leave Sierra behind.

Trembling uncontrollably, she whimpered, "Please, Sierra, hurry."

"Moselle, your home is magnificent," Sierra remarked, after recovering from the heart-stopping shriek.

"Thank you. We have nine bedrooms and eight baths, plus two libraries, and several offices and sitting rooms. The basement is where the general conducts the majority of his business."

"I hope we can see most of the house before dinner," Sierra remarked. But she was mainly interested in the general's office and the basement.

On the north side of the house, Sierra noticed a large door with a coat of arms, and she knew instinctively it was the general's private office.

"What a magnificent door," Sierra said, as she hurried down the corridor. "Did you design it yourself?"

"That's the general's office," Moselle replied. "I left that up to him."

Now we're getting somewhere, Sierra thought.

"Does he keep it locked?" she asked casually.

"Rarely," Moselle replied. "His important documents are kept in his safe at the office."

"Can I take a peek?" Sierra asked.

"I guess there's no harm in looking," Moselle said, opening the door but guarding the entrance.

Sierra needed to get inside the office to determine how it could be accessed from the outside, and she quickly sidestepped her host.

"You don't mind, do you?" she asked. Before Moselle could object, Sierra was in the room canvassing the windows leading to the outside.

Eyeing the computer, she eased her way to the large mahogany desk. "What a beautiful piece of furniture," she commented, running her fingers over its smooth surface.

"Please don't touch," Moselle said. "The general knows exactly how he's left things."

All the windows were locked, and Sierra wondered how she would get Monica inside.

"There's a lot more to see, and we don't want to keep dinner waiting," Moselle said, as she ushered Sierra from the room. "What would you like to see next?"

"I'd love to see the basement," Sierra replied.

"The basement underwent an extensive renovation a year ago, and even I haven't seen its completion," Moselle remarked. "Only Diablo and his cabinet are allowed underground. Well, we'd better get back."

"Thanks for sharing your beautiful home with me," Sierra said.

"Come anytime. I like you, and now I know why my son likes you. You're a lovely, intelligent girl. Not like some of his other friends."

They were heading down another dimly lit corridor when a ferocious animal…or something… appeared. It was baring its fangs and drooling.

It stood four feet eleven inches tall with bulging, bloodshot eyes that seemed to collide with his large ears. His talons were like those of a great eagle, which he incessantly tapped on the polished floor… and he smelled terrible. The creature suddenly let out a howl that almost sent Sierra to her knees.

"Don't be afraid," Moselle said. "His growl is worse than his bite. His name is Morpheus, and he's a gift from the Prince."

"I've never seen anything like it," Sierra replied. "Don't you find him and the creatures outside unnerving?"

"The Prince gifted Morpheus to us after the basement was completed. Ignore him; he won't attack. And even though the sentries outside can only be seen at night, they guard our home continuously. I'm alone a lot and, well, they protect me."

But Morpheus' penetrating eyes were riveted on Sierra, as if he knew what she was up to. She squeezed Moselle's hand until they rounded the corner and then sprinted back to the parlor.

"You look as if you've seen a ghost," the general remarked.

That was no ghost, Sierra thought, but she kept her opinion to herself.

"Dinner is served, madame," Barnard announced.

They retreated to the dining room, which was the size of a small ballroom. Sierra immediately noticed the table's immaculate white linens, and the place settings took her breath away. The general sat at one end of the table, and Moselle sat at the other end. Jackson sat to the general's right.

"Sierra, you sit here on my left," the general instructed. "I want to get to know you better."

"I'd be delighted," she replied.

Barnard entered the room and began filling the water goblets.

"Barnard, would you possibly have bottled water in that well-stocked kitchen of yours?" Sierra asked.

"I most certainly do, miss," he said, proud that he could offer anything she could possibly ask for.

"Our house water is well-filtered," Jackson stated curtly.

Well, well, Sierra thought, *the mute can speak.* "Barnard, I'd prefer bottled, if it's no trouble."

"None at all, miss."

Jackson's stare made Sierra uncomfortable. "I see you're not wearing the locket I gave you," he said coldly.

"It gives me a rash if I wear it too long," Sierra lied. Truth be told, wearing Diablo's image around her neck creeped her out.

"Sierra, your mother is an accomplished artist," Moselle said, "but what does your father do?"

"He's an engineer at the CCA," she replied.

"How long has he worked there?" she asked.

"Since I can remember," Sierra replied.

Sierra's mobile suddenly vibrated, indicating that Monica was outside waiting. She had to excuse herself without offending her hosts, then find her way back to the general's office without running into that ferocious hall monitor.

She waited for the others to begin eating, then gulped down her salad. When the lobster was served, she took only a few small bites.

"We were told you loved seafood," the general remarked. "Are you not hungry, child? We can fix you something else."

"This is fine, sir. I'm not a big eater. My father says I eat like a bird."

"Don't pay them any mind," Moselle remarked. "Small portions help us maintain our girlish figures."

While waiting for an appropriate time to excuse herself, Sierra made small talk and took a few more bites to be polite.

"Would you please excuse me?" she said. "My stomach's a little queasy."

"Would you like me to show you the way?" Jackson offered.

"No thanks. Your mother pointed out the restrooms on my tour."

"Meet us in the parlor," the general said. "We'll have coffee there."

She started down the dimly lit hall, stopping at the restroom in case she was being watched. She flushed the toilet and ran the water.

Then she climbed onto the toilet seat and opened the window, just in case. Her palms were sweaty as she hurried to the general's office. She had to get Monica inside. The walls seemed to breathe, and the figures in the paintings appeared to watch her every move, as she proceeded stealthily down the hallway. *What a beautiful but eerie home*, she thought.

She ducked into the general's office, switched on her mini flashlight, then opened the window behind his desk. She rotated the flashlight in a circular motion to alert Monica, but Monica's eyes were glued to the creature crouched on her windshield.

Sierra removed a red ribbon from her pocket and quickly tied it to the outside window latch as planned. She tiptoed to the door and eased it open. There stood Morpheus.

His nostrils flared, and he bared his teeth as if he hadn't eaten in years. Sierra's skin literally crawled as he slowly tapped his front talon on the floor, drool hanging from his nasty mouth. Her heart was pounding as she slowly closed the door and raced to the opposite end of the room. She waited and then peeked out, but Morpheus was there, as well, his eyes a fiery red. Horrified, she closed the door again.

She had been gone too long, and if discovered, she could never explain why she was in a place she knew she shouldn't be. More pressing, however, was escaping this creature.

She peeked out of the door, once again hoping Morpheus had returned to the pit from which he had come. Then she heard the dreaded tapping. He was standing behind her now, making low, guttural sounds as his beady eyes transformed from red to black and back again.

"Go away, nice doggie, or whatever you are," Sierra whispered. But the disgusting creature just clicked his teeth.

She remembered her dad's words. "*There's always a way out of any bad situation. If you let your head rule, fear can't get the upper hand.*"

Meanwhile, the general instructed Moselle to go and check on their guest.

"I'll go," Jackson said. "She's probably lost."

Meanwhile, the creature on Monica's vehicle finally flew away and she cautiously exited her auto. She strapped on her backpack, dashed across the street, then maneuvered her tiny frame over the wall before proceeding to the side of the house. She removed the red sash, climbed inside the window, and turned on her flashlight.

"Yikes," Monica whispered loudly. "What are you doing?"

"Trying to get past this creature before someone comes looking for me," Sierra replied. "But he won't let me out."

Someone was turning the doorknob, and Monica quickly doused her flashlight. Jackson could smell the creature. "Morpheus, are you in here?"

The monster's incoherent rambling tried to expose the intruders. But only Diablo could understand his dialect. As Morpheus started toward Sierra, she cautiously moved her half-frozen body behind a screen.

"There's no one here, Morpheus," Jackson said. "Now, go back to the basement and stay there."

Sierra didn't dare breathe as Jackson moved toward the swaying curtains. "I've told Barnard countless times about closing these windows," he mumbled in frustration. "He's becoming more and more forgetful."

Sierra hated leaving Monica alone, but she knew she could take care of herself. She eased from behind the screen and disappeared into the corridor.

Jackson closed the window, drew the drapes, and took one last look around the general's office. Wondering where Sierra could be, he turned off the light and closed the door.

Monica slid from behind the large palm tree near the general's desk, turned on her flashlight, and crawled into the general's large leather chair.

Sierra, meanwhile, was trying hard to appear indifferent about her long absence.

"Did you get lost?" Moselle asked. "We sent Jackson to look for you."

"I apologize," Sierra replied, "but I got lost admiring your breathtaking art."

"No apologies necessary," Moselle responded.

The general was casually reading the newspaper. "We thought you might've been eaten by Morpheus," he said, peering over his glasses.

"There you are," Jackson said, rushing anxiously into the parlor. "I've been looking all over the house for you. I thought you might've run into Morpheus again."

"I got turned around," she replied casually.

"Dad, you need to talk to Barnard," Jackson said. "The window in your office was open again."

Sierra noticed the quizzical look on Moselle's face, but she was grateful she didn't mention their earlier visit to the general's office.

"I'll speak to him later," the general replied. "Now, Sierra, let's get on with our visit. Because our son is interested in you, quite naturally we're interested in you, too, and your family.

"Tell us what your parents believe as it relates to our educational system, our illustrious leader, et cetera. In other words, are they loyal to the Establishment and the way things are run in our little country?"

Meanwhile, Monica was not having much success with the general's files. She knew they would be encrypted, but this was impossible.

She used every password she could think of, pulled out her electronic cryptogram, and tried every code breaker she thought might work. She finally leaned back in the massive chair, scratching her head.

Then she slowly typed in the word "light". Nothing. She entered "the light"; still nothing. Disheartened, she tried many other words before finally keying in "Uriel".

"Eureka!" She was in.

She pulled a flash drive from her bag of tricks and shoved it into the USB port. She then connected her wizard to the computer, enabling her to copy the general's entire files in record time.

Unfortunately, Barnard was on his way back to the general's office, after having been lectured again about windows he knew he had previously closed and locked.

"Weird things happening in this house tonight," he grumbled. "Windows opening by themselves, animals screeching, what's next?"

CHAPTER 12

The Lab

The general was tiring of Sierra. She was clever and intelligent, and the way she carefully chose her words assured him she was hiding something.

"What were you saying, child?" the general asked.

"I was saying that my parents are loyal…to their truth."

"And what truth is that?" the general asked.

"If everyone, especially the Establishment, would unite for the good of the people, together we could accomplish great things."

"Is that what *you* believe, Sierra?"

"Yes, I do."

The general eyed her sheepishly. He had to put a stop this ideology. It could contaminate the rest of the population and endanger the Great Commission.

Meanwhile, Monica had just completed bootlegging the general's files when she heard footsteps. She quickly turned off the computer and scampered under the desk. She heard Morpheus' guttural panting and immediately held her breath.

"Come back, Morpheus," Barnard instructed, shoving the creature back into the corridor. Barnard shuffled slowly toward the windows, reaching the desk just as the monitor blackened.

"Old age must be catching up with me," he chuckled, as he jiggled all the windows to make sure they were fastened. Morpheus meanwhile, was making a terrible ruckus in the hallway.

"What is wrong with that creature tonight?" the general asked.

"I'll have Herschel take him for a walk," Jackson replied.

Meanwhile, it was becoming more difficult for Sierra to fend off the general's numerous questions about her family's beliefs without revealing their secret.

"General," she said, trying to change the subject, "what's in the future for our nation?"

"We have many great things planned," he replied, "but I'm not at liberty to disclose them at this time."

"I'm hearing a lot about the Great Commission," Sierra pressured, "but only the elect seem to know its details."

"I'll tell you this," he continued, "it's a cause for which every man, woman, boy, and girl will have to sacrifice."

"What will we have to sacrifice?" she asked pointedly.

"The plan is still being refined," he lied, unwilling to reveal that the sacrifice would literally cost everyone their own blood.

Not about to let this self-important jerk off the hook, Sierra pressured him further. "Are you saying your own family doesn't know the concepts of the Great Commission?"

"The details at this stage are too complex for ordinary minds to understand, including my family."

Sierra smiled and took another sip of her coffee. *Whatever the Establishment is up to*, she thought, *it ain't good for the people.*

The general unnervingly stared at Sierra while sipping his after-dinner drink. She knew she should quit while she was ahead, but she couldn't help herself.

"General, don't you find that most people, when they understand the cause for which they're fighting, will fight harder and smarter?"

"In some cases, that's true," he replied. "However, when the intricacies of a cause such as ours are prematurely disclosed, you run the risk of sabotage."

"So, the Establishment expects the populace to sacrifice for a cause they know nothing about," Sierra replied, smiling.

Meanwhile, after having read some of the general's alarming files, Monica decided to go exploring. She moved cautiously down the dimly lit corridor and took the elevator to the basement. She stepped out into the stark white cellar and heard a soft drone. She turned the knob of the nearest door; it was locked. Drawn by the red double doors at the end of the corridor, she proceeded down the hallway. She shone her flashlight inside the room. The space was packed with large see-through refrigerators containing human remains.

The bodies were floating in a blue-green substance, and the stench was sickening. *Who are these people?* she wondered as she vomited into the nearest wastebasket.

The light from her flashlight began to fade and she headed for the door. She bumped into a large cage, shone her fading flashlight, and shoved her fist into her mouth. Hideous monsters with blank expressions were staring at her from their prisons. These grotesque creatures had been crossbred with humans, animals, and birds.

She groped her way toward the exit, wondering the purpose for these monstrosities. Suddenly, the door opened, and she quickly ducked into the closet.

Foreboding creatures moved effortlessly around the dark room, rustling papers and opening and closing file drawers, the unnerving clicking sound echoing on the tiles. She was trapped.

"Well," Sierra said, "it's getting late and I must be going." She had become weary of these cat-and-mouse games with the general.

"Must you leave so soon?" Moselle asked. "The conversation has been most stimulating."

"I don't want to wear out my welcome," Sierra replied, "and I don't want to worry my parents. I've thoroughly enjoyed myself and hope you'll invite me again," she lied.

"You're always welcome here," the general said. "You've made some interesting arguments."

Liar, Sierra thought. She hugged Moselle and wondered why she stayed so cold. They all escorted Sierra to the foyer, where Barnard appeared with her coat.

"Where's Morpheus?" the general asked.

"In the basement," he replied.

Sierra felt sorry for Moselle and promised to visit her again. *She'd probably have more visitors if she warmed up a little*, she thought.

She complimented Barnard on the delicious meal and his attention to detail, and the old man nodded in appreciation. She backed out of the driveway and gasped when she spotted Monica's car parked across the street. She quickly parked out of sight and changed into her tennis shoes. After checking her glove compartment for her gloves, pepper spray, and stun gun, she cruised down the lane directly behind the house, looking for the bathroom window she'd had the foresight to leave ajar.

She spotted the open window, but it was higher than she'd expected. However, the building's protruding stonework gave her a foothold. Her ascent was as difficult as she had imagined, but she finally made it through the window.

Sierra wanted to strangle Monica; her snooping had gone too far. She peeked into the hallway and spotted a light under the general's office door.

Terrified Monica was trapped inside, she listened at the door. She bumped a large potted plant and quickly stepped into the shadows.

"Is that you, Morpheus?" the general called.

Sierra held her breath until he closed the door again, then tiptoed to the elevator. Her heart was racing as she took the slow lift to the basement. She spotted a puddle of drool on the polished floor. Inhaling deeply, she headed toward the red door at the end of the hallway. Red was Monica's favorite color. She thought, *This could not be better staged if it was a horror movie.* She heard the dreaded clicking behind the closed door and sprinted to the end of the hall. She hid behind a sizeable post as Morpheus exited with a large scaly creature that walked upright. She stifled her screams, and when the ogres were out of sight, she quickly slipped inside the room.

She shone her flashlight around. "Monica, are you in here?" she whispered loudly. She observed the sizeable refrigerators and froze. Then she noticed a small door. Opening it carefully, she spotted Monica curled up on the floor.

"Are you all right?" Sierra asked.

"No," Monica whimpered.

"Needless to say, your curiosity has once again gotten us in hot water. Did those hideous creatures hurt you?" She was rambling, but happy to see Monica alive.

"I think the odor from the formaldehyde killed my scent," Monica replied. She paused. "My mom is in one of those tanks."

"Stop talking foolishness, and let's get out of here," Sierra scolded.

"Go see for yourself."

Sierra moved in the direction Monica was pointing and lifted her flashlight. She fell to her knees, and the two girls wept until they had no more tears.

"Sierra, Mom is floating in that…that stuff," Monica cried.

"I know, but we can't do anything for Auntie Liz now. Let's move it before we end up in a solution, too."

"Those creatures had me so scared, I almost peed my pants," Monica announced.

"I'm glad you didn't. I didn't bring any diapers," Sierra replied, trying to lighten a very dark situation.

"How did you find me?" Monica asked, ignoring Sierra's witticism.

"I'll explain later. Look for a window we can climb out of."

"How can I tell my dad about Mom?" Monica asked sadly.

"Maybe my dad can tell him. Meanwhile, stay at my house for a while, since I'll probably be grounded for life. But first, we have to get out of here alive."

"There's a window over there," Monica said, "but it's barred."

"This one isn't," Sierra replied. "It's small, but I think we can squeeze through. We need something to stand on."

Meanwhile, it was eleven o'clock, one hour before curfew, and Janu was pacing the floor.

"Where can she be?" he asked Ariana. "If she's not here in thirty minutes, I'm calling the general. We should never have let her go."

"Sierra is very responsible," Ariana replied. "And you've made her take every defense class there is. Now, have another cup of tea."

"I don't want another cup of tea. I want our daughter back in this house"

Meanwhile, Monica found a stool. "It doesn't look very sturdy," she whispered.

"Just hold it steady," Sierra replied.

She hoisted herself up and tried unlatching a window that clearly had not been included in the renovation. It was old and extremely hard to open. After much pushing and shoving, it finally gave way. Monica pushed from behind as Sierra twisted her body through the small opening. Although she was bruised and bleeding, Sierra was on the outside.

"Climb up, Monica, and I'll pull you through," Sierra whispered.

Halfway through the window, Monica cried, "Sierra, I'm stuck." Her shoulders were wedged in the narrow opening

"How did this happen?" Sierra cried. "You're smaller than I am."

"This is no time for an inquiry," Monica exclaimed. "Get me out of here."

Suddenly, they heard the dreaded clicking. Sierra pulled and tugged and managed to get Monica through just as the general switched on the light. However, there was no time to shut the window behind them. The girls raced to Sierra's waiting car and sped out of the lane with Monica hanging out the door.

"Are you trying to kill me?" Monica screamed.

"Shut up, Monica. Your snooping could've gotten us killed."

"If it wasn't for you, I wouldn't be here in the first place," Monica retorted.

"Okay!" Sierra shouted.

"What about my ride?" Monica inquired. "We can't just leave it here."

"We're not going anywhere near that car," Sierra replied. "We'll pick it up tomorrow."

"Why are you stopping?" Monica shouted.

"Be quiet," Sierra snapped. "Hi, Dad, please don't be mad. Monica and I are on our way home now," she reported in one breath.

"I didn't know Monica had been invited," a relieved Janu replied.

"She wasn't, but I'll explain when we get there. And, Daddy, I love you."

"Me, too," Monica shouted.

"I love you guys, too. Now, get home. You have some explaining to do."

"The girls are on their way in," Janu reported.

"And how did Monica get invited?" Ariana asked.

"She didn't. But they'll explain when they get here."

Meanwhile, the general was checking on his specimens in the lab when one of his winged creations began shrieking and pointing his talon at the open window.

"What have we here?" the general asked.

Mopheus roared, and every creature inside and out joined in concert; the sound was deafening.

CHAPTER 13

Synthetic Replicates

When the girls entered the house, they had never been so glad to see anyone in their whole lives. Sierra immediately ran into Janu's arms while Monica clung to Ariana. Their clothes were tattered and bloody, and they reeked of creatures and formaldehyde.

"Tell me everything," Janu said. "On second thought, take a shower and we'll talk in the morning."

"They'll be no sleeping until we hear this epic tale," Ariana announced. "Who wants to start?"

"Dad, before we start, would you call Mr. Stoner and let him know Monica's here. He's probably worried, too."

"If he even cares," Monica quipped.

"I'll call while your mother gets you some hot tea."

When Janu returned, Sierra and Monica were sitting on the sofa wrapped in blankets.

"Monica, Jacque said he'll deal with you tomorrow. His words, not mine. Now, start at the beginning. Were you physically assaulted?"

"I've never been so horrified in my whole life," Sierra blurted out.

"That's apparent," Janu replied, "but how did Monica get involved?"

"I told Monica everything, Dad. I know you told me not to, but I needed her help."

"Help with what, Sierra?" Janu snapped.

"While I was having dinner with the family weird, I had Monica sneak into the general's office and copy his computer files."

"You did what?" Ariana yelled. "Have you lost your mind? And Monica, do you do everything Sierra tells you to do? Are you both stupid or what?"

"You're scaring them," Janu said.

"That's not all I'm going to do," Ariana said, pacing back and forth. "Sierra, you're grounded for life. You two might have put this entire family in mortal danger, not to mention your own lives. And we're so close to going home."

"You've never done anything so stupid and irresponsible in your entire lives," she continued. "What were you thinking? I'm disappointed in both of you."

Exhausted from her trip around the room, Ariana flopped down on the sofa.

"I thought I could help by finding out if the Establishment knows of our plans. Then we could circumvent any traps they might be setting to hinder our escape."

"Precious, you can best help by staying alive and away from the general," Janu replied.

"But we did discover inhumane protocols being used that will negatively impact all Keresians in the near future," Monica remarked. "I even saw my mom."

"What are you talking about?" Ariana asked.

"I saw her, too, Mom. Auntie Liz was in a big cooler floating in a bluish-green substance in the general's basement. It was horrifying."

"This story is becoming more bizarre by the minute," Janu replied.

"Dad, I think all Keresians are in danger."

The girls told about the cross-bred creatures, Morpheus, and the numerous bodies floating in that awful-smelling solution.

They told of being trapped in the general's office, Monica's curiosity after reading a file, and Sierra finding Monica in a room in the lab, distraught after seeing her mother's remains.

Janu and Ariana stared at the girls as if they were aliens. "Are you two taking drugs?" Ariana asked.

"I've never lied to you before," Sierra replied. "And I wouldn't start with something this serious."

"Honey, why do you think they're preserving bodies?" Ariana asked Janu.

"I don't know," he replied. "But my first responsibility is to get our family out of Keres alive."

"But we must warn the other citizens," Ariana exclaimed.

Janu plopped down in a chair and held his head. "I just can't wrap my mind around this right now," he whispered. "Girls, please take a shower and go to bed. I promise we'll get to the bottom of this tomorrow."

"One more thing," Sierra said. "We had to leave Monica's vehicle at the general's house, and Jackson will recognize it."

"We'll talk about it tomorrow," Janu replied. "And if the general determines it was you in his lab, we'll have more important things to worry about than Monica's vehicle."

Meanwhile, Izaiah was at the top of the stairs eavesdropping. "Monsters and goblins and Auntie Liz floating around in a substance—now, that's bizarre," he murmured and tiptoed back to bed.

But what's more bizarre than a floating head that speaks? he wondered, as he turned off the light. He pulled the covers over his head, but he couldn't sleep.

He was meeting Jackson later that day, and this time there was no escaping him. He would have to turn his family in to the Establishment. *But what will happen to me?* he selfishly wondered.

He finally drifted off to sleep, but the recurring nightmare of the floating head was back again. He awoke terrified. His pajamas and bed linens were soaking wet, but he was afraid to get up lest the head was lurking in the corner. He lay in a pool of sweat, wanting sleep to come, but afraid the chase would begin again.

It was ten o'clock on Saturday morning when Izaiah finally awakened to the smell of sausage and blueberry pancakes. He envisioned eating the cakes with tons of butter, hot maple syrup, and ice-cold milk. *If I turn my parents in, who'll fix my favorite meals?* he wondered.

Meanwhile, the girls dropped Jordan off on the corner of Karrob Circle. He pulled his coat collar up around his ears and his baseball cap down over his eyes. Having been filled in on the previous night's horror show, he was now on the lookout for creatures great and small. He checked his surroundings one last time and unlocked Monica's vehicle. As he sped away from the curb, the blinds in the general's office closed slowly.

Izaiah headed for the Diner, rehearsing his lie and hoping he'd sound convincing.

"What's up?" he asked Jackson as he entered the eatery.

"I should ask you that," Jackson replied. "Have a seat. Are you hungry?"

"I already ate."

"Then we can get right to business. Several weeks ago, you raced into the Junction demanding my attention about something your parents had said. What was so urgent?"

"In retrospect, it really wasn't that important."

"Your parents were telling you and Sierra what?" Jackson pressed.

"They believe the citizens will have to sacrifice themselves to make the Great Commission, whatever it is, a reality, but only the Establishment and their families will reap the benefits. And that's why the Establishment is so secretive about the details. I thought that if anyone would know the truth, you would," Izaiah said, playing the ego card. "I wanted to reassure my parents that the Establishment always has our best interests at heart." Izaiah was surprised at how good he was at weaving this half-truth.

Jackson stared at Izaiah, knowing there was more to this tale. "I have an assignment for you," he said. "Unfortunately, you will not know what it is until it's time to carry it out. Failure to obey the instructions will revoke your membership in PsyOps, and there will be consequences."

"Will you prep me about the assignment?" Izaiah asked.

"No," Jackson replied, sipping his coffee. "By the way, how's your sister?"

"I didn't see her this morning, but I think she and Monica plan to hang out."

"They're thick as thieves," Jackson said pointedly.

"Yeah," Izaiah replied. "Go figure."

"Sierra had dinner at my house last night," Jackson said. "My mom's quite fond of her. Said she's smart and knows how to hold her own. But it seems the longer I know Sierra, the less I know about her." He sipped his brew. "Mobocracy," Jackson whispered.

Suddenly, Izaiah felt strange. He shook his head to clear his mind. "Well," he said, "if there's nothing else, I have a million chores to do."

"Keep your mobile handy," Jackson said. "I'll be calling regarding your assignment."

Izaiah made a beeline for the door, wondering why he was so antsy around Jackson lately. He arrived home and went straight to his room, questioning his loyalties. Despite everything, his parents and Sierra were his family. But his soul now belonged to the Establishment. And sooner than later, he would have to choose. Indecisiveness whirled in his head like leaves blown by the wind. Unbeknownst to him, a tempest of another kind was threatening, and he would soon find himself in the middle of the storm.

Meanwhile, Janu thought of the danger Sierra had put herself in for the family and questioned his decision to return to Fa'i. *Am I just being selfish?* he wondered. *Creatures, labs, and replicates…what in the world is going on?*

Suddenly, the wind began to howl, seemingly warning Janu that a storm of another kind was brewing. He called Malakh.

"Meet me at the Gallery," he said. "It's an emergency. The grove? Wear what? I'll make sure I'm not followed."

The clock in the square was chiming as Janu exited his vehicle. The grove was densely wooded and dark, and Janu didn't hear Malakh walk up on him.

"Geesh, Malakh, you scared the life out of me. What's with the getup, and why haven't I heard from you?"

"Good to see you, too," Malakh whispered.

"What are you doing?" Janu asked, as Malakh painted his face black.

"I want to show you something that will blow your mind." Malakh dropped to his knees. Janu followed suit.

"Why are we crawling?" Janu whispered.

"Stay low."

"If I get any lower, I'll be eating dirt."

"If you keep talking, you will be dirt."

The men crawled through brushwood and numerous prickly cactus plants before reaching the clearing.

"Put these on," Malakh said, and handed Janu a pair of round silver glasses.

"What are they for, and where did you get them?" Janu asked.

"They're called Electronoculars, or Converters, and I borrowed them from the lab that designs them. Turn the small dial on the side of the frame, and the magnified blue lenses will extend outward three inches." He pointed to the large tree across the highway. "Keep your eyes on the tree to your left."

"I don't see anything."

"Just keep looking."

Suddenly, the tree swung outward, the hedges slid back, and people in sky-blue uniforms and masks exited the compound.

Janu lowered the glasses, and the people disappeared. "I can't see them now."

"That's because the suits are made with electronic transmitters that transfer images to the Converters, enabling you to see what you really can't see. Without these high-powered binocs, the people in the suits are invisible."

"Incredible," Janu replied. "But why are we here?"

"To see what we can't see," Malakh replied.

"I'm not going anywhere near that tree thing," Janu whispered. "I told Ariana I was running an errand, not rendezvousing with death."

"I've been researching," Malakh replied, "and I believe this compound may be your way of escape to the Acheron River. And if our plan is to work, we need to find that out sooner than later. But if you're afraid..."

"Of course I'm afraid," Janu replied. "I'm terrified. I'll go as far as the hedges."

"Good enough."

The two men crossed the narrow highway, and just as they reached the tree, it revolved outward again, pinning them against the wall of hedges. With their Converters, they spotted a large figure and a small one approaching the entrance wearing blue suits. Janu lowered his goggles and the couple vanished.

"How neat is this?" he whispered.

The couple placed their left palms on the scanner at the entrance, and the tree began to close. Malakh grabbed Janu and followed them inside.

A ten-foot bronze statue of Diablo stood on a huge pedestal in the middle of the cemetery, glaring angrily at the intruders. Armed guards were moving about in a glass tower, and Malakh quickly pulled Janu down behind a large headstone.

Ten minutes had passed; Janu's knees were throbbing, and his back ached. As he stood to stretch, the ground quaked, and Diablo's statue began moving slowly backward on its track.

The guards shifted positions. One relocated to the south side of the tower, while the other moved to the window overlooking the spot where the two men were hiding. A searchlight was heading straight for them, and Malakh once again pulled Janu to his knees.

As if the bowels of hell opened, several people in blue suits emerged. The tree opened outward again, and the hedges slid back on their tracks. Once again, the people disappeared into the street.

"What *is* this place?" Janu whispered.

"We're among the dead," Malakh quipped, "but I'm going down to see what I can resurrect that might help us with our plan."

"Make it quick," Janu said, guardedly eyeing his surroundings.

"Watch the tower," Malakh instructed. "I'll be right back."

"If Ariana knew I was going to die, she'd kill me," Janu whispered, then chuckled at his ridiculous play on words. "But if I am going to die, what better place to be?"

Janu was sweating profusely in the chilled night air as Malakh disappeared underground. The statue completed its cycle, and the guards rotated their posts once again. He decided to ignore his fear and focus on the synchronized pattern of the guards.

Thirty minutes had passed, and still no Malakh. Janu thought all was lost when suddenly the statue began to move again, the guards rotated, and the tree revolved. With his Converters, Janu witnessed several people emerging from underground. He stopped breathing as one person headed toward him. He wasn't sure if he should run or surrender. Suddenly, Malakh whispered, "It's me, Janu."

Malakh turned around, waved to the group one last time, and quickly ducked behind the headstone just as the searchlight reached him. Janu laid his throbbing head on the cool dirt.

"Keep this up, and you'll have to bury me right here in this graveyard," Janu whispered.

Malakh removed the mask attached to his suit and laughed at Janu's histrionics.

"And where did you get the suit?" Janu asked.

"I borrowed it. What's going on down there is not good, Janu. We'll have to move our timetable up."

"Can we get out of here?" Janu asked.

"The tree rotates simultaneously with the movement of the statue," Malakh said. "And since the statue takes longer to complete its cycle, we should be able to get out of here before the others surface. We'll move closer to the tree so we can be ready."

"I don't care what we do as long as it's soon," Janu stated.

Fifteen minutes passed, and the statue finally rolled back on its track, the tree revolved, and the guards switched positions. The two men quickly dashed across the deserted highway. Just as they reached the brush, a trio emerged from the cemetery and turned left down the dark street.

"Let's follow them," Janu whispered, feeling a little braver now that he was on the outside. They were stalking the suits when the ensemble made a quick left and disappeared.

"Where'd they go?" Janu cried.

"I don't know," Malakh replied, "but I've seen enough for one night. You have a family to think about."

"So, *now* I have a family," Janu remarked. "What did I have before when you put my life in danger?"

"I was going to say, now that I have a suit, I'll come back another time. What I've seen is appalling, and I don't think I can take any more tonight."

"I know I can't deal with any more ridiculousness right now," Janu said.

"Goodnight, Janu. And by the way, we'll be meeting sooner than planned to begin Phase Two. Drive safe."

"Now he's concerned about my safety," Janu murmured as he unlocked his vehicle. His family's impending escape weighed heavily on him as he drove home. He couldn't stop thinking about the underground burrow. *One thing's for certain,* he thought, *we must leave sooner than planned.*

He pulled into his garage but didn't notice the black SUV parked across the street. Laying his head on the steering wheel, he wondered how one act of rebellion could cause so much misery.

CHAPTER 14

The Guest

The brisket and the green beans were perfect, and the buttered sweet potato pudding was awaiting the marshmallows. The chicken was frying a golden brown and the baked macaroni was gooey with cheese. The aroma from Sierra's apple pie filled the air, and Ariana was singing a tune from her homeland that Sierra hadn't heard since she was a little girl.

"Now this is a feast for a king," Ariana announced, excited about meeting Sierra's new friend. "Never did like that Jackson boy," she grumbled. "Evil, just like his father."

Meanwhile, Sierra's table-scape sparkled with Ariana's best table settings and the flowers Sierra hoped wouldn't fade during dinner. The doorbell rang.

"Are we ready?" she asked, meeting her parents in the foyer.

"Don't keep the young man waiting," Janu replied with a smile.

"Hey," Sierra said, as she opened the door.

"Hey, yourself," Jordan replied, and kissed her lightly on the cheek.

"Jordan Ancil, meet my wonderful parents, Janu and Ariana Calder."

"Nice to meet you both. I've heard a lot about you."

He gave Janu a firm handshake, then hugged Ariana gently. Surprisingly, he felt familiar, and she hugged him back.

"Come in," Janu said. "I hope you're hungry, my wife has cooked enough food for a king."

Jordan's eyes sparkled. "The food smells delicious," he replied.

"By the way, thanks for picking up Monica's vehicle. Did you meet with any opposition?" Janu asked.

"No, sir."

"The bathroom's at the end of the hall, if you'd care to wash up before dinner," Janu announced.

"Thanks."

He seemed familiar to Janu, as he headed down the corridor. "Can't be," Janu mumbled.

Dinner was served, and Jordan helped himself to thirds. Ariana periodically gazed at him throughout the meal, wondering where she had seen him before.

As they finished dessert, the Organism crackled, and Diablo began passionately reminding the citizens of their loyalty to him and his Great Commission.

"Can't we turn him off?" Sierra asked.

"Do you know how?" Jordan questioned.

Janu gave Jordan a quick look, wondering if he had been sent to trap them into a confession about their Organism's previous disconnection.

"Precious, you know that's illegal," Janu replied softly, and quickly changed the subject.

The rest of the evening went well. And despite their early misgivings, they all relaxed and found Jordan to be witty and good at playing games.

"Mrs. Calder, the dinner was delicious," Jordan said, as he prepared to leave. "I haven't had a meal like that in ages, or as much fun. My uncle works a lot, so we don't spend a lot of family time together."

"Well, you're welcome here anytime," Ariana said, and really meant it.

"Your parents are really cool, and funny," Jordan said, as he and Sierra stepped out onto the porch. "And quite serious when it comes to winning," he chuckled. "But where's Izaiah?"

"He's at Korey and Dazmin's for a sleepover."

"I'll call you tomorrow," Jordan replied, and skipped down the stairs two at a time.

He thought the night went well and planned to visit often, for reasons known only to him and his uncle. Suddenly, his vehicle door was wrenched open, and he was immediately dragged out. A hood was placed over his head, and he was forced so hard to the ground he thought his kneecaps were broken. He was punched and kicked until he almost lost consciousness. Something hard came down on his right hand, and he grimaced in pain but refused to cry out.

"Stay away from Sierra," someone screamed in his face, "or it'll be worse the next time."

It started to rain as the thugs raced off. Jordan snatched the hood from his head and tried to see the license plate, but the blood in his eyes blinded him. He lay in the middle of Polk Court, watching his lifeblood wash down the street. He took his handkerchief and wiped the blood from his eyes, then pressed it to his nose. But the blood was running as fast as the rain poured. Suddenly, he doubled over in excruciating pain, and he knew he was in trouble. It was close to curfew, and he had to get home before losing consciousness, but he wasn't sure he could make it in time.

He inhaled and exhaled small puffs of air until he finally managed to get behind the wheel and drive away. He took the back streets to avoid Enforcers, weaving in and out of traffic, barely conscious. He finally pulled into his driveway but was unable to come to a complete stop. The car staggered like a drunk into a tree, and Jordan slowly rolled out onto the wet pavement. If he didn't move quickly, he could die a few feet from his home. He groaned like a wounded animal as he crawled up the porch steps to the front door.

He couldn't get to his door key, nor could he lift his swollen hands to ring the doorbell. Turning slowly, he raised his left arm and pressed the bell with his elbow, then slumped down and rolled onto his side. When Malakh answered the door, Jordan was lying in a fetal position soaking wet, with blood oozing from his eyes, nose, and mouth. He gently picked his nephew up and carried him inside.

He gingerly laid Jordan on his bed and quickly called his friend, Dr. Chamberlain. The doctor diagnosed Jordan with a severe concussion, two broken ribs, and a broken bone in his right hand. The doctor insisted Jordan go to the hospital for tests and x-rays, but Malakh refused, assuring the doctor he could take care of the boy himself.

The doctor cleansed Jordan's wounds, tended to his broken ribs and hand, and gave him something for the pain.

"Who did this?" he asked.

"I don't know," Malakh replied, "and the boy's in no condition to say. But I will get to the bottom of it."

"Be careful," the doctor replied.

Malakh wondered what he meant, but he wasn't interested in the answer right now. He was more concerned about his nephew, who was like a son to him.

"I'll check on him after my rounds tomorrow," Dr. Chamberlain said. "In the meantime, keep him warm. His mouth is badly swollen inside and out, but try to get some liquids in him. Have him breathe into this machine four times a day to prevent pneumonia, and make sure he gets plenty of rest. Take his temperature every four hours, especially around midnight, when his fever will likely peak. Can someone look after him while you work?"

"I can work from home. And, Doc, I'd appreciate it if you'd keep this to yourself."

"I hope you know what you're doing," the doctor mumbled, then headed for the door. "I'll honor your request for now, but this should be reported to the Establishment. Call me if you need me."

Jordan, coughing and wheezing, motioned for Malakh to come closer. "I know who they were," Jordan whispered through throbbing lips. "But if we do anything, it'll jeopardize our mission."

"You're right, but I don't like it. You could've been killed."

Malakh gave Jordan the liquid medication the doctor left and tucked the covers in around him. He sat quietly in the chair beside his bed and watched him sleep. *How much longer?* he wondered. Malakh pulled a blanket up around himself and fell asleep.

For two days, Sierra waited for Jordan's call. *Was it something I said?* she wondered. *Couldn't have been the food; he ate three helpings. Maybe he lied about having a good time.*

She was pacing back and forth in her bedroom when her mobile chimed. She knocked over the books on her nightstand to get it.

"Hello," she said breathlessly.

"You're certainly hard to reach these days," Jackson remarked.

"Oh, it's you. How are you?" She could've kicked herself for not checking the caller ID.

"I'm fine. How's your cold?" he asked, sarcastically.

"Better, thank you," she replied, faking a cough.

"Well, since you're feeling better, have dinner with me Friday night."

"Okay," she replied. "Anyway, I have something to tell you."

"I'll pick you up around six."

"Why don't I meet you at the restaurant?" she quickly replied. "I have an errand to run after dinner, and I'll need my car."

"It's a long drive," he insisted. "And afterward, I can take you wherever you need to go."

"All right," Sierra agreed, not at all comfortable with the arrangement.

She called Jordan again, but it went to voice mail. "I'm having dinner with Jackson Friday night to end our relationship," she said. "I'll call when I get back."

Jordan heard the message and was uneasy. He had warned her to be careful around Jackson after that horrific night at the general's house. But if he returned Sierra's call, she would sense something was wrong, and then he'd have to reveal what had happened to him. She would confront the perps and possibly put herself in danger.

Meanwhile, Izaiah's mobile chimed.

"It's time," Jackson said.

Izaiah had been dreading the call, but when Jackson muttered "*mobocracy*", he was again willing to prove his loyalty to PsyOps. He dashed to the back porch so his parents couldn't eavesdrop on his conversation.

"PsyOps and the Establishment are depending on your demonstrated willingness to carry out orders," Jackson said, "no matter the assignment."

"What do they want me to do?" Izaiah asked.

"First, convince some of your friends to assist you with a project you know nothing about. Afterward, your loyalty will be tested."

"What do you mean?" Izaiah asked.

"The Masters usually ask something quite unexpected of the apprentices," Jackson continued. "After you've completed your initial assignment, call me on my mobile for further instructions."

Jackson hung up, leaned back in his father's chair, and clasped his hands behind his head. He felt confident that the general would be proud of the assignment he had fashioned for Izaiah.

"That chair's too big for you, son," the general stated, as he entered his office. "You still have a lot of growing to do, and I don't mean physically. Your smart-aleck girlfriend was in my basement, and she tampered with my computer. Her father probably put her up to it. In any case, I can't have her come into my home and disrespect me."

"Find out what she knows," he continued. "If the details of the Great Commission come out prematurely, Diablo will have my head…literally." The general glared at his son. "Or would you rather I give Jason the assignment?"

Jackson was tired of having to compete with his replicate. "I can handle it," he said.

"If I didn't know better, I'd think Sierra's got you by the nose, boy. Either you handle this, or Jason will. And he won't be as polite." The general was annoyed that after all this time Jackson had not uncovered the Calders' plot.

"I said I'd handle it," Jackson replied. "After Friday night, I'll know exactly what her family's up to. Count on it."

Meanwhile, Izaiah phoned Korey and Dazmin, brothers who had been his best friends since grade school. The three were thicker than thieves, a moniker they would soon live up to.

"It's your dime," Korey said.

"Meet me at the clubhouse tomorrow after school, and bring Dazmin. I need your help," Izaiah stated.

"You okay?" Korey asked. "You sound strange."

"Will you meet me or not?"

"We'll be there," Korey stated emphatically. "Seriously, are you in some kind of trouble?"

"I'll meet you tomorrow at three," Izaiah replied, "and don't be late." He had wanted to tell his best friends about PsyOps, but Jackson had warned him there'd be serious consequences.

Meanwhile, Janu phoned Malakh to inform him about the general's borrowed files.

"Have you reviewed them yet?" Malakh asked.

"No."

"What are you waiting for?"

"I'm afraid to see what's in them."

"Man, read the files, and call me afterward."

Janu hung up and nervously rubbed the infamous thumb drive between his fingers. He called Monica and invited her to dinner.

It was only fair that she be involved in the unveiling, since she had risked life and limb to copy the documents. Plus, he would need her genius to open the heavily encrypted ones.

Monica arrived at six, and after the meal, Janu ushered the ladies into his study. He noticed the dark SUV outside in the shadows and quickly drew the drapes. He pressed a button under his desk, and a large picture on the wall shifted to the right. He removed five miniature boxes from his safe, handed one to each of the ladies, kept one for himself, and laid the other box on the table. He put a finger to his lips, sat Monica down at the computer, and pulled a metal gadget the size of a cigarette pack from his box before moving across the room. He pressed the green button on the gizmo and motioned for the ladies to insert their earpieces.

"Can you hear me?" he whispered.

"Yes," they responded.

"Ladies, I present the *Laisser-Faire*."

"The what?" Sierra asked.

"It means a state of noninterference," Janu replied proudly. "Ariana, remove your earpiece. Can you hear me?"

"No," she replied, reading his lips.

"Girls, can you hear me?"

They both nodded.

"Now, Sierra, remove your earpiece. Monica, talk to me. Did either of you hear her?"

Reading his lips, Ariana and Sierra both shook their heads. Janu motioned for them to reinsert their earpieces.

"When the component is activated, your words are no longer audible to the human ear," he said. "They're captured like fireflies in a jar, then transmitted to another Laisser-Faire."

"You're kidding," Ariana said.

"Now we can speak freely in our homes or if we're miles apart from each other. This baby will help us stay under the radar while we execute our plan."

"Way to go, Uncle J," Monica wailed, always excited about the newest technology.

"They'll be kept in the safe temporarily. Now, let's see what unholy mess is on this disk."

Janu inserted the disk and Monica took out her little black book. She entered one code after another, trying to open the files not previously opened. Pacing nervously back and forth, Janu asked, "Can you get in?"

"Yes, but I'm having problems decrypting the red-flagged files."

Finally, when prompted by her decoder, she keyed in six digits followed by six capital letters. The screen turned bloodred, and various titles appeared in black.

"Good girl," Janu cried. "Guys, listen to this."

Project: I	***REPRODUCE***
Project: II	***ANNIHILATE***
Project: III	***STRIKE***
Project: IV	***RECROWN***
Project: V	***NEW ORDER***

"What does it mean?" Sierra asked.

"I believe these are the strategies of the Great Commission," he replied. "Monica, can you open them?"

She tried everything she could think of, but nothing worked. She reached into her backpack and pulled out a flat device the size of a mobile. She plugged it into the port and hit a series of buttons. Red, green, and yellow lights ran up and down the side of the gadget until only the green light remained.

"Eureka!" Monica shouted.

Janu kissed her forehead. "You truly are a genius."

Suddenly a large black door appeared on the monitor, and the word *REPRODUCE* emerged one letter at time, followed by an animated Prince Diablo. He was surrounded by fire, and his mouth began to move, but there was no sound.

"We need sound," Janu whispered anxiously.

Monica ran her fingers over the keyboard like a maestro, turned several knobs on the gizmo, and then there was sound.

Janu quickly plugged the fifth Laisser-Faire into a port to mute the sound. They, however, could hear the potentate clearly.

"My fellow comrades and supporters of the Great Commission," he began. *"Our goal, one nation under Diablo, will only be achieved when I take back what is rightfully mine. Only then can I bless you with the life you deserve."*

"As previously discussed, your prompt submission of the blood and tissue samples of your District's most highly intelligent citizens will aid in the creation of a people that will help my endeavor."

"I understand some in your Districts are opposed to giving us these samples; report them immediately to General Armon. They will either be eliminated or re-created and programmed to follow me without question."

"We've recruited dynamic men and women, as well as boys and girls, who've joined our forces. Now is the time to implement Phase One of Project Light. The policies and procedures have been mailed to you under separate cover."

"You will have one week to complete your review, at which time you will be notified of the date, time, and location of the ratification summit."

"And when I come into my kingdom, you will each be given a noble position for your loyalty and faithfulness. I look forward to all of us enjoying the benefits of Fa'i in the very near future. Goodbye for now."

"This is more serious than we imagined," Janu replied. "Have you girls been recruited?"

"No," Sierra replied, "but I'm not so sure about Z. He's been acting really weird lately. And those runs he's making two and three times a week are not with Korey and Dazmin."

Ariana's heart melted. After much snooping, eavesdropping, and watching Izaiah become more distant and rebellious, she was confident he was somehow mixed up in this lunacy.

CHAPTER 15

The Breakup

The day had arrived for Sierra's final date with Jackson. Flirting with danger seemed to be her norm lately. She knew she shouldn't meet with Jackson alone, but the recent events at his home had prompted her to immediately end their relationship.

"Sierra," Ariana called.

"I'm in the closet."

"I don't like this one bit," she said. "Why don't you take Monica along?"

"Monica's busy, and we'll be in a public place. Don't worry."

"I wish you'd drive your own car. What if he decides to take you to his awful house?"

"He won't, I promise. I can take care of myself."

Sierra wanted her parents to know where she was going, but Jackson wouldn't tell her.

Ariana squeezed her tight. "You've always been too brave for your own good. It's okay to fear some things. Sometimes it keeps you safe. Call and let us know when to expect you."

"Mom, please don't worry. You and Dad have enough on your minds with Z."

"It's my job to worry," Ariana said softly, then left the room.

Sierra donned black jeans, a red-studded pullover sweater, and her favorite black tennis shoes. Dressing to impress was not her goal. Before heading downstairs, she pulled her hair up in a ponytail.

Leaving with her parents' many instructions resounding in her head, she found Jackson leaning on his sports vehicle and pretended she was glad to see him.

"How are you?" he said, giving her a hug.

"I'm good," she replied, and climbed inside.

"How's your mom?" Sierra asked, breaking the lengthy silence. "I've been meaning to call her and thank her for an interesting evening."

I bet it was interesting, Jackson thought.

"Oh, she's great," he replied. "She wants to know when you're coming over again. I told her I hadn't heard from you lately."

"Tell her I said hello," Sierra replied, ignoring his sarcasm. "How long before we get there?" she asked.

"Not long," he replied.

An hour later they pulled up to an upscale eatery. Nicely dressed couples were coming and going, and Sierra wished she'd dressed more appropriately. Before Jackson could open her door, she quickly freed her ponytail from the rubber band. The ambiance was great, the music played softly, and Sierra almost forgot why she was there. They were ushered to a table, and Jackson placed their order. When the salad arrived, Sierra picked at hers. Neither said a word, and by the time their entrees arrived, Sierra's stomach was in knots.

"So, what did you want to tell me?" Jackson asked.

Not remembering anything she had rehearsed, she blurted out, "Our relationship is over."

"What makes you think I'd allow that?"

"You don't own me," she whispered.

Jackson stared at her, and she stared back.

"No one leaves me until it's convenient for me," he stated. "You should speak with your new boyfriend, Jordan, before making such a decision."

"YOU DON'T OWN ME," she stated loudly, drawing stares from the other patrons.

"We'll see," he said. "Now finish your meal so we can leave."

"And stop telling me what to do. I'll leave when I'm ready."

"But you're not driving, remember."

"Cabs are running, and my dad will come get me, if necessary."

She was shaking all over, but she still needed information. Having been taught that she could catch more flies with honey than vinegar, she took a deep breath and put her fork down.

"I'm sorry for the outburst," she said. "I hear your father and Diablo have great plans for our nation. I'm interested in hearing about them."

"What are you talking about?" Jackson asked rudely.

"You know, the Great Commission. I heard it's going to benefit all of us, and the general has included you in the scheme of things. Aren't you excited? About time he recognized your worth."

Jackson took his time chewing and swallowing his food. "I *have* been included in helping Dad implement the Great Commission, and I'm learning a lot. Like how to recognize a phony, and to accept that not everyone is loyal to the Prince or his cause. I've even discovered how to expose those pretending allegiance."

Sierra knew Jackson was talking about her, but this was not the time to lose her cool and panic.

"You really are maturing," she replied.

"Finish up," he said. "I have another stop to make."

They left, and Jackson got into his car, leaving Sierra on the sidewalk until he was ready to unlock her door.

Annoyed, she said, "I hope this stop won't take long, it's getting late and I'm tired." Suddenly she had an eerie feeling and spotted birds in the air.

"Why are we going in this direction?" she asked.

"I told you I have a stop to make."

Meanwhile, Izaiah was at the Club House waiting for Korey and Dazmin. "You're late," he barked.

"Calm down," Korey said. "We're here to help you, remember. What do you need us to do?"

"I don't know yet. I'm waiting for a call."

"Who from?" Dazmin asked.

"That's confidential. And you can't tell anybody about tonight."

"You're awfully touchy," Dazmin replied.

"Look," Korey said, "if I get into any more trouble, my dad will make the Enforcers look like kittens."

Izaiah's mobile rang. He was given an address and told that they should wear ski masks. "Whatever you do, do not turn on the lights," he was ordered.

"How are we supposed to see?" Izaiah asked.

"Figure it out," the caller replied.

Korey, driving his dad's truck, found the address across town. They parked in front of the abandoned-looking house, and Dazmin slammed the door as he got out.

"Will you please be quiet?" Izaiah whispered.

"If anybody *is* in this old house," Dazmin replied, "they can't hear us, because they're probably dead."

The boys slowly climbed the stairs to the front door. "Man, this place is creepy," Korey remarked.

"Isn't it too late for birds to be out?" Dazmin asked, pointing to the creatures in the leafless tree.

"And they look weird," Korey replied. "Izaiah, I don't know about this."

"I'll go in first," Izaiah replied, equally afraid.

He turned the squeaky doorknob, and they stepped inside. Suddenly a loud shriek filled the house. The boys grabbed one another and screamed like little girls.

"What was that?" Korey asked.

"I don't know," Dazmin replied, climbing Korey's back. "But…but let's get out of here."

"It was just a little noise," Izaiah replied.

"That was not a 'little noise'," Korey replied. "And it's getting close to curfew."

"Wait just a little longer," Izaiah whispered loudly. "If nothing jumps off soon, you can go."

"Better be soon," Korey replied.

They surveyed the foyer with their flashlights. "This place is huge," Dazmin said.

Izaiah opened a door on the left and peered inside. "We'll wait in here until it's time."

"Time for what?" Korey insisted.

Meanwhile, Sierra was growing more impatient. "Look, Jackson, I'm tired, and I want to go home now. "

"We're here," Jackson said, pulling up in front of a three-story building. "This is not the greatest part of town, so keep the doors locked. I'll be right back."

"You're not leaving me alone," she said. "I'm coming with you." He had hoped she would.

"This place is unnerving," she said, as they entered the vestibule.

"I won't be more than ten minutes," he said. "I have a call to make."

As Sierra waited alone in the dimly lit hall, thumping and screeching sounds came from beneath the floor. This was as good a time as any to call home. She reached into her purse for her mobile, but was suddenly grabbed from behind. A hood was pulled down over her head, and she was carried up a flight of stairs. She tried to get free, but to no avail.

A squeaky door opened, and she was violently shoved inside. Unbeknownst to her, she kneed Dazmin in the groin, and he fled from the room groaning.

"You're a real spitfire," Izaiah said, his voice disguised by his mask. He slammed her into a chair. "Now, sit there and be quiet."

Because of the hood and the darkness of the house, the boys didn't know Sierra was their hostage. They yanked the cover from her head, quickly blindfolded her, stuffed a rag into her mouth, and tied her arms behind her back.

"Let's get out of here," Izaiah said. He and Korey hurried from the room, locked the door behind them, and waited in the hall for further instructions.

Sierra knew this was Jackson's doing. He could be a little crazy when he didn't get his way, but all this over a breakup?

The house was inundated with weird noises and screeching sounds, and Sierra knew the creatures were nearby. She tried freeing her hands, but the rope was tied too tight.

No one knew her whereabouts. She was alone, she was terrified, and she had no way out.

Jordan sensed something was wrong. It was getting late, and Sierra hadn't called as promised. With swollen fingers, he dialed Sierra's home number.

"Hello," Ariana said.

"Hello, Mrs. Calder, this is Jordan. How are you?"

"I'm well, thank you. And you?"

"I've been better."

"You sound awful, son. Are you all right?"

"I'll be okay. But I didn't call about me. Did Sierra keep her date with Jackson, and have you heard from her?"

"Yes, she did, and no, I haven't. Why?"

"I think she might be in trouble."

"What makes you think that?" Ariana asked.

"It's getting late, no one has heard from her, and I don't trust Jackson. I think we ought to call her."

"Sierra's good at taking care of herself," Ariana replied, trying to waylay her own fears.

"If she's caught unawares, she might not have time to defend herself," he stated, unconsciously rubbing his ribs.

Ariana admitted she hadn't felt comfortable since Sierra left. "It wouldn't hurt to call her," she said. "If you reach her first, have her call me."

"I will," Jordan replied.

"And, Jordan, I hope you feel better soon."

He quickly disconnected and dialed Malakh, who wasn't picking up.

"Uncle M, please call me," he pleaded. "I need your help."

Meanwhile, the two thugs Jackson had hired to force Sierra to confess to the theft of his father's files and the invasion of their basement entered the house.

"Are you part of the initiation, too?" Izaiah innocently asked the two goons who were climbing the stairs.

"Don't know anything about that," Dark Horse replied.

Suddenly, loud moans echoed throughout the house. "This place is really creeping me out," Korey stated. "I'm leaving."

Suddenly, Sierra's mobile rang, and Tony pulled it from her purse.

"Idiot," Dark Horse growled. "What are you going to say? I've just kidnapped the person you're calling, can I be of assistance? Put that thing away."

"But if we don't answer, the caller will think something's wrong," Tony replied.

"Or maybe they'll think she forgot to turn it on," Dark Horse snapped.

"When do we get our money?" Tony asked, as Korey and Dazmin rushed from the building.

"When we finish," Dark Horse replied.

"What money?" Izaiah asked.

"None of your business," Dark Horse retorted.

Meanwhile, Jordan was listening to Sierra's message. *"Sorry I missed your call. Don't be shy. Leave a message after the beep, and I'll get back to you by the by."*

By now, Sierra knew this was not a joke. It was late, and she knew her parents were worried. Her arms ached terribly, and if she didn't bring them around the front of her body soon, she feared they might snap off. She worked the rope until her fingers were numb, then stood with the chair tied to her back. She wriggled her arms and shoulders up and over the back of the chair, nearly fainting from the excruciating pain, but only the blindfold came loose.

She crept around the dark room trying to find the light switch, but she couldn't. She groped the doorknob, but the door was locked. Yelping and loud footsteps suddenly penetrated the night.

"What was that?" Izaiah whispered.

"I don't know," Dark Horse replied, "but the hounds are out tonight."

"Look, Horse," Tony stated emphatically, "I agreed to help you, but I didn't agree to babysit the living dead."

Izaiah's mobile rang. "Are you guarding the package?" Jackson asked.

"Just like you told me," he replied, "and the others are here, as well. Where are you? And who's the package?"

"I'll be there shortly, and the package is not your concern," Jackson replied.

"Well, hurry, it's near curfew, and I need to get home," Izaiah said.

"You and your friends can leave when I get there," Jackson replied.

But Korey and Dazmin were already burning rubber down the street. Suddenly, an earsplitting sound rang out throughout the house.

"That guy can't pay me enough," Tony said. "I'm out."

He and Dark Horse scurried from the house, leaving Izaiah alone. Soon after, the front door flew open. The dim light from the street cast an eerie shadow on the tall man standing in the entrance. Izaiah shone his flashlight in the man's direction and stood trembling at the top of the landing.

"Jackson, is that you?" he whispered.

"Yes," Jackson replied robotically. But his hair was uncombed, his face was unshaven, and his clothes appeared as if he'd just gotten out of bed. Izaiah couldn't worry about Jackson's strange appearance right now, though; he had to make curfew.

"Can you give me a lift? My parents will be on my case if I'm late."

"We'd better hurry. I've got to get back," he said, glancing toward the upstairs room.

Meanwhile, Sierra was kicking the door, but no one came. She managed to spit out the rag in her mouth. The front door slammed, and she stumbled to the window in time to see a young man climb into Jackson's pickup.

"WAIT," she screamed. "PLEASE DON'T LEAVE ME." She banged as hard as she could on the window with her forehead, but they couldn't hear. *Why would Jackson leave me here?* she wondered.

"Are you okay?" Izaiah asked, after climbing into Jackson's truck. "You seem preoccupied. By the way, there's *weird* howling and screaming going on in that house, like animals caught in a trap."

They rode in silence. Jackson had the package on his mind, and Izaiah had Jackson on his mind.

Izaiah peered at his friend from the corner of his eye and knew something wasn't quite right. This person wasn't anything like the Jackson he knew.

"Turn here!" Izaiah yelled. "Did you forget where I live? You've only been to my house a thousand times."

"Not quite myself tonight," Jackson replied.

No kidding, Izaiah thought.

"Can you give me the directions again?" Jackson asked, ignoring Izaiah's accusatory stare.

Meanwhile, Ariana was near delirium. Neither she nor Jordan had been able to reach Sierra, and Janu was heading out to find her.

"Honey, *please* be careful," Ariana pleaded. "I don't know what I'd do if anything happened to you or Sierra."

"Nothing is going to happen to either one of us," Janu said and hugged her tight. "Remember, we're all going home."

Izaiah put his key in the door, shaking his head as Jackson drove away. "Never would've believed him to be into drugs," he mumbled.

"Sierra," Janu shouted, "is that you?"

"It's me," Izaiah replied.

"Son, your sister's missing."

"What do you mean she's missing?" he asked, displaying his usual I-couldn't-care-less attitude.

"She went to dinner with Jackson hours ago and hasn't come home yet," Janu replied. "It's past curfew, and she hasn't even called."

"Have you tried her friends?" Izaiah asked. "You know how they are when they get together."

"Yes," Janu said. "We called Monica first, of course, thinking she was there. But Monica hasn't seen or heard from her either."

"She would never miss curfew," Ariana said, tears streaming down her cheeks.

Izaiah knew Miss Goody-Two-Shoes would never do anything to break the law.

"Have you tried her mobile?" Izaiah asked.

"Numerous times, but it goes to voice mail," Janu replied.

Now Izaiah was worried. Sierra lived and breathed with her mobile attached to her ear. She would never intentionally ignore it.

"I'll call my friends, see if they've seen her," Izaiah offered.

"Thanks," said Janu.

Sierra wasn't one of Izaiah's favorite people right now, but he still didn't want anything bad to happen to her. He called all his friends, including Korey and Dazmin, but no one had seen or heard from her.

Izaiah lay on his bed going over the events of the evening, especially Jackson's strange behavior, and the secret package he wasn't allowed to see or ask questions about.

Meanwhile, with the help of the streetlamps, Sierra spotted a wooden table in the corner. A half-filled soda can was surrounded by spiders and other crawling bugs, but lying alongside it was the most beautiful can opener she'd ever seen.

She writhed in pain as she walked her fingers backward toward the metal, sending bugs scurrying back to their hiding places.

Sierra gently eased the can opener between her fingers, picking at the rope until it gave way and her hands were free. She brought her arms around the front of her body and screamed in agony.

Sierra was trying to unlock the door with the can opener when she heard a car pull up outside. She cautiously moved to the window and spotted Jackson. He looked maniacal.

The front door opened, and as Jackson slowly climbed the creaking stairs, Morpheus appeared from nowhere. Sierra grabbed the ropes and lay on the smelly cot in the corner, adjusting the blindfold so she could peek from beneath. Pulling the covers up to her chin, she hid her untied hands and lay very still.

The door creaked on its hinges as Jackson and Morpheus loomed large in the entryway. She was sure they could hear her heart beating. Jackson shone his flashlight on her, and she let out a snort to convince him she was asleep. Sierra watched as he stared at her, left the room, then locked the door behind him.

Quickly removing the blindfold, she eased from the cot and immediately went to work on the lock again. She finally jiggled it loose and carefully opened the door.

The peeling wallpaper in the dimly lit hallway seemed to have a thousand eyes, and a chill ran up her spine. A door opened at the bottom of the stairs, and she quickly stepped into the shadows. Jackson was holding a sinister-looking metal rod in his hands, and she wondered if he was planning to use it on her.

She grabbed a lit candle from a wall sconce and crept quietly down the hall. She heard the familiar *click, click* sound on the floor, and she felt faint.

The corridor was lined with several doors on the left and right, but they were all locked. But the door at the end of the passageway was ajar, and the stench of formaldehyde took Sierra's breath away. The farther she descended, the stronger the stifling odor became. But she couldn't go back; Jackson and Morpheus were probably searching for her.

Izaiah was dozing off when suddenly he jumped straight up. Was Sierra the package, the ultimate test of loyalty to which Jackson had referred?

His stomach was in knots. If he told his parents his suspicions, he would have to expose his affiliation with the PsyOps. Instead, he decided to sneak back to the haunted house and find out for himself.

Meanwhile, Janu called Malakh.

"Must be important if you're calling me here," Malakh said.

"My daughter's missing," Janu replied. "She went to dinner with Jackson and hasn't returned home. She's never out after curfew."

"Jordan's worried, too," Malakh replied. "How can I help?"

"Meet me at Valiance Diner," Janu replied. "Wait. Is Jordan Ancil your nephew?"

"Yes," Malakh replied. "I'll be there in thirty minutes, and bring your Laisser-Faire. We must remain as discreet as possible."

Izaiah had been eavesdropping at the top of the landing. "Who was that, Dad?"

"He's someone who's going to help me find your sister."

Meanwhile, Jordan willed his body out of bed.

"Where are you going?" Malakh asked.

"I have to help find her."

"Son, you're in no condition to help anyone. Her father and I will handle it, I promise. Stay by the telepad. I'll keep you posted."

"I know she's in danger."

"How do you know that?"

"She left a message that she was breaking up with Jackson tonight and he was taking her to dinner, but he wouldn't tell her where. He thinks she's his property. If anything happens to her, it'll be my fault."

"Is she the reason you were badly beaten?"

"Yes," Jordan replied. "You and Mr. Calder might have to separate. And since you've never met Sierra, you'll need me for recognition."

"Can you handle the ride, son?"

"I have no choice."

"Do you have any idea where she could be?" Malakh asked as he helped Jordan dress.

"No," he replied. "None of her friends have seen her either."

Malakh shook his head. "You're breaking up with an egomaniac, but you don't drive your own car. Does anyone know Jackson's whereabouts?"

"No, but I'm going to find out. And if he harms a hair on her head, I won't be responsible for my actions."

CHAPTER 16

The Lab

When Sierra first saw the old house, it appeared to be an ordinary three-story building. Now, as she descended deeper into its bowels, she realized there was nothing ordinary about it.

Sierra reached the bottom landing and thought of turning back as her trembling hand touched the ice-cold doorknob. Instead, she opened the large door, stepped inside a rotunda chamber, and gasped from the acidic stench. Suddenly, the floor quaked and the wall she faced revolved outward. She spotted a door to her left and slipped inside a small room. People in sky-blue uniforms emerged from behind the moving wall. Their feet were shod with matching booties, and they wore masks and silver goggles with blue lenses.

The overwhelming stench made her eyes water, but her only way out might be in through the opened wall.

The partition began to reclose, and she quickly slipped inside. She grabbed a pair of goggles and a mask from a box nearby and quickly slipped them on. Hundreds of people dressed in sky-blue uniforms were carrying pads and pens and scurrying about like squirrels.

She was in a lab the size of a small city. As she gazed in awe at the hustle and bustle, motorized cars and mini trucks zipped by on overhead rails. Coolers similar to the ones in the general's basement held human remains. "This is not good," she whispered.

Meanwhile, Jordan remained in the car while Malakh went inside the diner.

"Nobody's seen her," he reported to Jordan in frustration, "but we'll find her."

Just then Janu arrived, hoping for good news, but there was none. "Jordan, I thought you weren't feeling well."

"I'm not. But you and Uncle M will have to split up, and he's never met Sierra."

"When Jordan left your house the other night, he was brutally beaten. He has been confined to bed ever since," Malakh reported.

Janu was shocked. "I'm so sorry. Does Sierra know about this?"

"No," Jordan replied, "and I never want her to. We've got to find her, Mr. C."

"Where do you think we should look first?" Janu asked.

"The general's home," Jordan replied. "If Jackson is there, then where is Sierra, and why didn't he see her safely home?"

"The general hates me," Janu replied. "If he did know something, he wouldn't tell me."

"You have to try," Malakh stated. "Your daughter's missing, and you have a right to be concerned, especially since Jackson was the last to see her."

The thought of seeing the general again made Janu's blood boil.

Meanwhile, Monica was frantic with worry. She had warned Sierra to never be alone with Jackson again. She immediately thought of that heartbreaking night more than a year ago when her mom was taken from her. They had just finished dinner when the Enforcers kicked in the door.

"Evening, Jacque," the Commander had announced, "we need to speak to you and your wife in private."

Jacque quickly ushered Monica into her bedroom. "Stay here, sweetheart, and don't come out until I come for you," he had instructed.

She had eased her door open and heard the Enforcers accuse Elisabeth of treason against Prince Diablo and the Establishment. *Never*, Monica had thought. *Mom wouldn't hurt a fly.* She sank to the floor and covered her mouth to hold back the screams. But when the angry men handcuffed

Elisabeth, she bolted from her bedroom screaming, fighting the Enforcers, and clinging to her mother. As a shocked and sobbing Elisabeth was dragged from their home, Monica was backhanded by an Enforcer she had kicked in the shin. And just like that, her mother was gone forever.

She watched as her father became bitter and hard to get along with. A once vibrant, fun-loving man who made her laugh had become a shell of himself who paid her little or no attention, leaving her to fend for herself.

Normally, she stayed out of his way, but not tonight. Her mother loved Sierra, and she would want Jacque to do everything in his power to help find her.

She went to her father's study, but the door was closed. She spotted a light underneath and tapped lightly. When he didn't answer, she knocked harder.

"Come in," he responded angrily.

"Hi, Daddy, what are you doing?"

"I'm busy, what do you want?" he replied, never turning to acknowledge her presence.

"I wouldn't bother you, but it's important."

"What is it, Monica?" he asked impatiently.

"Sierra's missing, and no one knows where she is."

"And how's that my problem?" he asked.

"She's mysteriously disappeared like Mom, and I was wondering if you could help."

"Why would I do that? It's after curfew, and she should be home. Maybe she's being held for criminal behavior. I warned you to stay away from that family."

"But Sierra's my friend, and I thought Janu and Ariana were yours."

When he turned to face her, she saw he was disheveled and hadn't shaved in days, and his cold, lifeless eyes frightened her. It hurt her to see him like this. *He's been lost for some time*, she thought, *but Sierra hasn't been, and I'm going to find her.*

"Thanks for nothing," she mumbled, and left the room.

Who are you to tell me to stay away from that family? she thought as she headed back to her room. *That family has been my lifeline ever since you abandoned me.*

Monica's emergency tone rang on her mobile.

"Sierra, is that you?" she asked.

"No, it's Izaiah. I think I know where she is. Pick me up."

"Are you crazy? You know the penalty for breaking curfew."

"If you want to find Sierra, do as I say. There's no time to lose."

"Boy, what have you gotten yourself into?"

"Just hurry."

Monica grabbed her mobile and threw her laptop into her carryall. Jacque wasn't aware she was leaving the house, nor would he care if he did know.

She opened her squeaky car door and slipped behind the wheel, cringing as she raised the garage door that needed oiling. Using her low beams, she slowly backed into the street, barely missing the car parked at the curb. She was driving down Hollow Lane, a small alley many teenagers used to avoid the enemy, when she spotted an Enforcer cruising about two hundred yards in front of her. She slammed on her brakes and doused her low beams.

He turned left out of the alley, and she quickly backed up. A good decision, because he was waiting around the corner. After much dodging and maneuvering, she reached Izaiah. He was hiding behind a tree. He ran and jumped in her vehicle.

"Boy, what have you done?" Monica immediately asked. "If you had anything to do with this…"

"Don't start. I feel bad enough."

He told her everything: his recruitment into PsyOps, and the initiation assignment given him that day. He even mentioned Jackson's creepiness earlier, and how he had had to direct him to their house.

"The guy practically lives at my house, and he needs directions? Go figure."

"Creep," Monica replied. "If he's done anything to Sierra… Where to?"

"Swear you won't tell my parents about this," Izaiah begged. "They'll kill me."

"Not if I kill you first."

"And if PsyOps find out that I revealed their secrets, they will kill me…and you, too."

"You've really gone and done it this time," Monica stated. "Just what is PsyOps, anyway?"

"It's a secret society formed by the Establishment to determine who's loyal to Diablo. We have taken an oath to spy on friends and family and each other. Somehow they got into my head and made me think my family is my enemy."

"Izaiah, very peculiar happenings that we don't understand are going on in this nation. Sierra and I have both witnessed things that I don't have time to go into now. Let's just say that it would be wise and healthy for you and your family if you disassociated yourself from Jackson and PsyOps…sooner rather than later."

"I don't know if I can. They have some kind of hold on me. Once you're in, you can never get out."

"Well, you'd better find a way out, mister." She hesitated. "On second thought, maybe you could be a PsyOp inside the PsyOps and find out something about this Commission thing. You might be able to help your family with their plan."

"You know about that cockamamie revelation?"

"What I do know," Monica said, "is that the Establishment's planning something big, and the fallout for the people is going to be pretty bad. Geez, Louise, Izaiah—are we almost there? If I had known it was this far, I would've charged my vehicle."

"Turn left at the next corner," he said. "It's the house on the right at the end of the block. Turn off your lights. We don't want to be seen."

"By whom?" Monica wailed. "It looks abandoned."

"When we were here earlier, we heard loud noises coming from below."

"And who is 'we'?"

"Korey and Dazmin helped me abduct the package."

"And you think Sierra is the package?"

"Yeah."

"How do we get inside this creep-hole?"

"I haven't had time to think that through yet."

"Izaiah, I know you don't want to call your dad, but somebody should know where we are and what we're about to do. If these people are as dangerous as I know they are, we're going to need some serious backup."

"No," Izaiah said emphatically. "Janu will kill me."

"Don't call your dad by his first name again. Understand?"

"Yeah, yeah, now stop nagging and help me figure out a way to get Sierra out of here."

"If she's even in there, Izaiah. We have only your hunch to go on."

"Monica, I'd bet my life on it. I've thought it through, and all the pieces fit. What better way to test my loyalty to PsyOps than for me to be a part of my own sister's abduction?"

"Well, are we going to walk up the steps and ring the bell?" she asked sarcastically, as they stood staring at the house.

"No, silly," he whispered. "But a house this size must have a basement. Let's go around back. Maybe we can find a window or something to crawl through."

"Over here," Monica whispered, pushing and tugging on a window that wouldn't budge. She found a crowbar in her bag of tricks and placed the flat end under the window.

"You over there with the muscles, give me a hand."

Izaiah gave the bar two good shoves, and the window frame gave way.

"The last time I went through a window," Monica quipped, "I was crawling out, not in."

She shone her flashlight into the basement as Izaiah climbed through the window, then handed him her backpack.

"Geez, Monica, this thing weighs more than you do," he said as he helped her down.

"Shhh," she said. "Someone's coming."

She pulled Izaiah into a stairwell just as the basement door opened. *Click, click.* Monica wanted to puke. She peeked through the door.

"Let me see," Izaiah said.

"Only if you don't scream," she replied.

"I'm not a child," he said.

Izaiah peered through the crack and quickly covered his mouth. "What the devil is that?"

"That is Morpheus."

"You know that thing's name?"

She ignored the question. "Jackson appears androidish or something," she remarked.

"I told you he was acting weird," Izaiah replied. "Let's go before that thing picks up our scent. He's even uglier than you."

"Oh, shut up," Monica snapped, "and go find out where these stairs lead."

Meanwhile, Janu felt weighed down as he climbed the steps of the general's estate. He didn't want to falsely accuse Jackson, but he was sure he knew Sierra's whereabouts.

He rang the doorbell, and a sickening moan pierced the quiet night. He looked skyward and stared into the eyes of a strange creature perched on the eaves.

"What the..." The possibility of his little girl being trapped inside this house infuriated him.

"May I help you?" Barnard asked in his low, gravelly voice.

"My name is Janu, I'm Sierra's father, and I would like to speak with Jackson, if he's home."

"One moment, please."

It was evident that Janu would not be invited in as the door slowly closed in his face. He peered upward again. Now there were three pairs of eyes staring at him. Finally, Jackson opened the door.

"Hi, Mr. C," he said, "is everything okay?"

"No, everything is not okay. You took my daughter to dinner tonight, and she hasn't returned home."

"I dropped her off long before curfew," Jackson lied. "What she did after that, I have no idea."

"I think you do," Janu replied. "What restaurant did you take her to, and what time did you leave there?"

"We went to the bistro in the canyon. We talked, we ate, and we left around nine thirty. She said she was tired, so I drove her home. That's the last I saw of her. Have you checked with Monica or some of her other friends? Maybe she's with one of them."

"Jackson, you know as well as I do that Sierra never stays out after curfew unless she's with me or her mother."

"Well, I don't know how I can help you," Jackson replied. "Now, if that's all, I have guests."

Before he could ask to speak to the general, the door was quickly shut in his face. Janu was furious, but finding Sierra was more important than fighting with this sadistic family.

Monica, meanwhile, was leading the way down the dimly lit stairwell of the old house with her flashlight. "How many floors did you say this joint has?" she asked.

"Three, I thought," Izaiah replied.

"Well, we were *in* the basement, and we've gone down five more flights," Monica stated. "What kind of place is this?"

"I was never given the grand tour," Izaiah replied.

"You used to be such a sweet kid," Monica said, rolling her eyes, "but you're becoming more obnoxious by the minute. What was that?"

"It's coming from in there," Izaiah said, pointing to the big black door.

"Well, open it," Monica said.

"You open it," Izaiah said.

"You want to be treated like an adult, so now act like one and turn the knob. Plus, you're bigger than me and I can hide behind you."

"Not funny, Monica."

CHAPTER 17

The Brethren

Meanwhile, the general, the High Council, and the governors from the twelve districts had been summoned to an emergency late-night meeting at Prince Diablo's estate.

They were exquisitely dressed in uniform as they entered the eloquent banquet hall. Some had as many as thirty bars and stars across their stuck-out chests, their various colors indicating their rank within the Brethren.

Diablo slowly stood to his feet, adjusted the much-too-opulent headdress and moved toward the dais. He brought the gavel down hard on its stand and announced, "This meeting is now called to order."

All activity ceased, including that of the waiters and busboys, and the Brethren stood to salute their prince. Diablo whispered something in the general's ear, then took his seat.

The general slowly moved to the podium and stated in his most prince-like manner, "I have some good news and some not-so-good news." The crowd murmured.

"Somehow, someone outside the Brethren has obtained our strategy for the Great Commission," he stated. "And if this information is prematurely released to the populace, it could end our mission before it begins."

He failed to mention that the strategy had been stolen from his home under his very nose.

"Also, some of you have not yet identified the rebels in your districts, as requested. As I speak, these insurgents are plotting to undermine and overthrow our objective to expand our territory across the river.

"The good news is that together we can ferret out every insurrectionist, no matter their age, and bring them to justice on our way to victory. One such person has already been apprehended and is being held captive as I speak."

"We cannot be stopped," he continued. "What say you? Will we accomplish this for him?" He turned and pointed to Diablo.

The men stood to their feet, and with thunderous applause, they whistled, cheered, and chanted Diablo's name until they were nearly hoarse. Finally, when Diablo's thirst for praise was somewhat quenched, he waved his hand and the room fell silent.

"Prince Diablo has commissioned us to cross the river and take back our inheritance," the general shouted. "Abundant life for eternity."

The general managed to work the Brethren into a frenzy once again, and pandemonium erupted as they remembered their former home. They, along with Diablo, had been ousted from Fa'i because of their rebellion against Uriel. Now they shouted and stomped their feet, as they envisioned returning to paradise.

"Remember the days we drank from the fountain of youth," the general bellowed above the din. "There was no aging or dying. Imagine once again living forever?"

Old men waved their frail arms, others kicked their tired legs, and some rubbed their bald heads.

"I'll have the energy of a teenager," an elderly governor cried from a table in the middle of the room. "My hair will no longer stay in bed when I get out," another shouted.

Even thePrince thought that was funny, and the men roared with laughter. Finally, when they were somewhat composed, Monica's dad stepped to the mike.

"Your Worship."

"Yes, Colonel Stoner," Diablo replied, enjoying the many superlatives with which his subjects honored his deity.

"With all due respect, how do you plan on accomplishing this monumental task? The forces in Fa'i have great powers, and I doubt if they will sit back and let us take their country without a fight."

Moving to the edge of his seat, the Prince replied, "The element of surprise will be our greatest weapon, but we'll explain later."

The general leaned into the mike. "The red-tagged items in your packets need your immediate attention. The dates and timelines are crucial to the success of our mission.

"You must familiarize yourself with every aspect of Sector I and be ready with your input at our next meeting, one week from tonight.

"In addition," he continued, "advise your district PsyOps to quietly but expeditiously search out our enemies, including family members, friends, and coworkers, and reveal those enemies at our next meeting. They're out there; now go and find them. Anyone who is not with us is against us. Are there any questions?" Silence.

"My fellow comrades, in closing, no suggestion or tip from the least in your communities should be overlooked. We're on our way to paradise, gentlemen. Let's go with oneness of heart, mind, and spirit."

The applause and foot stomping caused the floor to shake and the chandeliers to dance from the ceiling. Tired of the raucousness, Prince Diablo waved his hand, and all fell silent.

"There are refreshments in the rear of the auditorium for all who wish to partake," the general said.

But as was customary, no one moved until Prince Diablo did. He stood and waved to the Brethren as he left the dais. They leapt to their feet, cheering once more.

Meanwhile, Sierra was in the mystery lab trying to find a way out. With the high-tech Converters, she watched people clad in blue uniforms perform their duties in robotic fashion.

Suddenly the wall began to revolve again. She thought about running, but where would she go? Resembling a deer in headlights, she sat crouched in a corner, wishing she was at home in her warm, comfortable bed. She quickly pulled her knees to her chest and covered her head with her arms.

She sat motionless, her insides quaking. She squeezed her eyes tight and held her breath as the people in blue uniforms headed her way, the swishing sound of their lab suits closing in on her. But they passed her by.

"Geesh," she mumbled. "They were so close they could've stumbled over me. Am I invisible or what?" Suddenly, someone whispered from behind, "What are you doing here?"

Expecting it to be Jackson and Morpheus, she turned slowly. But it was Izaiah, disguising his voice, and she had never been happier to see him and Monica.

"You idiot," she whispered loudly. "You scared the life out of me. What are you doing here? And how did you two find me?"

"We'll explain later," Monica replied. "Meanwhile, we have to find a way out of this madhouse before we end up in a glass cooler like my mom."

"Auntie Liz?" Izaiah asked.

"We'll explain later," Sierra whispered. "You know, I don't think these guys can see us while they're wearing those binoculars.

"How come?" Izaiah asked.

"I was in this corner, thought I was dead in the water when two people walked right past me. They didn't even notice me. There must be a connection between the blue uniforms and the funny eyewear."

"I don't care what the connection is," Izaiah remarked. "Let's get out of here. What is this place, anyhow?" he asked, surveying the city-like compound.

"Whatever it is, it's giving me a headache," Monica squawked.

"Izaiah, there are goggles and masks in that blue box," Sierra whispered. "Get a set for you and Monica and be careful. I think this is a lab where they're manufacturing humans."

"They're procreating people?" Izaiah asked.

"Looks like it," Sierra replied.

"How can they do that?" Monica asked.

"It appears they're crossbreeding some and freezing others after death to bring back to life at a later time."

"You're kidding, right?" Izaiah asked.

"I'm not."

"Do you have a plan of escape?" Monica asked.

"Don't think I'm crazy," Sierra whispered, "but I say we find some creep suits and take a tour of the place. We need to know what we're up against, what's really going on here."

"And I say you're out of your mind," Izaiah stated firmly. "Mom and Dad are worried sick about you. Dad's out now with some friend of his searching for you, and he'd be furious if he knew what you were planning. And, what about that menacing creature I saw with Jackson? He could be sniffing us out as we speak."

"We've got to do this, guys," Sierra stated. "Maybe this is *our* great commission. Who knows whose body and identity they plan to steal next? It could be one of us, a family member, or a friend."

"My point exactly," Izaiah exclaimed. "I like myself just the way I am. I say we leave while we're still intact."

"What do you think, Monica?" Sierra asked. "Should we investigate or leave with our tails between our legs?"

"Uh, okay," she said distractedly. "Anyway, I owe it to my mother to find out what really happened to her."

"What does Auntie Liz have to do with all of this?" Izaiah asked.

"I'll tell you later," Monica replied. "I've been noticing several robot-like people go in that room on the other side of the railing without suits and then come out with the blues. Sorry, I couldn't resist. If we slip into a suit, and move about freely, who knows what we'll find."

"We'll appear less conspicuous if we go in one at a time," Sierra said.

"Who's going first?" Monica asked.

"I'll go," Sierra whispered. "You two work out who'll be next. Once I'm inside, I'll let you in. Be careful and don't draw attention to yourselves."

Sierra moved stealthily to the door that read *Classified Personnel Only.* As she turned the knob, she felt a tug from the other side. She quickly hid behind a cabinet as two men in blue suits emerged and headed toward the escalator. She slipped inside before the automatic door closed.

Blue suits were hanging on racks in the most sterile room she had ever been in. She slipped into a jumper and was zipping it up when she heard the secret knock.

Yanking the door open, she thrust two suits and headgear equipped with transductors at her cohorts. "Hurry, put these on," she said. "Monica, this one is a little big, but it'll cover your backpack."

They donned the goggles and the masks and quickly left the room. The transductors in their headgear allowed them to communicate with each other, as they made their way through a maze of corridors. While the goggles allowed them to witness things they could not have otherwise seen, Monica had her own mission. "I'm going in there," she said, pointing to the Operations Room. "The heart of this setup is probably in there."

"All I want is a way out of this crazy place," Izaiah retorted.

"Monica's right," Sierra whispered. "Most citizens aren't even aware this place exists. What if the Establishment plans to get rid of us all and replace us with replicates? I think that's something we all need to know."

"We need to know how to get our crazy selves out of this crazy place," Izaiah snapped.

"Well, go then," Sierra replied, "but Monica and I are staying. This is our only opportunity to discover what's really going on in this demented town of ours."

"Not only that," Monica interjected, "but we stand a better chance of getting out safely if we all work together. Plus, Izaiah, I need you to be my lookout while I hack into the lab's computer system."

"Have you both gone mad?" he retorted.

Monica slipped into the pristine Operations Room that housed numerous computers. Red, green, and orange lights were flashing at the many workstations. "Where do I begin?" she mumbled. Suddenly, she heard someone coming and quickly ducked into an adjoining room. "I'm going to strangle Izaiah," she murmured. "Some lookout he is." She cracked the door and saw a person in blue sit down at a computer labeled *The Great Commission*. Monica eyed the keyboard as the worker typed in a user name and password. After much input, the person left the room, his posture straight as an arrow.

She ran to the same computer and was about to enter the codes when the door opened again. She subtly pulled her mask down over her face and froze.

"There you are," the man in blue said in a severely monotone voice. "I was looking for you. I need some information from the VP file, and I might as well do it while you're logged on."

Beads of sweat were running down inside her mask as the man leaned over her shoulder. Her hands were shaking, *and* she had forgotten the password.

If I input the wrong code, he'll know I'm a fraud. "I'm going to kill Izaiah if I don't die first," she mumbled.

"What was that?" the man asked.

"Uh…nothing," Monica replied.

"Z, why are you out here pacing up and down drawing attention to yourself?" Sierra asked. "And where's Monica?"

"She's in the Operations Room with a man in blue. I saw him when he went in, but I couldn't warn her. I've been hanging around in case she needs my help."

"She *needed* you to be her lookout," Sierra replied sharply.

"I only turned my back for a minute," he lied, failing to mention his little tour of the floor.

"I'm going in, Z, and you'd better not move," Sierra warned. "This is not some game we're playing."

He knew she was right, and now Monica could be in danger.

Monica typed in what she thought was the password and held her breath. After what seemed like forever, the logon was complete. The files were heavily encrypted, and a tremendous number of symbols appeared on the screen; symbols Monica couldn't make heads or tails of.

Suddenly, the man's hand was on Monica's shoulder, and she went rigid, wondering if he was on to her. "Would you pull up the VP6 files, as well?" he asked.

She was ready to execute some of her defensive moves and dash for the door, when it opened and she heard a familiar voice.

"Anna, do you have that information I requested?" Sierra asked.

"Yes, I do," Monica replied, pretending to be Anna. "Sorry," she told the man, "I'm needed elsewhere." The puzzled man stared at the two women.

Izaiah was still pacing outside the door when Monica walked over to him and whacked him hard in the back of his head.

"You're a terrible lookout," she cried. "Oh no. I left my bag inside."

"I'll get it," Izaiah offered. "That's the least I can do for leaving you alone."

"I knew you had left the area," Sierra scolded. "Things are really piling up for you, Z."

"Make it quick," Monica said. "This place is really freaking me out, and the people are even freakier. We'll meet you in the corridor on the other side. Now, hurry."

Izaiah slowly stepped inside the room. He located the door to the adjoining room and started in that direction, hoping to get in and out without much ado.

"Can I help you?" the man sitting at the computer asked without turning around.

"No...no," Izaiah stammered. "I left something behind earlier. Won't be a minute."

He retrieved Monica's bag, and just as he reached the door, the man turned. He looked Izaiah up and down and spotted his tennis shoes.

"You know it's against the sterilization policy to be anywhere in the facility without booties!" the man scolded. "What is your name and number?"

"My...my name and number?" Izaiah hedged. "Uh, my name is Jonathan, and my number is two-four-six-eight-ten." He yanked the door open and ran toward the east corridor to warn Sierra and Monica.

"We need to leave," he whispered. "My cover's blown."

"What have you done now?" Sierra whispered harshly.

He pointed to his feet.

"You idiot," Monica yelled.

"We have to get out of this un-human factory... *now*," Sierra said.

The man in the Operations Room ran a check on Jonathan and his number, and neither was in the system. He immediately notified Protocol of a possible security breach.

Meanwhile, Jason, Jackson's replicate, was running from room to room with Morpheus, sniffing out Sierra's scent. They were responsible for finding out, by any means necessary, whether or not Sierra had hacked into the general's computer. But their prisoner was nowhere to be found.

Suddenly, Morpheus pulled Jason in the direction of the stairwell. "Is she down there, boy?" he asked, patting the creature's grisly head. "Let's go find her."

CHAPTER 18

The Facility

The telepad rang. "Hello," Ariana said. "No, I haven't heard from her yet, and I'm really worried. By the way, Jacque called. Apparently, Monica's missing, too."

"Please come and get me," she pleaded. "I'm going stir-crazy."

"I know you're afraid, but I need you there in case Sierra calls," Janu replied. "Anyway, Malakh wants to bring Jordan by, if you don't mind. He could use some mothering, and you could use the company."

"No, I don't mind. But how does Jordan know Malakh?"

"I'll explain when we get there. In the meantime, wake Izaiah. I'll need his help."

Ariana knocked on Izaiah's bedroom door, but he didn't answer. She opened the door and switched on the light. His bed was empty. She sank to her knees and cried until she was exhausted.

Janu arrived shortly thereafter and called to her, but she couldn't respond. He ordered Malakh to look around downstairs while he checked upstairs. He found her in the middle of Izaiah's bedroom floor and gently took her in his arms.

"Where's the boy?" he whispered.

"I don't know," she sobbed. "I don't know where either of my children are. How's that for a mother?"

"You're the best mother any child could ask for," Janu told her. "We'll find our children, if I have to turn this evil city upside down."

"There you are," Malakh said, surprised to see Janu and Ariana on the floor. "Is she all right?"

"She will be," Janu replied. "Would you mind putting water on for tea?" Janu rinsed a washcloth in cool water and wiped Ariana's face.

"We'll be in Fa'i soon," he said soothingly.

Meanwhile, their children were across town in a morgue-like facility with alarms pealing all around them.

"What do we do now?" Izaiah asked as they ducked into the nearest stairwell.

"I choke you," Sierra said.

"No fighting. We've got to find a way out of here," Monica interjected. "Sierra, one of us can sneak back into the uniform room and get Izaiah some booties. Then we can mix in with the hullabaloo and walk right out."

"What about me?" Izaiah asked.

"Find a hole and crawl in it," Sierra said.

"I'm sorry, all right?" he replied.

"No, it's not all right," Sierra remarked. "Monica, I'll go, since it was my brother who screwed up."

"We'll both go," she replied. "And don't worry. I'll be a better lookout." She glared at Izaiah.

"What about me?" he asked again.

"Remove your tennis shoes," Monica said. "They stand out like a sore thumb. No one will notice you're missing booties in the chaos. Stay in the stairwell. We'll be back shortly."

The girls opened the door and eased into the corridor. People were running helter-skelter all over the place, so they ran, too, straight into the uniform room. They found the booties and were ready to leave when they heard a *click*.

"No more uniforms will be stolen tonight," said someone on the other side of the door.

Sierra turned the knob; it was locked. "Now what do we do?" she cried.

"We'll bang on the door until someone hears us," Monica said. "The uniforms will hide our identity."

They banged and yelled until they were breathless. Finally, they heard a welcomed *click*.

They opened the door, and there stood Jason and Morpheus.

No one moved. Finally, Sierra said, "Thank you, someone locked us in by mistake."

Morpheus sniffed the air, attempting to pick up the girls' scents, but the uniforms were a deterrent. However, the duo's eyes were riveted on the terrified girls as they hurried across the platform. When the teens reached the stairwell, Izaiah was nowhere to be found.

"Where is he?" Sierra cried.

"He wouldn't have gone quietly, and there are no signs of a struggle," Monica replied.

Just then, three people entered the stairwell. "What's going on?" Monica asked innocently.

"There's been a breach in security," the tall gentleman replied breathlessly. "Notify Protocol if you see anyone suspicious."

"Do we know what he or she looks like?" Monica asked.

"No," a woman said. "But the culprit stole a uniform and mask, and he's wearing tennis shoes. Can you believe that?"

Monica joined in the laughter. "Thanks for the heads-up," she replied. "How many did you say there are?"

"One…that we know of, but there could be more. Be careful."

This was one time when Sierra was glad Monica had the gift of gab; she wasn't sure she could've pulled that off. Suddenly, the alarms stopped.

"They've probably caught the intruder," one gentleman stated. "We should get back to our stations."

Meanwhile, Izaiah was in the sub-basement checking out various rooms. One door was marked *Authorized Personnel Only*. Inside that room was an inner sanctum with the inscription *Synthetic Reproductions*.

"They *are* re-creating people," he mumbled.

He tiptoed from one see-through refrigerator to another, trying to recognize the bodies floating in the stench-filled solution, wondering if they had had a choice in the matter. As he slipped back into the hallway, a door opened. He quickly hid behind a large white cabinet and tried not to hyperventilate. The girls were searching for him.

"This place reminds me of the general's mausoleum," Monica whispered.

"Let's hope there's a window to climb out of," Sierra replied.

"And where are you going?" Izaiah whispered as he stepped into view.

The girls screamed and clung to each other.

"Shhhh!" Izaiah said. "Somebody will hear you."

"Boy, have you lost your mind?" Sierra whispered loudly. "Put these booties on and let's get out of here before you get us all replicated."

"First, come and see what I've found," he replied.

As they slipped back into the Reproduction chamber, Monica began to shiver. She was a diabetic and should have eaten hours ago. She found two granola bars in her bag.

"Can I have one?" Izaiah asked. "I'm starving."

"That's nothing new," Sierra quipped. "Did you recognize anyone in the tanks?"

"No," he replied, "but there are more creatures in there, and I wasn't going in by myself."

They crept toward the closed door. "You go in first, Z," Sierra said, pushing him in front.

"Why do I always have to go first?" he whined.

"I told you, you're the biggest and the strongest, and we can hide behind you," Monica replied.

They huddled together as they entered the dimly lit room. "Look at this one," Izaiah whispered.

"That's a nasty-looking mole," Sierra said. "I'd hate to be around when he wakes up."

"Let's get out of here," Izaiah announced.

Meanwhile, Malakh was heading out the door.

"You can't go without me," Janu said. "You've never seen my children."

"I'll find them," Malakh replied. "Anyway, you're needed here."

Janu knew Malakh was right. Jordan was ill, and Ariana was crazy with fright. He reached into a drawer and pulled out a device.

"What's this?" Malakh asked.

"I've been so upset lately with all that's happened, I forgot I had these tracking monitors," Janu replied. "Since this town has become so bizarre, I borrowed several from the Agency to keep up with my children. I attached one to Sierra and Monica's vehicles and Izaiah's motor bike. This should help you locate them."

"But Uncle M, you don't know who you're looking for," Jordan said helplessly.

"As long as I have this…thingamajig, I'll find them. Now, stop worrying, I'll be back soon."

"Malakh," Janu interjected, "those are my children."

"I'll call you when I've located the vehicle," Malakh replied. "By the way, whose vehicle are they in?"

"They must be in Monica's, because Sierra was picked up by Jackson and Izaiah's motor bike is in the garage."

Malakh got a description of the vehicle and headed out the door.

Meanwhile, the trio had left the Reproduction lab and was turning a corner when they spotted Jason and Morpheus roaming the corridors.

They hid behind a column until the duo disappeared. As they tiptoed into another long corridor, Sierra spotted a large grate in the wall.

"Monica, do you have a screwdriver?" she whispered.

"Yes. Why?"

"We're going to climb inside and follow the air."

Izaiah vigorously unscrewed the grate and helped Sierra climb in. He was about to hoist Monica up when he heard the *click, click, click* of Morpheus' talons. He quickly shoved Monica inside, then climbed in and held the grate as steady as he could.

"Don't move a muscle," he whispered.

"Are they coming?" Sierra asked.

He nodded his head and tried hard not to move the screen. The disgusting pair stood by the grille for what seemed like an eternity. Izaiah watched as Morpheus continuously sniffed the air, grateful the uniforms masked their scents. Finally, the duo moved on, and the *click, click, click* slowly faded.

"Who has bubble gum?" Izaiah asked. Monica pulled a wad out of her mouth.

"I don't want that nasty thing."

She shoved it at him. "It's already pliable."

He pressed the gum between the grille and the wall to temporarily hold the grate in place, then squeezed past the girls to lead the way.

"Stay close," he whispered. "If we follow the air, it should lead us to the outside."

Monica was feeling really bad by now, but she didn't want to let on. Finally, she said, "I'm burning up in this suit."

Malakh, meanwhile, was searching the city with the tracking monitor. But it was way past curfew and not a teenager was in sight.

Suddenly, he had a horrifying thought. As he sped down the highway, an Enforcer flashed his lights and pulled him over. The uniformed man slowly approached his vehicle.

"License and Statistic," the Enforcer said.

Malakh handed him the necessary papers, and the Enforcer immediately apologized.

"I'm so sorry, Grand Master Malakh," the Enforcer said. "I'll escort you across town, and you won't be troubled again."

"Thanks," Malakh replied. "Time is of the essence."

Back at the madhouse, Izaiah and the girls were literally frying in their suits. The space was tight, and their knees were raw and bleeding inside their uniforms from crawling on the hard steel floor.

"Where does this thing end?" Sierra complained. "My back is killing me."

"I don't want to die in this place," Monica moaned.

"Stop complaining and keep going," Izaiah said.

"You don't have to bite our heads off," Sierra snapped.

"You're sucking up all the good air with your jibber-jabber," Izaiah retorted.

With no signs of getting closer to the outside, they were all on edge. And the higher they climbed, the hotter it became. Their strength waned, and they had little air to breathe. They knew they were in trouble, but they couldn't turn back.

"Mom and Dad will be so disappointed when they hear of our deaths," Sierra panted.

"Nobody's dying," Z wheezed. "We'll get out."

"How? We don't know where we are," Sierra replied. "We could be captured and replicasized… or worse."

"Replicasized?" Monica whispered.

"I made it up."

"Please stop talking," Izaiah begged.

"You're right," Sierra agreed. "We'll just quietly die in this tube."

"No, I mean it. I think I hear something."

Suddenly, a surge of air rushed over them, and they clung to each other to avoid being blown backward down the chute.

"Let's keep going," Sierra cried.

"I don't know if I can make it," Monica whispered. "You guys go on without me."

Monica had removed her mask and was turning purple; blood was dripping from her nose.

Sierra gasped. "Monica, you're scaring me. Z, do something."

"She's got to have air," he replied. "Quick, remove your belt, hook it to mine, then tie them to the rope in Monica's bag."

"But I can hardly move in this small space."

"Just do it," he said. "Put her on my back and tie the belts around the two of us as tight as you can."

"I didn't know she was this sick," Sierra panted. "She's in this mess because of me. If we lose her, it's my fault."

"We won't lose her," he replied. "Are you finished?"

"Yes."

They crawled toward the draft until their knees and legs were numb. Pushing through another gush of strong air, they came to an elevator shaft.

Izaiah was trembling and could hardly breathe when they finally reached the grille. He was sweating profusely, and his hands were raw and bleeding.

"Sis," he whispered, "I'm not sure I can make it. Go for help. We'll wait here until you get back."

"I'm not leaving anybody behind," Sierra replied. She kicked the grille until it came loose. It seemed to fall forever before hitting the bottom. Once inside the shaft, they would still have the insurmountable task of getting out while the elevators were ascending and descending at bullet speed.

Sierra knew Monica couldn't climb the ladder to the upper landing by herself. And although Izaiah was strong, she wasn't sure he could carry Monica's dead weight. She stepped out onto the ledge to assess the situation as an elevator was fast approaching. Unfortunately, there was no time to crawl back inside. She pressed her back as close to the wall as possible, hoping there was room for the lift to pass without taking her with it. Suddenly, Izaiah grabbed her arm.

"Quick," he shouted through the screeching noise. "Grab that bar on the left and be as still as you can."

She held her breath as the elevator rushed by and every fiber of her being shook. She was almost pulled from the platform.

She had heard that death was like crossing the street, but when she slowly opened her eyes, looking up at her was a smiling, teary-eyed Izaiah. She started to cry as he told her with a quivering voice, "I knew you could do it."

He helped her inside and held her close. "You really had me scared," he whispered.

"Me, too," she sobbed. "How's Monica?"

"While you were playing superwoman, I found a prescription bottle and a lemon bar in her bag. I stuck a pill under her tongue and a bar in her mouth, but she still looks pretty bad."

"What are we going to do, Z? We've got to get her out of here."

"You go up the ladder first, and I'll hoist her up from behind."

"Don't you think we should strap her to your back?"

"What if the harness breaks and she falls? For once, let's do it my way."

Brush with Death

Sierra and Izaiah hurriedly dragged Monica along the narrow ledge of the shaft. If the elevators started upward again, this time there would be no escape.

Sierra proceeded up the ladder first, followed by a very weak Monica, who was certain she was going to "die in this awful place." Suddenly, the nightmare they all dreaded became a reality.

"Go faster," Izaiah shouted.

"Monica can barely move," Sierra countered.

Izaiah pushed her up from behind as Sierra shouted, "Monica, move your behind or we're all going to die."

"Just leave me," she wailed.

"That is not an option," Sierra bellowed. "Now, move it."

"Would you two stop yakking?" Izaiah whispered. "This elevator is about to bite me in the butt."

The elevator started upward again and stopped at the floor just beneath them. From the conversations inside the lift, Izaiah knew they were still being hunted.

As he quickly moved to the next rung, a piece of rebar protruding from the underside of the step tore through his uniform, slicing his left shin.

Sierra pulled Monica to the top, then spotted the blood. "Z, you're bleeding," she cried.

"Shhhh!" He grimaced. "The people in the lift will hear you."

The elevator ascended again, and Izaiah swung his bleeding leg up to the last rung. But his blood-soaked bootie detached from his sock and fell on to the elevator cable.

"Sierra, I lost my bootie," he whispered.

"The *bloody* one?"

"Yeah."

"No one will find it," she replied.

"I hope you're right."

Monica moaned as Sierra replaced her mask. "I know it's uncomfortable," she said, "but we're going to try to leave the way we came in."

"Where's my bag?" Monica wheezed.

"I have it," Sierra replied, then force-fed Monica another lemon bar.

"Can you walk on your own?" Izaiah asked Monica, as they eased into the corridor.

"I think so."

"Head for the exit on the other side of the escalator," Izaiah said, "and I'll follow." Sierra and a slow-moving Monica headed for the stairwell. Once inside, they heard running on the stairs.

"What do we do now?" Monica whispered.

"I have no idea," Sierra replied.

Izaiah was following the girls when he heard someone shout, "Stop, young man."

If he turned and ran in the opposite direction, that would draw unwanted suspicion. "Are you talking to me?" Izaiah asked, as the man trotted toward him.

"I think I know where the intruder may be, and I need you to come with me," the portly gentleman panted.

"But I spotted someone suspicious running in that direction," Izaiah said, pointing opposite the staircase the girls had entered.

"Where are your shoes and booties?" the man asked.

"In the uniform room." Izaiah chuckled lamely. "I heard the alarm and didn't have time to put them on. The mission was more important."

"We'll have to carry on without them," the man replied. "Protocol has ordered us to find this interloper. Maybe the person you saw is still on the premises. If we hurry, maybe we can catch him."

"I think we should split up," Izaiah suggested.

"I don't," the man replied. "If we find him, I might need your help in containing him."

"Monica, how are you holding up?" Sierra asked.

"I don't think I can make it."

She lifted Monica's mask. "Here, grab some air."

"We've got to find a way out, Sierra, or I'll die."

They were already on the top landing with nowhere else to go but the roof, and Sierra was terrified. "Z, where are you?" she cried.

After much insistence, the officer agreed to separate from Izaiah, who rushed to the staircase where Sierra and Monica were hiding.

He quickly climbed the stairs, but just before reaching the top landing, a door swung open, and he faced his pursuers.

"Have we found him yet?" Izaiah quickly asked, as if he was part of the search.

"Not yet," a woman replied. "But he can't escape. The facility's on lockdown."

Izaiah joined the group and was leading them up the stairs when he spotted Sierra quickly replacing Monica's mask.

"What's going on here?" he asked authoritatively. He was wearing his mask, but Sierra recognized his bare feet and was momentarily relieved.

"We were pursuing a suspicious character when my friend suddenly took ill," Sierra replied.

"Take her to the lab, her wires might be crossed," a man in the crowd instructed.

"She's better now," Sierra quickly responded.

"Keep going," Izaiah bellowed to the group as if he was in charge. "The perp could be getting away and we're standing here gabbing. I'll escort the ladies down."

Izaiah's authoritative behavior amazed Sierra. "What do we do now?" she asked, as they watched their predators retreat.

"We're going to get the heck out of here," Izaiah replied.

Meanwhile, Malakh waved off the Enforcer escorting him across town. His mobile rang as he turned left onto Crescent Street.

"No, I haven't found them yet. I'll call when I do."

"They didn't just disappear," Janu barked. "Apparently, this is a two-man job." He was taking his anguish out on Malakh. "I'm sorry," he said. "I know you're doing all you can."

"I haven't given up," Malakh replied. "Must the vehicle be moving for the tracker to locate it?"

"No. Why?"

"I might be going about this the wrong way. I'll call you later."

He jumped on the expressway heading north, suddenly driving like a crazed man. He had a feeling that if he didn't hurry, he might not find the kids alive or unharmed.

He sped down Clariot Street until he reached the facility center, then stared up at the old house. Suddenly, the tracker began to beep, confirming his worst nightmare.

He paraded up and down the street until he spotted a flashing red light under a small green vehicle partially hidden by a large oak tree. It was Monica's…and it was empty.

Screeching sounds suddenly pierced the night. He spotted the humanlike creatures in the nearby trees and knew the kids were in that house and in serious trouble.

From his trunk, he retrieved the blue suit, mask, and booties he had stolen in the cemetery and quickly donned the outfit. He then proceeded to the rear of the old house.

He jiggled the lock open with a small knife and stood in the basement of a place he had sworn he would never reenter.

Meanwhile, the fugitives reached the basement and eased into the long white corridor. "Someone's coming," Izaiah whispered.

Click, click, click. They ducked into a dark room until the *click*ing disappeared. Suddenly, Monica moaned. “Someone’s holding me, and I can’t move.” When Sierra found the light switch, they all screamed.

“Shhhhh!” Malakh whispered, “or we’re all dead.”

The man in the refrigerator was now in the room. And that sickening mole with the hair protruding out of it was even more gross up close.

“Please, let me go,” Monica begged.

“I’m sorry I frightened you,” he said, “but you need to be very quiet.”

“And how did you think we’d manage that after scaring us half to death?” Sierra asked.

“Weren’t you just floating in a disgusting liquid?” Izaiah asked.

“Are you alive or NOT?” Sierra questioned.

“I’m very much alive, and my name is Malakh. Your father sent me to find you. What are you guys doing here?”

“We’ll ask the questions,” Izaiah replied.

“And just how do you know Uncle J?” Monica asked.

“We work together. And when you, Sierra, didn’t come home before curfew and Izaiah wasn’t in his room after curfew, and when Monica’s dad called your house looking for her, Janu called me for assistance.”

“Why didn’t he come himself?” Sierra asked.

"He's taking care of your worried-sick mother and my ailing nephew, Jordan.

"Jordan… Jordan Ancil?" Sierra asked. "Is he your nephew?"

"Yes, and he was assaulted after leaving your house."

So that's why I haven't heard from him, Sierra thought.

"Look," Malakh said, "the longer we stay here, the more dangerous it becomes." He eyed the children. "The uniforms are good, but where are your shoes and booties, Izaiah?"

"My shoes are inside Monica's backpack, and I only have one bootie," Izaiah replied, eyeing the stranger suspiciously.

"Put your shoes on," Malakh instructed. He searched the room, then handed him a fresh pair of booties.

"Are you the man who was floating in the tank across the hall?" Izaiah asked again.

"Let's try to get out of here in one piece," Malakh replied, ignoring the question.

"And how do you propose we do that?" Sierra asked.

"I'm familiar with this place," Malakh said.

"Now…why does that not surprise me?" Izaiah commented.

Malakh was already annoyed with these kids, who had lured him back to a place he didn't want to be. "Do exactly as I say," he said, "or we might not get out alive."

"But Monica's sick," Sierra replied.

Malakh reached inside his uniform and pulled out a wafer. "Eat this," he said. "We're going to walk out the front door, and we don't have time for you to be sick."

"Are you insane?" Sierra whispered. "It'll be heavily guarded."

"Probably," Malakh replied.

"Then you *have* lost your mind," Sierra countered, forgetting her manners. "Or do you want us to be captured and turned into the walking dead?"

"If I wanted that, I wouldn't be here to rescue you," he replied. "Izaiah and Monica will go out first, and Sierra and I will bring up the rear. Now, let's go."

"Why can't we get out the way you got in?" Sierra asked.

"It would take too long," Malakh replied.

Sierra mouthed to Izaiah that she wasn't sure about this guy. But Monica was amazed at how fast the wafer had worked. Her energy was already off the charts, and she was once again her old self. She needed a year's supply of that stuff.

Someone was running in the corridor. "Stay calm," Malakh whispered as they eased their way upstairs to the front entrance.

"My car is parked down the street on your right," he said. "Sierra, start the engine and keep it running until I get there."

"What are you going to do?" she asked.

"I don't have time to explain. If the guards ask where you're going, tell them you've been assigned by Protocol to canvass the neighborhood."

"What kind of car are you driving?" Izaiah asked.

"It's a dark blue Shinei."

"And just how are we supposed to find a dark blue Shinei in the dark?" Monica questioned.

"By the gilded angel on the hood," he replied.

"An angel?" Sierra questioned.

"Just go. You kids will be the death of me with your interrogations. And keep your eyes on the trees," Malakh cautioned.

"Why the trees?" Izaiah asked.

"Creatures are lurking in them."

"If they're anything like Morpheus, I want Mommy," Izaiah replied.

"Stop being silly," Sierra scolded.

"I'm serious. I really want Mommy."

CHAPTER 20

The Zenith

As suspected, the Enforcers outside the facility were still on watch for the trespasser.

"Let's go," Malakh told the youngsters, and shoved Izaiah and Monica through the door. Izaiah nodded at the Enforcer guarding the entrance and quickly proceeded down the steps.

"Where are you going?" the Enforcer asked.

"We've been ordered to scour the neighborhood for the intruder," Izaiah replied.

Sierra had just reached the bottom step when Malakh took the kids and the Enforcers by surprise. "The intruder has been spotted behind the building," he shouted. "Come with me," he told the Enforcers as he ran down the steps.

"We can't leave our posts," the young Enforcer stated.

"What's your name, Officer?" Malakh asked.

"Rafael, sir."

"Well, Rafael, you could be dismissed for insubordination to a Senior Enforcer's command." As Malakh distracted the officers, the teens hurried down the dark street.

"Sir, I have to get permission to leave my post," the young Enforcer declared.

"And your supervisor will have you arrested when he finds out you let the enemy get away," Malakh snapped.

Izaiah, meanwhile, was frantically searching for the Shinei. "Could he have parked any farther down the street?" he whined.

Monica spotted the car under a tree. Izaiah pressed the unlock button on the key fob several times, but to no avail.

"There's a keypad on the side of the door," Monica stated. "We probably need the code."

"He only gave me the key fob," Izaiah replied.

Monica tried several combinations, then noticed the cherub on the hood. She keyed in the letters *a n g e l.*

"Now press the key fob," she told Izaiah.

"You drive, Sierra," Monica said as she opened the door and leapt into the back seat with Izaiah quickly hopping in behind her.

"Malakh didn't tell me to drive," Sierra replied. "He said to start the car. And we can't just leave him. If it wasn't for him, we would still be in that tomb."

"We don't even know who he is, or if he's telling the truth," Izaiah remarked. "This could be a trap."

"Call Uncle J and ask him," Monica suggested.

Meanwhile, Janu was wearing a hole in the carpet pacing back and forth. He hadn't felt this helpless since his trip across the river. Jordan lay quietly, nursing his sore ribs while Ariana sat motionless.

Tears streamed down her face as she remembered the battle Sierra had waged in her womb to survive. And now all of her children were lost. It was too much to take.

"Are we just going to sit here?" she suddenly cried. The telepad rang, and they stared at it as if it had leprosy. Finally, Janu snatched the receiver from its cradle.

"Daddy, it's me," Sierra cried. "We're on speaker."

"Are you all right?" Janu screamed. "Have you seen Izaiah and Monica?"

"We're all here," Izaiah offered, "and we're okay…for now."

Sierra started to cry, then tried to pull herself together. She didn't want to upset her dad any more than he already was.

"Z and Monica came to rescue me," she sobbed.

"Just come home," Janu shouted, tears of relief warming his cheeks.

"We're trying, Daddy. We're in a car belonging to a man named Malakh. He says he's your friend, but we don't know if we can trust him."

"I sent him to look for you while I stayed with your mother and Jordan."

"I heard what happened to Jordan," she said. "Is he all right? And how is Mommy?"

When Sierra referred to him and Ariana as *mommy* and *daddy*, Janu knew she was frightened. "Jordan is fine, and your mother wants you kids to come home. Where's Malakh?"

"He's distracting the Enforcers at this strange house so we can get away, but we're not sure whether we should leave him here."

"Don't leave him," Janu said. "We need him if we're to escape this crazy place alive. Why didn't you girls contact me on your Laisser-Faire?"

"I forgot mine, and Monica almost died."

"What is a Laisser-Faire?" Izaiah asked. "And why don't I have one?"

"What was that about Monica?" Janu asked, ignoring Izaiah.

Suddenly, the kids began to scream. Out of nowhere, a huge winged creature flew overhead and lifted Malakh off the ground, carrying him away into the night.

"What's happening?" Janu asked.

"This is not good," Izaiah shouted.

"Daddy, one of those bird-man-creature-things with huge wings just flew away with Malakh!" Sierra cried. "Now what do we do?"

"Calm down and come home," he replied. "Don't drive past the Enforcers; you'll draw attention to yourselves. You could all be arrested for curfew violation, so be on the lookout for Enforcers."

"We'll be home within the hour, if all goes well," Sierra cried.

"All will go well because the King cares," Janu replied.

How King Uriel would know of their situation, Sierra had no idea. But her dad's words were comforting nonetheless.

"Can we ditch the sweat suits?" Monica asked as they turned around and headed home.

"We need them in case we get stopped," Sierra replied.

"Well, if anyone's interested, I'll be the puddle of water in the back seat," Monica quipped.

"How do you feel, Monica?" Izaiah asked sincerely.

"After tonight's horrific events, I'm shaking like a leaf. But physically, I've never felt better. I must find out what was in that wafer."

"If we ever see him again, we can ask," Sierra replied sadly. "Malakh was trying to save us, and now we can't save him."

"Just get us home in one piece," Izaiah stated. "And remember what Dad told you."

"Don't preach to me, Z. I have enough to worry about without listening to your back-seat driving."

"Would you rather I preach to you in the front?" he teased, trying to lighten the situation.

"Just be quiet. I'm nervous enough."

In Malakh's efforts to rescue the youngsters, he had once again underestimated his archenemy, Cerberus. He tried freeing himself, but the creature's talons dug deeper into his shoulders, like sharp knives slicing through raw flesh. The temperature of the ice-cold wet clouds sent shock waves through Malakh, and he felt as if he'd been stripped naked. The flapping of the bird-man's huge wings gave Malakh a migraine, and he felt like an ant being carried off by an elephant.

"Where are you taking me?" he shouted.

Before Malakh could brace himself, the bird-man and playmate of Prince Diablo sent Malakh crashing headlong into the side of a mountain before he tumbled onto a nearby ledge.

"Why were you at the facility?" Cerberus roared in a voice that sounded like a strong wind.

"I could ask you the same," Malakh replied. "And who's guarding the gates of Hades while you're up here visiting?"

"You were warned," Cerberus replied, his foul breath permeating the clean, fresh mountain air. "You made a binding contract with our Prince that if you were released, you would expose his enemies. And if you did not, you would be destroyed. As yet, he's received no intel from you regarding his adversaries."

"The Prince has kept the details of his Great Commission secret, so how can the citizens be against something they know little or nothing about?" Malakh replied.

"Don't play games with me," Cerberus roared, baring his ugly fangs. "You've had enough time to determine who our enemies are. Tell me, or you won't leave this mountain alive."

"There are a lot of people who seem suspect," Malakh replied. "But I won't accuse anyone falsely. I need more time."

"Do you think the Great Commission is a game?" Cerberus roared.

"Dethroning Uriel and enslaving Fa'i's inhabitants is most certainly not a game," Malakh replied.

"And you will help us succeed, whether you like it or not," Cerberus hissed.

"I'm not intimidated, Cerberus. I need more time."

"You're out of time, Malakh. The Great Commission is soon to be launched, and we have knowledge of several citizens who could prematurely leak our plans to Uriel. You have until Wednesday next to confirm who those citizens are."

Cerberus bent low, and Malakh stared into his fiery eyes. "I know I can count on you," the creature whispered, dragging his sharp talon under Malakh's chin.

Malakh was furious, but now was not the time to retaliate. "I'm at your disposal," he replied.

"You speak the truth," the creature hissed. "And don't you forget it."

"You mentioned suspects," Malakh said, wiping the blood from his chin. "I need names. I can't deliver if I have to constantly play guessing games."

"They're right under your nose," Cerberus roared. "Now, get us what we want."

Malakh suddenly covered his ears. Out of the thick darkness came a host of bird-men, and the sound was deafening. Led by the chameleon-like Prince Diablo, who had once again changed his persona, they settled on the mountain above.

More hideous than his feathered comrades, Diablo spread his wings, and six large bloodshot eyes on the inside of each wing glared at Malakh. He knew the Prince could be obnoxious, but this was nauseating, even for him. *What a loathsome creature*, Malakh thought.

Diablo's ruby-red eyes protruded from his much-too-large forehead. And the wisps of black hair sitting on his bald head were dangling in front of his ugly face. His drooling mouth was in the form of a large beak, displaying enormous fangs.

"Malakh, my comrade, what a displeasure," Diablo said. "How have you been? Just as *fowl* as ever?" he asked, and pointed to the birds, who joined in a chorus of laughter.

"I've been better," Malakh calmly replied.

"Why were you at my facility center?" Diablo asked pointedly.

"I was checking on my other self."

"You mean the one who's floating in a big vat of chromazium?" the Prince bellowed. "Thanks to your other self, we will soon have our master race."

"And what will happen to the current citizens?" Malakh asked. He knew the Prince planned to eliminate most, if not all, of the population.

"That will not be an issue, I promise," Diablo replied.

"For the record," Malakh stated, "I don't appreciate being flown to this zenith against my will."

"Your will is my will," Diablo replied.

"Then what is this really about?" Malakh asked, feigning frustration.

"It is about you taking way too much time to deliver on our agreement," the Prince stated.

"As I explained to Cerberus, these guessing games are beginning to bore me," Malakh replied. "Just tell me whom I should be focusing on."

Diablo hesitated. "A student at the Academy by the name of Jordan Ancil, a know-it-all, tried to embarrass me in front of the entire Gathering. Anyone brazen enough to challenge me has to be up to no good."

Malakh wondered if the Prince had ordered the attack on Jordan.

"In addition," Diablo continued, "a young lady by the name of Sierra Calder, who also attends the Academy, and her parents, have subversive ideas about me and my Establishment. Check them out, as well."

"Sir, her brother has been recently inducted into PsyOps," Cerberus offered. "He could be a spy to discover and expose our secrets."

Malakh was stunned. *Izaiah a PsyOp? Does Janu know?* Hiding his dismay, he said, "Now, that's the kind of information I need."

"You see my dilemma," the Prince stated. "These people must be caught, and you're the man to do it."

"How much time do I have?" Malakh asked, trying to sidestep Cerberus' deadline.

"Yesterday," Cerberus answered for the Prince.

"I *can* report that I recently removed a traitor from inside the CCA," Malakh announced. "He was about to blow my cover."

"How did you handle it?" Diablo asked.

"I planted on him the evidence he intended to plant on me, and his plan backfired. It all worked to my—I mean our—benefit."

"It's only a matter of time before they're all flushed out," Diablo insisted. "And should you attempt to cover up or aid any conspirators in any way, I will consider you a traitor and a threat, as well."

"And what do I get for my allegiance?"

The Prince folded his eye-encrusted wings around himself.

"You get to keep your head," he roared. "Now, get him out of my sight," he ordered Cerberus.

CHAPTER 21

Annihilation

They were two blocks from home when Sierra missed the stop sign behind a large tree.

"Watch out for that car," Izaiah yelled.

"I almost wet my pants," Monica shouted.

"Oh, shut up and watch out for Enforcers," Sierra snapped.

"Just trying to help," Izaiah retorted.

Suddenly, they spotted a parked red and black. Sierra quickly dimmed her headlights.

"We can't go pass them," Monica stated.

"Make a right here, and take the alley behind Brookshire," Izaiah instructed.

The teens finally pulled into the driveway, unaware of the creatures lurking nearby.

Meanwhile, Janu, Ariana, and Jordan were gathered around the computer, aghast, as they perused more of the general's files.

"Mom, Dad, we're home," Sierra cried.

Janu and Ariana rushed the children.

"I can't breathe," Sierra complained. But her parents' arms felt warm and safe, and she had never been so glad to see anyone in her whole life. Even Izaiah welcomed Janu's hug, something he hadn't experienced lately because of their differences.

"You okay, boy?" Janu asked.

"I'm fine, but I had to rescue your daughters from extreme danger, and now I'm hungry," he quipped.

"He's fine, if he wants to eat," Ariana said, then kissed him on the cheek.

"What are you guys wearing?" she asked.

"Getaway suits," Izaiah joked.

"Well, take them off. They stink."

There were three puddles in the middle of the floor, but Ariana didn't mind. Instead, she fetched towels and dry clothes for her three prodigals.

"Where's Jordan?" Sierra asked.

"In the hallway, and in no condition to be squeezed," he replied, stepping forward.

Sierra hugged him gently. "How are you?" she asked, eyeing his bandages.

"I'm okay," he replied. "Now, come and see what we've discovered."

Sierra and Monica were dumbfounded as they read of the Establishment's experimentation with cross-breeding.

"That explains what we saw at the facility center," Sierra remarked sadly.

"And the general's basement," Monica added.

"And the cemetery," Janu mumbled.

"What cemetery?" Ariana asked.

"I'll explain later," Janu replied. "But, there's one file we'll need Monica's magic to open."

"First, change into these dry clothes," Ariana commanded.

She made turkey sandwiches and hot tea for everyone, grateful her children were safe. But she wouldn't know how grateful she was until she heard the whole story.

"Did you guys find out what happened to Malakh?" Janu asked.

"No. And after what we saw tonight, we didn't want to," Izaiah quickly responded.

Monica returned, sat down at the computer, and after cracking her knuckles, announced, "Let's get started."

Meanwhile, Malakh and Cerberus were airborne once again. The creature literally dropped Malakh off in a tree near the facility, and when he climbed down, he was covered with cuts and bruises.

The leaves in his hair gave the appearance of a green wig, and he smelled like Cerberus. It was midnight when he called for a cab.

The Calder household was asleep in their chairs as Monica created an algorithm to break into the unopened file. It was taking forever to work, and she, too, started to nod off. Finally, the computer beeped long and loud and woke everyone except Izaiah.

"He'd sleep through a hurricane," Ariana exclaimed with a smile.

Monica read a portion of the file and cried, "Oh boy."

"What is it?" Sierra asked, jumping to her feet.

"It's the general's personal diary."

"Read it out loud," Janu said.

"I don't want to read any more," she said.

"I'll read it," Sierra replied. As she perused the file, she began to weep.

"What's the matter?" Ariana asked.

"Among others, our family's listed for annihilation," she cried. "And because Jordan and Monica associate with us, they're included. We've been labeled subversive, disloyal, and treasonous," she continued. "All except Z." She turned and stared at Izaiah, who was snoring softly.

"Let me see," Janu said.

"She's right," he remarked sadly. "We'll have to leave sooner than planned."

Meanwhile, Malakh was hiding behind a tree. When he spotted the cab, he ditched the blues. But the cabby wasn't sure he wanted a fare from a man discarding a weird uniform with an ugly mole. Malakh, however, quickly leaped into the back seat.

"Take me back across the bridge," Malakh ordered. "And hurry."

"Are you gonna hurt me?" the cabby asked.

Malakh knew how he must look and smell, not to mention how hideous his infamous mole was. "No," he replied, smiling.

"Can you pay the fare for such a long trip?" the cabby asked.

"I can," he replied. "And there's extra, if you get me there in record time, without being stopped by Enforcers."

The cabby left the curb at record speed, throwing Malakh back in his seat.

"I'd like to get there in one piece," Malakh shouted.

"Then strap yourself in, sir. I have a lot of mouths to feed, and I can use the extra dough."

Janu, meanwhile, was almost finished scanning the general's diary when he exclaimed, "I knew

Malakh was too good to be true. He's in bed with the Establishment."

"That's not true, Mr. C," Jordan declared.

"Then how do you explain the general's knowledge of private conversations your uncle and I have had?"

"I don't know," Jordan replied, "but my uncle would never betray you. Soon you'll know the truth."

"What truth, Jordan?"

Jordan didn't answer. Meanwhile, Janu was so overcome by Malakh's betrayal he'd forgotten Izaiah wasn't on the list. But Sierra hadn't. She walked over and kicked him in the shin.

"Ouch, Sierra, what is wrong with you?"

"How is it that your name doesn't appear on this, this…death list?" she asked.

"What 'death list'?"

She dragged him to the computer. "READ," she shouted.

Finally, he confessed. "I… I joined PsyOps, Diablo's covert organization, and I guess I'm protected."

"Protected from what?" Sierra shouted.

"From *everything*? I don't know."

"You did something that stupid without talking to your mother and me?" Janu screamed. "Are you insane? These people are trying to kill your family for no other reason than we disagree with their sick philosophies. And they're planning war against my King."

"I don't believe your King exists," Izaiah retorted, "but I know Prince Diablo does, and I want to be a part of his Great Commission."

"Read it for yourself, son," Janu shouted. "If my King doesn't exist, then why is your Prince creating a futuristic army to overtake a king and a kingdom that…isn't?"

"Yelling is not helping," Ariana said. "We must find a way out of this mess."

"Let Mister Wonder Boy find a way out," Janu shouted.

"Z, how could you?" Sierra asked.

"You guys don't know anything about it," Izaiah replied. "PsyOps gives me the respect I never get around here. Dad, you never listen to my views or try to understand how I feel. You only dictate how *you* want me to feel. Well, I don't feel about a lot of things the way you do, and when Jackson approached me…"

"Jackson?" Sierra asked. "What does he have to do with this?"

"He and the general sponsored me. Without their support, I never would have gotten in."

"Jackson knew about this and didn't tell me?" she asked.

"My understanding," Jordan interjected, "is that among other things, PsyOps' purpose is to expose family and friends who don't agree with Diablo's ideologies and then turn them in to the Establishment."

Janu was in Izaiah's face. "I've been working for years to free this family from demonic rule, and you've been reporting our comings and goings to our enemies? You've put this entire family, and our friends, in mortal danger, and I'm ashamed of you."

The doorbell rang, and they thought they had awakened the neighbors.

"Who is it?" Janu all but shouted.

"It's me," Malakh whispered.

Janu opened the door. "You look and smell a mess," he said.

"It's a long story," Malakh replied. He stepped into the room and greeted everyone. Nobody responded.

"I see you guys made it home safely," he remarked. Still no response. "Is everybody deaf? What's going on?"

"Maybe you should tell us," Sierra said sarcastically. "Better still, read what's going on." She pointed to the computer. "Have a seat."

He examined the document. "I was certain this is what was being planned, but I had no way of proving it," he stated.

"Can you explain how the general knows secrets that only you and I have shared?" Janu accused. "I didn't tell him."

"Me neither," Malakh replied. "You've got to believe me."

"I believe you," Jordan replied.

"You would," Sierra snapped.

Malakh put his finger to his lips. "It could mean one of two things," he whispered. "You've got a mole in your home, or our homes and devices are bugged."

He turned to Izaiah. "Do your parents know you're a PsyOp?" he asked. "More importantly, are you eavesdropping on your father and me and divulging our conversations?"

"No," Izaiah countered. "Why is everyone ganging up on me? I have a right to live and believe as I choose."

"But you don't have a right to jeopardize the lives of your family and friends," Janu snapped. "You've been deceived and influenced by an evil force."

"Look," Malakh concluded, "it's been a long, arduous day and night for all of us. Let's get some sleep, then we'll be able to think clearly."

Malakh took Janu by the shoulders. "I would never betray you," he whispered. "From now on, I'd use my Laisser-Faire when speaking in this house. We'll talk later."

"I'm exhausted, I'm going to bed," Sierra said.

She kissed her parents and slowly ascended the stairs with Monica in tow, followed shortly by Izaiah, who did *not* want to be alone with his dad.

Janu and Ariana sat quietly holding hands, not knowing who or what to believe. Although physically and mentally exhausted, nothing compared to the pain of their son's betrayal.

Early that morning, Ariana awakened Janu from a ghoulish daydream. "It's okay, honey," she whispered. "We'll be home soon."

He lay on his damp pillow, mindful of the guilt she must be carrying, knowing it was initially her idea to cross the river. He'd heard her weeping many nights when she thought he was asleep. But by morning, she would smile and say, *"One day, honey, we're going to see the King."*

He fell asleep again, and when he awakened, he could smell the coffee brewing and the bacon cooking, and he realized how little he'd eaten yesterday. He sat on the side of the bed and was reminded of the horrors of the past day and night. He showered and dressed, dreading the unavoidable confrontation with his son. He loved his children overwhelmingly, including Monica, who had been fighting for her life since she lost her mother. *What a mess our lives are*, he thought, as his mobile chimed.

"I'll be there within the hour," Malakh said. "If we're to quickly finalize our plan, it's time to get your family involved."

Meanwhile, General Armon was at the Diablo Strategic Center, holding an emergency meeting with the Brethren.

"Unfortunately, our beloved Prince could not physically be with us today," he announced. "But he wanted you to know that he's here with you in spirit."

Diablo had transformed himself into an elderly gentleman who was sitting in the rear of the auditorium, hoping to uncover any Brethren opposing his quest.

"When we last met," the general continued, "you were told to report all insurgents within your precincts. Please drop those names in the basket at the end of the meeting."

"I know some of you, if not all, may have been shocked to learn that the replication process of our citizens has already begun, as I outlined in your packets. But be assured, this is the only way to win a victory for our prince."

"In our attempt to create a stronger species, we ran into a few obstacles when cross-breeding some humans with certain animals and reptiles. However, those obstacles have been surmounted, and we are now on point."

"Can you duplicate my wife?" one man shouted. "I'd gladly swap her for one who'd act right."

Everyone laughed, including the elderly gentleman in the rear.

"See me after class," the general replied, "and I'll see what I can do. Tonight, however, you will witness what we've kept hidden for decades. With an open mind, you'll be able to see our new future, our new world and its new order. We'll view the processes of Synthetic Reproduction, and how it has and will continue to play a major role in the success of Diablo's Great Commission."

While Janu waited for Malakh, he viewed one of the general's files not previously examined. As fate would have it, he would read the identical information the general was preparing to share with the Brethren.

Back at the DSC, the lights were dimmed, the projector lowered, and various silhouettes and dimensions danced on the screen.

"My fellow compatriots," the general began. "We all know of the paradise across the river, which was once our home, along with many others not in attendance tonight."

"And in case you've forgotten, we've reminded you of Fa'i's magnificence in your manuals. For ages, our great and powerful prince has strategized to take the throne of that city, and we're going to help him. This paradise has eluded us far too long."

Great applause followed.

The general's voice swelled. "Most of all, Diablo's heartfelt desire is that our families, friends, and loved ones have access to the River of Life that will keep our youth young and erase years from our elderly."

The Brethren whistled and cheered. The Prince had failed to inform the general that the river would also reverse his hidden and mysterious curse.

The elderly gentleman in the rear stood to his feet and cried, "Long live our prince and soon-to-be king."

General Armon echoed the cheer until every man was on his feet chanting the mantra. When the general thought the old gentleman was satisfied, he waved his hand, and order was restored.

"Although our beloved prince has experienced some resistance," the general continued, "he will not give up his right to possess Fa'i, or our right to live forever." More thunderous applause.

"Brethren, you are about to witness firsthand the creation and re-creation of life as you've never known it." The general clicked his remote, and the presentation began.

"What you're seeing, gentlemen, is the replication of cells, often referred to as Synthetic

Reproduction. Simply stated, it is the process of duplicating human cells in order to reproduce a human. It is a repeatable process whereby an original cell can be grown outside the human anatomy and duplicated multiple times."

"Are we *now* in the business of manufacturing humans?" Governor Miramar called out in disbelief.

"This sounds like crazy talk," someone else replied. "And what does this have to do with us, anyway?"

"I know this seems extreme," the general continued, "but when you get the full understanding of what we can accomplish with these beings, you, too, will be as amazed as I am."

"In the beginning, we learned too late that the cells and the recipient eggs must be compatible. They were not. Thus, these monstrously large beings were created, as seen here on the left."

"Yuck," one governor cried.

"The Establishment then hired Amalgam Research Protocol, or ARPRO, a highly competent organization in this field, to aid us in producing super humans and mammals. ARPRO has taken the human DNA we submitted, along with research and other processes and procedures too technical to explain, and they have reproduced random humans in their exact form."

"Fascinating," another governor whispered to the gentlemen at his table.

"In an attempt to produce super-powerful human beings, we crossbreed humans with large animals and birds." The general pointed to the screen. "This process is called infusion. We were unsuccessful, but after discovering the creatures possessed superior intelligence and could speak various languages, we decided to use them to our advantage."

"Double yuck," the man cried again.

A hand went up in the back of the room on the right side, and it was clear that the general would not be able to finish his presentation without questions.

"Yes?" the general said halfheartedly, annoyed by the interruption.

"This is very fascinating," Governor Laitan said, "but how does this affect us and the people in our precincts?"

The general had hoped to avoid that question until much later in his exposé. "Great question," the general replied. "But hear me out. Then, at the end of the presentation, if you still have questions, I'll do my best to address them."

Meanwhile, Janu was reading with his mouth agape the same information the general was presenting at his meeting. "No way," Janu cried. He continued reading.

ARPRO will use only the highest quality genes to create and/or reproduce humanoids and creatures. These beings will be controlled by our great prince and programmed and trained to obey him without question or reserve.

Back at DSC, questions were being hurled at the general from around the room. Finally, Governor Childress stood. "I've studied only a little about this subject, so correct me if I'm wrong. But won't these changes to the genetic structure of humans and animals unfavorably affect their offspring?"

"Unfortunately, Governor, for the purposes of our Great Commission, descendants are not a primary concern or a priority at this time." The room was buzzing. "Gentlemen, please, once I've completed my presentation, I promise to open the floor for questions and answers."

Janu read on: *A secret warehouse has been erected solely for the purpose of storing these rare, superior genetic materials, which will be labeled and guarded twenty-four hours a day.*

Human traits and capabilities such as intelligence, creativity, strength, athletic prowess, and artistic talent will be enhanced. The Establishment will be able to shop, if you will, and choose the genomic makeup of its citizens that will benefit our new world. Without these protocols, the Establishment would have no control over how these beings would think or behave.

All designs must first be approved by a vetted board of overseers.

"I must be losing my mind," Janu murmured. "A genetic storehouse? Are humans to be chosen like groceries?"

Meanwhile, Governor Stoner, Monica's dad, ignored the general's request, and asked, "How would this storehouse operate?"

The general forced a smile and thought, *What part of "hold your questions" didn't you understand?*

"As I said before, by avoiding the normal reproductive process and shopping at the storehouse, we can design individuals or create families of our liking. But the designs must first be approved by and kept under the control of the Establishment, of course."

"How would that affect the created or re-created being's thinking and behavior?" Governor Raydor questioned, not yet convinced about this whole duplicating business.

"The brain is very complex and cannot be changed by the process of infusion," the general stated. "A chip, specifically programmed with obedience properties, will be injected into the brain, causing that individual, or mammal, to willingly conform to the purposes and desires of the Prince."

As Janu continued to read, he could hardly contain himself.

"I hope that answers your question, Governor Stoner," the general said.

"No, sir, it does not."

"Think, gentlemen. From our storehouse, we can create horses able to ride like the wind without tiring, and soldiers able to fight without growing weary. Species doing only what they have been programmed to do. I won't apologize for my enthusiasm—I could go on all night. But I have taken up enough of your valuable time."

"Before we open for questions and answers," he continued, "there will be a mandatory meeting next week to wrap up this phase of the Great Commission. Two weeks following that meeting, the process of genomic alteration will begin nationwide. It will be our primary focus. Within the next eight weeks, every citizen, including children and animals, will be called in for a mandatory examination, at which time their blood will be drawn and a series of tests performed to determine their DNA and genetic makeup."

"Does this mean our immediate families, as well?" Governor Jacque Stoner asked with a smirk on his face. *How nice it would be to keep Monica physically and mentally away from the Calders' influence*, he thought.

"Yes, it does," the general replied. "You want obedient wives and children, don't you? Well, now is your opportunity."

"What about us?" Governor Childress questioned.

"The exams of the Brethren will be slightly different. In addition to your mental and physical exams, your loyalty to our beloved prince and his Great Commission will be tested and judged."

"So, if you're apprehensive about our quest, I suggest you bow out now. There will be no negative consequences," he lied. "We just need to know whom we can count on."

That statement caused quite a stir. "Governors, please," the general shouted. "It's up to you to notify your people of the importance of these exams. Tell them what you will, but get them to the facility at any cost."

There was considerable murmuring throughout the auditorium as the old gentleman in the rear tried to assess his subjects' allegiance.

The general breathed deeply and continued, "Transportation will be provided, if needed, and if anyone resists, arrest them. If they are not already on your subversive list, notify us immediately with their names and addresses."

Janu continued reading. *The common people will be obligated to submit to a physical and mental exam, and their IQs will be tested and reviewed. These will aid the Establishment in determining the "category" into which each person will be placed, as well as how to proceed in creating their duplications.*

"As if things couldn't get any worse," Janu moaned, staring at the monitor in disbelief. "They are literally planning to create a perfect society—a flawless people."

"Gentlemen," General Armon screamed into the mike, trying to further convince them of this debauchery, "imagine a people without defects or shortcomings, an obedient and strong people who will do our bidding and win the battle for our beloved prince. Imagine not having to spend your budget on crime prevention, but being able to use the excess money on your own personal desires," he said, hinting at bribery.

"Now, I know you have plenty of questions and concerns," the general continued, offhandedly. "As promised, I will address any fears or anxieties to the best of my ability. So that everyone can be heard, please come to the mike in the front of the auditorium and speak clearly."

"Good evening," Governor Boudreau began. "I want to be clear. You're saying the Establishment is duplicating its citizens in order to create exceptional people to govern the city of Fa'i?"

"That is correct."

"This might be a silly question, but what happens to the citizens you propose to replicate, or the ones who don't meet your strict protocols?"

"We have a place for them," the general replied. "There's much work to be done before our prince can sit on the throne of Fa'i, and we'll need all the help we can get. Are there any more questions?"

Governor Boudreau retreated to his seat more confused than before. Then Governor Childress walked slowly to the mike.

"I have a question, General. Shouldn't our people have something to say about their other selves, their new destiny, and this new world we're taking them to?"

"Once we reveal the Great Commission to our citizens, they'll welcome a twin who can accomplish all they cannot in order to afford them eternal life in Fa'i," the general replied. "They'll appreciate what we're trying to accomplish...for them, of course."

"Won't we be somewhat confused bumping into ourselves on the streets?" Governor Childress continued. "How will anybody know who's real and who's not? I don't know about the others, but I'd feel mighty strange meeting myself in the marketplace...or at work."

No one noticed the elderly gentleman in the rear taking notes.

"Governor Childress, not all of the details have been finalized yet," the general replied. "When the research is completed and the final report distributed, all your concerns will disappear... I promise. For now, trust our great prince and father. He knows what's best for all Keresians."

CHAPTER 22

The Plan

Janu was still reeling from the file he had just read when the doorbell rang.

"Who is it?" he asked.

"It's me…and Jordan."

Malakh wore a blond wig and black-rimmed glasses. He had somehow, *overnight*, grown a mustache and beard, and his hideous mole was covered with makeup. Jordan was bent over with gray hair and a beard, and he was carrying a cane. Meanwhile, Sierra and Monica were washing up the lunch dishes and chatting nonstop. Ariana was amazed at how they never seemed to come up for air. Izaiah had gobbled down two turkey sandwiches, an entire plate of fries, a large glass of apple juice, and a huge bowl of ice cream. *A bottomless pit*, Ariana thought, as he retreated to his room.

"Are you ready?" Malakh whispered to Janu.

"Why are you whispering?" Janu asked.

"Did you sweep your house for bugs?"

"Not yet."

"I swept mine this morning and found five devices," Malakh replied. "So, I brought you my sonarmeter."

"What's a sonarmeter?" Sierra asked as she entered the room. "And who are your guests?"

Janu put his finger to his lips. "It's Malakh and Jordan," he whispered.

"If I'd seen you on the street, I wouldn't have recognized you," she said, giggling softly.

"Then we've succeeded," Malakh replied. "My sonarmeter is a sensor of hidden devices. If any are here, this baby will find them."

"What kind of devices?" Monica asked, peeking out from behind Sierra.

"The spying kind," Malakh whispered.

Janu pulled Malakh to the side. "Before we start sweeping," he whispered forcefully, "I'm still not sure whose side you're on."

Malakh replied, "I have enough evidence to put you and your whole family away for the rest of your lives...but I'm here. And someday you'll understand how much I want you to succeed. Now, let this be our last conversation about this, because time is running out and we've got a lot of work to do."

Janu wanted to believe him. One thing was certain: he would take Malakh out in a heartbeat if it meant protecting his family. But time was running out, and he had already invested too much of it to give up now.

Everyone except Izaiah followed Janu around the house as he moved from room to room, sweeping the detector from left to right.

Suddenly, a red light flashed on the sonarmeter as it inspected the cabinets under the kitchen sink, behind the refrigerator, and finally, under the dining room table.

Janu was furious. In total, he found seven bugs: three downstairs, and one in each of the bedrooms upstairs. Quickly and quietly removing each bug, he handed them to Malakh, who put them in a water-filled baggie and placed them in a container with a lid. Satisfied that all bugs had been removed, Janu called everyone into the family room. Izaiah was sitting in a chair with his legs crossed. Janu snatched the container from Malakh and threw it at him.

"You see these?" Janu yelled. "Your so-called friends have been spying on your family."

"Janu, we must keep our heads if we're going to get through this," Malakh said.

"Izaiah," Ariana cried, "I'm disgusted that you're part of this treachery. These evil demons have corrupted you."

"Son, whatever game you think you're playing…it's over," Janu whispered. "We're all going back to Fa'i. Is that understood?"

"And just how do you plan on doing that?" Izaiah asked.

Janu squelched his anger and disappointment in his son, but he was crushed.

"We've called you all together," Janu announced, "because if our mission is to succeed, we need everyone's cooperation. I opened another of the general's files entitled 'Genomic Alteration', and my hair stood on end. Later, I'll read you some excerpts from the file, and then you'll understand the urgency of our quickly moving ahead with our plan."

"Sierra and Monica, thank you for having the foresight to copy the general's files," he continued. "Otherwise, we'd be sitting ducks, like the rest of the Keresians."

"You are taking me with you," Monica blurted out. "You're the only family I have now."

"Absolutely," Janu replied. "First, we'll talk to Jacque. He might want to go with us."

"I'm not so sure," Monica replied. "He's been really weird since Mom disappeared." She still couldn't believe Elisabeth was dead.

"Come, sit down, girls," Janu instructed. "It's time you learn how we came to be in this evil place. As you know, we once lived in paradise across the river. We thought life was better on this side, and our curiosity caused us to rebel against the king's command.

"We were lured to Keres by trickery and deceit, like many other Fa'ites, including your parents, Monica." Her mouth was agape, but she kept silent. "Unfortunately, we found out too late that Keres was not all we believed it to be. And, since before you were born, Sierra, we've been trying to return to our home."

"When did all this happen?" Sierra asked

"Seventeen years ago, when I was pregnant with you," Ariana replied, tears welling up in her eyes. She told of her deception, naivete, and vulnerability, leading to the disobedience that brought about their current situation.

"We wanted to tell you and Izaiah earlier," she whispered, "but we were ashamed. We still are, but it's time you know the truth."

Izaiah sat in the chair with his head back and his eyes closed, indicating he wanted no part of this confession. By the time they had finished, the girls were teary-eyed, and Malakh and Jordan dropped their heads. Everyone except Izaiah was moved.

Malakh added, "Diablo has cleverly convinced his foolish followers that Fa'i is rightfully his, and he's creating a so-called invincible army by cross-breeding and replicating the citizens and animals of Keres.

He plans to remove Uriel from his throne and take over the nation of Fa'i. But that will never happen."

"Has my mother been replicated?" Monica asked.

"It's possible," Janu replied. "If she's alive, I promise, we will find her." Sierra squeezed Monica's hand trying to absorb some of her friend's pain.

"That explains the strange creatures we've been running into lately," Sierra said.

Izaiah sat up in the chair, smirking. "You all have got to be kidding," he said. "This sounds like a horror movie."

"Where do you think the creatures you saw came from?" Sierra asked. "They weren't born like that."

"Son," Malakh said, "Diablo is an evil being. And because you've submitted to his will, it's hard for you to understand."

"Oh, I understand," Izaiah replied, and stood to his feet.

"Sit down," Janu commanded. "I'm not finished with you."

"Son," Malakh said gently, "you don't believe what we're saying because you're under Diablo's influence. In order for us to help you, you must tell us what happened the night of your induction."

"I've been sworn to secrecy—that's why it's called a 'secret society'. But tell me, Malakh. If you're not one of them as you profess, how did you return unharmed after being carried off by one of the very creatures you're speaking of?"

"Watch your tone," Janu scolded, although he'd been wondering the same thing.

Malakh stared at Izaiah with hurricane-like eyes. That was a question he couldn't answer right then. Instead, he asked, "Are you guys ready to return home?"

"Yes," Ariana replied. "When are we leaving?"

"A week from Friday," Malakh replied.

"That soon?" she asked, grinning broadly.

"The sooner the better," Janu stated.

Ariana's smile suddenly faded. "Janu," she said, hugging him tightly, "You promised to take us back to Uriel, and you have kept that promise."

"We're not there yet," he continued. "There are obstacles to overcome and hard work to be done before we see Fa'i again."

"How will we cross the river without being killed?" Sierra asked, glancing anxiously from one parent to the other. "Remember what happened when we first came across."

Her parents were stunned. How could she know what had happened in the river? She was still in Ariana's womb!

"Precious," Janu said, hiding his shock, "you don't have to be afraid—you're a great swimmer. I prepared you for this day."

She didn't have the heart to tell her parents that even though she was a good swimmer, she was still terrified of the water. The memories of her mother fighting for both their lives in the river were deeply imbedded in her subconscious mind, but they resurfaced now and again to haunt her.

"Anyway," Janu continued, "I didn't know then what I know now. Malakh has located the hidden caves that will take us back to Fa'i. They're treacherous and heavily guarded, but we can get through them if we follow the plan and stick together." He gave Izaiah a fierce look.

"You will encounter some water," Malakh interjected, "but it should take you around the Acheron River of Woe, not through it."

"There's something I've been waiting forever to reveal," Janu said with excitement. "Malakh, will you give me a hand?"

"How much does this table weigh?" Malakh asked, massaging his back. "I feel like I'm carrying two mules uphill."

Janu pulled the rugs back, and they stared at a trapdoor. Ariana gasped. Janu lifted the door and climbed down into the hole. Several minutes later, he handed Malakh a large rolled-up parchment, then emerged with a large metal box.

He emptied the contents on the table. There were water boots of varying sizes, numerous flashlights, batteries galore, headgear with lanterns attached, and lots of heavy rope with heavy metal hooks attached to them. There were water canteens and enough rations in sealed containers to last, it seemed, a lifetime.

Malakh spread out the large parchment on the table. "Gather 'round," he announced. "But first, Janu, I think it would be wise to engage the Lassier Faires."

"Let's go underground," Janu said. "The tunnel is soundproof, it has light, and we can take as long as it takes."

Amazed at what Janu had accomplished in secret, Ariana giddily declared, "My husband's a genius."

"Where's Izaiah?" Janu barked, as he helped the women into the tunnel.

Izaiah, confused, was heading to his bedroom. "They're crazier than I thought," he mumbled as he climbed the stairs. "Underground caves, rivers, a king, unending light…foolishness."

"Jordan, would you please find Izaiah?" Janu asked.

"Let's get started," Malakh said. "Time is short."

"I'm not starting without my son," Ariana stated firmly.

"I don't want to start without him either," Janu replied. "But I won't allow anyone or anything to stop us from going home." He wiped the dust from the table, rolled out the map, and told Malakh to begin.

Sierra had tried to talk with her brother earlier, but he wouldn't listen. She knew Janu loved Izaiah, but she believed he would leave him behind, if necessary.

A few minutes later, Jordan was dragging Izaiah in by the arm.

"Listen carefully," Malakh began.

They moved to either side of the table and leaned over the large brown paper. The map was covered with a matrix displaying colors of red, black, green, and blue, along with what seemed like hieroglyphics.

"What's all this?" Sierra asked.

"A map of the underground caves and waterways leading to the river," Janu replied.

"Looks like Greek to me," she said.

"You don't have to worry about the details," Malakh assured her. "Your dad and I know what all of it means. All you guys have to do is focus on your individual assignments."

"Malakh is going to explain our plan of escape," Janu said.

"Guys, we can do this," Monica exclaimed.

"You're a girl after my own heart," Janu said, smiling. "Now, if you don't understand something, we'll go over the plan as many times as necessary until everybody's comfortable with their responsibilities."

Malakh began, "You'll be wearing black clothing and boots so that you're not easily detected. You'll find a pair in this box to fit you." He leaned over the parchment and traced a path. "You'll stay in this underground until you reach Kinetic Boulevard, which is as far as this tunnel goes."

"I can't believe you did all this, honey," Ariana stated, looking around the tunnel. "When did you find the time?"

"May I continue?" Malakh asked.

"Sorry," she said, "but this is too exciting."

"When you reach the end of the tunnel," Malakh continued, "emerge carefully. A car belonging to the Establishment will be waiting for you… here." He stuck a pushpin on the map where a small black car was drawn.

"Why can't we take our own car?" Ariana asked.

"Only those who know of its existence use this road," Malakh replied. "If you show up in an unmarked car, you would be immediately spotted. Take the back route along Chanel Street until you reach this road bearing left." He tapped his finger on the makeshift map. "Continue along its path until you come to what looks like a dead end, then get out and move quickly."

"You won't be able to see the entrance to the cemetery because it's covered by trees and hedges," he continued. "Janu will know the place. Directly behind the bushes is a large gate that opens by voice activation or a registered thumbprint. At the entrance to the tunnel that leads to the river, you'll find a scanner that photographs irises. If either mechanism does not recognize you, the silent alarm will go off, and all will be lost."

"But our voices, thumbprints, and irises are not registered for access," Janu stated.

"I anonymously taped a meeting with Diablo earlier this week," Malakh said. "I removed all voices but his from the tape, then extracted certain key words, turning them into the code words. They've been transferred to Sierra's iPhone, which she'll play at the entrance to the cemetery."

Ariana was beginning to show signs of apprehension. Sierra looked her right in the eyes. "Mom, I don't know how I know, but Uriel wants you to come home."

"You're right, Sierra. It's now or never."

Malakh continued his briefing. "Once inside the graveyard…"

"Janu, you seem to know a lot about this graveyard," Ariana stated. "When were you there?"

"Not now, honey," he replied.

"You'll see a large marble statue of Diablo in the center of the yard," Malakh continued. "Izaiah will climb the statue and press the fourth button from the bottom on the coat. If you press any other button, the alarm will sound, and it will be game over."

"I don't consider this a game," Ariana said.

"Wrong choice of words," Malakh replied. "As Janu knows, the statue is on a short track that slides back and forth. I suggest that you not wait until the passageway is completely open before climbing down into the tunnel. I've allowed ten minutes for the opening and your descent."

"And, Janu, remember to keep a close eye on the armed guards positioned in the tower. You're also going to watch for the electromagnetic beam that shines on various parts of the yard at different intervals. Move quickly and quietly, and only when the beam is not focused in the area of the statue."

"Once you're all in the tunnel, Monica can press the green button at the bottom of the stairs located on the wall to your left. That will close the statue, hopefully, before the searchlight reaches it. You don't want the guards discovering the open statue without anyone ascending or descending from the underground."

The women stared nervously at each other.

"I never said this would be easy," Malakh stated, "just doable. Every minute detail has been worked out. Otherwise all our efforts would be in vain."

"Do you people really think you're going to get away with this?" Izaiah questioned.

Malakh stared at Izaiah, then handed Janu a compass.

"Once underground," he continued, "travel east until you reach the bronze gate, which leads to the caves. The iris scanner is located here." He tapped his finger on the map. "I've taken care of that, as well. The trek shouldn't take you more than twenty-five minutes. We're using a compass rather than a GPS so you can't be tracked."

"Make sure you check the compass regularly," he continued. "You can easily get lost down there. You'll recognize the second gate; it'll be engraved with a large *D*, and we know what that stands for." All but Izaiah chuckled nervously.

"Once inside the caves," Malakh continued, "use your flashlights. The caves are long and arduous, and you'll need to preserve your headlamps for the dark crypt. You should have enough batteries to get you to the clearing."

"You said you've taken care of the eye scanner?" Janu questioned.

"I'm saving that for last," Malakh replied. "Now, this is where it gets treacherous. As you leave the caves, you'll come upon a great precipice that looks uncrossable. When you look down, you'll see nothing but darkness and void—a large chasm, if you will."

"I know this sounds crazy, but if you'll step out on what looks like nothing, a foundation will be there to support you. This was ingeniously engineered by Diablo for those clever enough to get that far. Seeing nothing on which to cross, they would likely turn back. Once you cross the chasm, climb down the stairs, and you will be facing two roads. There's an invisible presence in that region that has been very effective in pulling people in the direction that seems right. But you must resist following that road, because it will lead to destruction. Many have lost their lives following their natural instincts."

"You mean we're not the first?" Sierra asked, now uncertain about this seemingly impossible journey.

"Once you make it over the chasm," he continued, "you'll be at the mouth of the river, where a motorboat will be moored. It should be eight fifty-five at that point."

"Again, move quickly and quietly. Don't turn on the engine until you're out from under the bridge—you'll have to row your way to the clearing. There will be enough paddles inside the boat for everybody to help with that task. The last hurdle will be getting the boat into the calm waters. This will take some maneuvering and concentration, because the river will try and lure you toward the dark, raging tide. Keep both hands on the wheel, Janu, watch your gauges, and hold your course steady. You should make it through safely."

Janu remembered how they had almost lost their lives seventeen years before in that very river.

Now, having to face that same river again made him tremble. But he would muster the courage needed… for his family's sake.

"I can't express enough the importance of you being at the mouth of the river on time," Malakh continued. "Once I release the gate to let you cross, it will remain open for precisely three minutes, then it will automatically close again. If you're a second late, I won't be able to help you. You'll be trapped, and you will be caught."

"Janu and I will lock in the time frame from this very spot to the cemetery. You'll only have one shot at this, so we'll go over the plan until everyone has the details embedded in their minds. Your life and the lives of your family members depend on it."

"Getting to the first gate on time seems to be very critical," Jordan said. "How much time should they allow?"

"They?" Sierra questioned. "Aren't you coming with us?"

"I plan to," he replied, "but you never know what can happen." He whispered in her ear, "Don't worry about me. Your family needs you to stay focused."

Sierra nodded, but she wasn't sure she could keep her heart and mind in this plan knowing that Jordan might be left behind.

"It should take about forty-five minutes to get from our house to the yard," Janu remarked.

"It'll take no more than four minutes for the statue to move back on its track," Malakh exclaimed. "If all goes well, and depending on what the guards are up to that night, it shouldn't take more than three minutes for all of you to get underground—four at the most."

"It's approximately half a mile to gate number two," Malakh informed them. "It'll be treacherous, so let's assume another thirty minutes—no, thirty-five to be on the safe side. Be sure to wear your water boots, because you'll be wading through knee-deep water."

"So, figure roughly two hours from your home until you reach gate number two," Jordan interjected.

"Is there any special reason you chose this particular day for our exodus?" Sierra asked.

"Did you forget? That's the National Feast of Celebration Day," Malakh replied. "In addition, Diablo will be hosting a banquet at the Diablo Community Center for all the Brethren and armed forces in preparation to launch the Great Commission."

"That should keep the Establishment and the citizens distracted for hours," Janu replied.

"But we still have to be extremely careful and alert at all times," Malakh stated. "They know something's up and have increased their manpower. Guards will be posted everywhere, not to mention those obnoxious flying creatures."

"The majority of the night guards at the Agency will be in the cafeteria having dinner at that time," he continued. "The computer lab should be minimally guarded, allowing me the time to program the mechanism that opens the gate."

Suddenly, Ariana did a little jig. "We're really going home!" she sang. "We're really going home. After all these years, we're really going home."

Ariana's jubilation made everyone laugh, all except Izaiah. Sierra had never seen her mother so happy. *Fa'i must truly be wonderful*, she thought.

Suddenly, Ariana stopped. "Janu, what if Uriel hasn't forgiven us?" she asked.

"That's a chance I'm willing to take," he replied.

"Mom," Sierra said, "if the King is all you and Dad say he is, I think he'll welcome you with open arms."

"I hope you're right," Ariana replied, her face aglow with a smile of remembrance. "I know I'll be glad to see him. Nobody knows how much I miss his love."

"All right," Janu said, feeling some of the apprehension Ariana was feeling. "We've got a lot of work to do before our departure. Malakh, can we go over the plan one more time?"

"Yes. We won't have many more opportunities to review the details before your departure, so it's important that everyone's on point. Where's Izaiah?" Malakh asked. "He could stand to hear this again."

"He was here a minute ago," Monica replied.

"What time are we leaving next Friday?" Ariana asked.

"Six o'clock sharp," Janu replied.

"You don't think Izaiah will do anything stupid, do you?" she asked.

"He'll be okay," Janu replied, not truly convinced.

Everyone's attention was again focused on the large parchment when Izaiah returned with part of a sandwich stuck in his mouth.

Janu tried not to show his anger. "We'll go over the plan one more time, then entertain questions."

"I don't have any questions," Izaiah said with his mouth full. "I crawl up a statue and push a button. How hard is that?"

Sierra wanted to punch him in the face, but because of their guests, she held her peace.

Janu calmed himself. "It's vital we understand our individual assignments, but it's equally important to understand each other's responsibilities, in case someone can't carry out their task."

"Just when is all this supposed to take place?" Izaiah asked nonchalantly.

Ariana started to answer, but Janu shook his head. "Haven't you been listening?" he asked. "Oh, I forgot, you left the room. Just familiarize yourself with the plan so we can move on."

Izaiah walked somberly to the table and peered at the map, pretending interest. He had no intention of leaving his home and friends, escaping in the middle of the night like a common criminal, going who knows where. He had already made arrangements to stay with Korey and Dazmin whenever his family left for their make-believe world.

"Why, of course you can stay with us while your parents are vacationing," Mrs. Hakiim had told him, *"as long as it's okay with them."*

I'll worry about parental consent later, he thought as he stared at Malakh. *Where did he come from anyway, and who gave him the right to suddenly show up in our lives and tell us what to do? And, how does he know so much about everything? Maybe he's the real enemy. He never did explain how he returned unharmed after being carried off by Big Bird.*

He peered at his family. *They've lost their minds*, he thought. *Even Monica, one of the most brilliant people I know, believes this other-world mumbo jumbo. Who else will they brainwash? I've got to stop them. They'll thank me when they realize it's for their own good.*

CHAPTER 23

Sierra Revealed

Sierra woke the next morning with her assignment on her mind. Her heart was racing like a runaway train, and she dreaded getting out of bed.

Malakh had announced the previous evening that he had programmed a device that would convince the scanners at the cemetery that Janu was a member of the authorized personnel. The challenge, however, was removing the mechanism from the CCA. Months ago, Malakh had diverted suspicion about Janu's Organism shutdown from himself to his assistant, who was dragged from the Agency cursing him and vowing revenge. Since then, his department has been under close scrutiny, and everyone and their personal belongings were scanned before they could leave the building. The only way to get the device out was for someone beyond suspicion to remove it, and Malakh had chosen Sierra.

Janu had raved like a madman. But Malakh guaranteed him that as long as Sierra followed his instructions, she would be safe. If she needed help, he would be at her side at a moment's notice, and he would *not* sacrifice her to save himself.

"Sierra's intelligent and a quick study," Malakh had argued. "Not to mention, I can get her into the Rotunda Hall a lot easier than I can you—she's much prettier." The humor was lost on Janu.

"Daddy," Sierra had pressed, "if I escaped the general's house of horrors, I can handle this."

Still not totally convinced, Janu had reluctantly agreed. "If anything happens to my daughter," he had whispered to Malakh, "I will hold you personally responsible. Are we clear?" Understanding Janu's passion, Malakh had ignored his threat.

"Once the device is removed and we initiate the plan, there'll be no turning back," Malakh had informed them.

By midnight, their tasks had been etched into their brains—everyone's except Izaiah's, who had long since gone to bed.

Fear currently mocked Sierra. *You'll never make it out alive.* But she couldn't turn back; everyone was counting on her. She would have to be focused and alert today, putting on the best performance of her life.

She wanted the day to be over as she slowly got out of bed. Used to cutoff jeans and T-shirts, she stared at the chic navy-blue suit Malakh had given her to wear. She found her navy pumps, and because it was raining, pulled out her navy beret.

She dressed hurriedly, applying her makeup heavily to mask her youthfulness. The suit fit her perfectly, and she looked like a true CCA employee. Her long, curly hair pinned atop her head gave her an air of refinement.

Everyone in the family knew about Sierra's assignment, except for Izaiah; he was no longer to be trusted, and she was stunned at the loss she felt. She hardly knew her little brother anymore, and his drastic change was beginning to frighten her. She couldn't believe he had gone to bed before the training was complete. It was too early for him to be up, but Sierra had to be certain. She wanted to be long gone before he came downstairs. As she clipped the phony ID badge to her lapel, she recalled Malakh's words: *"I have faith in you, Sierra. You can do this. No one will suspect someone they're not looking for. I've scheduled a mandatory meeting tomorrow morning at nine. This will keep most of my staff out of your way. Get a good night's sleep and I'll see you tomorrow."*

Sierra took one last look in the mirror, and again she had to beat back her fears. Her hands were shaking as she grabbed the purse Malakh had given her.

"Familiarize yourself with the contents," he had told her. *"They're your ticket into the Rotunda Hall."*

A month ago, I never would have agreed to do anything so dangerously foolish, she thought. *But after recent events, I have no choice.*

She quietly left the house and climbed into the car Malakh had provided with CCA tags. Before raising the garage door, she checked for her parking permit.

As she peered through the sheets of rain blanketing her windshield, she reminded herself to stay calm. When she finally reached the massive CCA building, she noticed twelve flags with various motifs attached to the front portico and blowing in the wind, each representing a Keresian precinct.

Malakh's final instructions were: *"Act like you belong, like you know where you're going and what you're doing."*

"Easy for him to say," she mumbled as she drove around the block twice trying to calm her nerves. She finally pulled into the parking structure, located her designated parking spot, and turned off the engine. She was early, but she had things to do, like slowing down her heart rate.

She looked in the mirror and fixed the flyaway strands of hair that had wilted from the dampness before pulling her cap down close to her eyes. What little confidence she had was giving way to doubt, as she tried to ignore the inner voice reminding her of her tragic fate if she was caught.

Suddenly her fears surrendered to courage, as she reminded herself that this was not just about her, but that it could be the purpose for which she had been born.

Someone tapped hard on the window, and her newfound courage quickly faded. "Are you all right?" a middle-aged woman asked.

"I'm… I'm fine," Sierra sputtered.

The woman left, and Sierra scanned the parking structure. She pulled a small, compartmental box from her handbag containing two fingers made of silicone rubber. She quickly slipped the pliable casts on her left thumb and right index finger, then donned her navy gloves to hide the bogus digits. She checked the special watch that would alert Malakh if she was in trouble. Lastly, she slipped on nonprescription eyeglasses containing a tiny Lassier Faire.

She looked in the rearview mirror one last time, then slowly emerged from the vehicle. As she approached the many steps of the bronze structure, she realized no expense had been spared by the Establishment in constructing this magnificent edifice.

Huge lions constructed in dark granite and baring ferocious fangs were perched on either side of the portico. Sierra thought their eerie eyes were following her every move.

The noise from her pounding heart blocked out the hustle and bustle of the people around her, and she wanted to turn and run. Instead, she courageously stepped inside the main entrance.

CHAPTER 24

Rotunda Hall

She immediately headed for corridor B, located to the left of the escalators. *"It's the least traveled,"* Malakh had advised.

The few people Sierra met smiled and spoke cordially. She responded in kind, briefly glanced their way, then quickly headed for the elevators.

As she turned the corner into the adjoining corridor, she collided with a young security officer in a mobile cart. He smiled and apologized.

"I'm sorry," he said. "You were coming so fast I didn't have time to get out of your way. Are you okay?"

"Yes, yes, I'm fine," Sierra replied. "Now, if you'll excuse me."

It was eight twenty-five, and she had to be at the meet and greet before eight forty-five. Afterward,

Rotunda Hall would be secured until the meeting concluded, and then it would be too late.

"I haven't seen you around here before," the SO commented, as she hurried toward the elevators. "Can I give you a lift?"

She had no time for idle chitchat and punched the up button several times. But not wanting to draw attention by being rude, she replied, "Thanks, but I'm late for a meeting."

"All the more reason I should give you a lift. Hop in," the young man said.

"I'm headed for Rotunda Hall. Do you know where it is?" she asked.

"I most certainly do," the young officer replied. "It's my business to know where everything is so I can help damsels in distress like yourself."

The officer winked, and Sierra smiled lamely. *What a crock,* she thought.

"You must be pretty important, meeting in the Rotunda…and so young."

"I'm not as young as you think," Sierra said. "I'm the Director of Special Agents, but this is my first meeting in the Rotunda."

"By the way," the SO said, "I didn't get your name."

"I didn't give it," Sierra responded coyly. "My name is Sie…uh, Alaina."

"That's a nice name, Sie…uh, Alaina; not like those odd names people have nowadays." He laughed at his own wit.

"I didn't get your name," Sierra said.

"I didn't give it," the SO replied. This time Sierra laughed, a little too loudly.

"It's Lamar, and I have to take you to Special Clearance. Anyone going to the Rotunda has to go through Special Clearance."

Are you serious? Sierra thought. "But I've already been cleared," she replied nervously.

"Must follow protocol," he whined, mimicking his supervisor. "Won't take but a minute."

"But that's why I received clearance yesterday," Sierra complained, "so I wouldn't be delayed today. Look, Lamar, this is my first meeting since my new assignment, and I don't want to be late. That would make a bad first impression. You know how the Establishment feels about punctuality." She was desperate and jabbering way too much.

"Show me your clearance badge," he said, "and I'll take you right to the Hall."

Malakh didn't say anything about a clearance badge, she thought. She was trembling and wanted to throw up, but she remembered Malakh's words. *"Stay calm; you'll be able to think through a crisis." Well, this is a crisis*, she thought, *and I can't think of a thing.*

She frantically rummaged through her purse, but she didn't know what she was looking for. "It's here somewhere," she said, smiling weakly at the young man. "I promise to have it before we reach the Hall."

Lamar eyed her suspiciously, and she expected to be shot on the spot. *I've been watching way too many late-night movies*, she thought.

While she continued her search, the SO continued toward the Clearance Department. She started to leap from the cart and run for the exit, but in her heels, she knew she might fall and break both her legs.

She had been so on edge, she'd forgotten to familiarize herself with the contents of the purse as Malakh had instructed. Now ready to go quietly to the guillotine, she spotted a small pale-yellow envelope hidden in the inside flap of the purse—and inside of it was her clearance badge.

"I found it!" she bellowed.

"You're supposed to wear that above your ID at all times. You did know that, didn't you?" Lamar's tone was not as friendly as before.

"This is a new position, and I'm not totally familiar with all the protocols regarding Rotunda Hall," Sierra replied.

"This is not a minor infraction, Alaina. There are serious consequences for being anywhere in the CCA without proper clearance, especially the Rotunda Hall."

Sierra could tell he was not totally convinced about her naïveté. She waited breathlessly while he examined the clearance badge, staring at her, then at the badge several times.

Time was running out. What would she do if she was locked out of the Hall? Lamar finally returned her badge and headed for the Rotunda.

Before she could breathe a sigh of relief, he informed her she'd have to show her registration papers at the entrance to the Hall. "You don't want to be fumbling around up there," he warned. "They take clearance matters much more seriously than I do."

"Thanks for the heads-up, but I have my papers," she said.

With shaking hands, she quickly searched the purse again. The papers were at the bottom in another envelope, and she breathed deeply. Finally, she could sit back and enjoy the splendid architecture of her father's workplace.

Having only minutes to find Rotunda Hall, she walked swiftly to the end of the corridor and turned left. As instructed, she took the last elevator on her right to Mezzanine C, where several guards were stationed.

She had her papers in hand as she crossed the corridor to the glass elevator. Placing her bogus left thumbprint on the security pad, she watched as the car ascended like a snail.

Her knees shook as a guard approached. She willed the elevator to move faster, and when the doors opened, she all but leapt inside. But before the doors closed again, a hand reached in and held them ajar.

"Papers please," the guard requested.

Sierra quickly handed them to the officer and just as quickly retrieved them.

"When you leave the elevator," Malakh had advised, *"turn left. The curved passageway will take you to Rotunda Hall. It's a large oval annex encircled by offices and an obscure corridor. Unfortunately, the device is located in the hidden passageway, which can only be accessed through the lounge."*

"Don't arrive too early; you want enough people in the lounge so you can get lost in the crowd. But don't arrive late, either. Once the doors to the Hall are locked, no one will be allowed in or out of the area until the meeting is over; then it will be too late to get the device."

"Coffee and doughnuts will be served in the lounge before the meeting, so mingle with the staff. Introduce yourself as the new kid on the block, but don't spend too much time with anyone. Before entering the conference room with the others, discreetly familiarize yourself with the Hall."

"Sit in the back to avoid drawing attention to yourself when you slip out. Keep your eyes on the clock

behind the podium. Ten minutes after the meeting commences, leave quietly."

"In the corridor, take the zigzagging passageway to a door marked 'Off-Limits–Executive Special Agents Only.' Place your silicone-covered fingers on the security panel and hold them there until the indicator light turns green. If you remove your fingers too quickly, you'll set off the silent alarm. Punch in 8286 and turn the doorknob counterclockwise."

"With your clearance badge, you shouldn't have any trouble. But if you are stopped, you're Director Alaina Yves, Special Agents' Processing Department, third floor."

Meanwhile, Janu was in his office on the tenth floor pacing up and down. His baby girl was putting herself in harm's way for the family, while he sat idly by. He glanced at his watch for the umpteenth time. "I'm the head of this household," he mumbled. "I should be taking the risks."

Sierra finally made it to the lounge in Rotunda Hall and networked the room like a professional, meeting and greeting staff as if she belonged. She didn't stay too long with any one group, but she circled the room, always heading toward the corridor that would lead to the device.

The coffee hour would end in seven minutes. She had to hurry if she wanted to be in her seat before the doors were locked.

She slipped unnoticed into the corridor and hurried past the restrooms until she spotted the passageway that zigged and zagged. She found the door that read, "Off-Limits–Executive Special Agents Only." But where was the panel?

She feverishly searched the area until she located the panel hidden in a small niche just left of the door. Malakh was right; knowing where things were would save a lot of time later. She had three minutes to get back.

"Young lady," an elderly woman called. "What are you doing?"

"I'm… I'm new here, and I was trying to locate the restrooms," Sierra stammered. "I'm attending a meeting in the Hall."

"This area is off-limits to unauthorized personnel, and you passed the restrooms on your way here." The woman eyed Sierra's ID suspiciously, and Sierra quickly retreated.

"You'd better hurry," the old lady said with a snicker. "Once those doors are locked, they won't be opened for anyone, not even for someone new."

The lounge was empty. Sierra quickly opened the conference room door just as the guard was inputting the security code. He stared at her disapprovingly.

"I'm new here," Sierra told the guard, and she gave him a big smile.

The sentinel was not impressed. “Take your seat,” he growled.

She quickly found an empty chair in the rear. When Malakh spotted her in the back of the room, he gave a sigh of relief. “This meeting is now called to order,” he announced. It was exactly nine o’clock.

Ten minutes later, the guard left his post, and Sierra slipped behind the wall into the forbidden corridor. The old battleax wasn’t roaming the halls, and Sierra stealthily made her way to the “Off-Limits” area.

She quickly removed her gloves and placed the silicone-covered right index finger onto the blue screen, and the silicone-covered left thumb onto the red screen. When the panel turned completely green, she entered the code, the door opened, and she slipped inside.

She didn’t turn on the light for fear someone might spot it from the hallway. Instead, she pulled out her mini flashlight and searched the room until she located the file cabinets.

She doused the light, groped the walls, and bumped into furniture until she reached the cabinets. Her heart was racing like a locomotive as she tried every file drawer until she found the one left unlocked. “It would have to be the last one,” she mumbled.

Under the manila folders was a small package marked *Precious*. It contained the device and enough security cards and ID badges for the entire family.

She slipped the package into her purse and headed for the door.

Suddenly, she remembered to deactivate the security cards so as not to trigger the silent alarm. She shone her flashlight around once again and spotted the deactivator across the room.

She wiggled through a maze of file drawers, desks, and machinery, bumping her knees and shins along the way. She was neutralizing the fourth card when she heard someone at the door.

She thought about sneaking out the back entrance, but the activated cards would set off the alarm, and she wasn't about to leave them behind. She turned off her flashlight and hid.

The door slowly opened, and she felt sick. "I'll get the light," a man said.

"Maybe we should leave it off," said another man. "It'll be spotted from the hallway. I brought a small flashlight."

Sweat oozed from Sierra's pores as she lay curled in a fetal position behind a desk. The two men stood talking in the dark.

"What's on your mind, Drake?"

"I think we have a grave situation in our town, Zen, and I'm not sure what to do about it."

"What do you mean?" Zen asked.

"There seems to be an epidemic going around, and now every family has to be tested, given some kind of shot, and examined like guinea pigs. There's even talk of replications? What is the Establishment doing?"

"You sound disgruntled," Zen replied. "Don't you trust our leadership?"

"Of course, I trust them. I'd just like to know what they're up to."

"All citizens have received notice," Zen replied. "My family has already taken the shot. You give a little blood, take a written and oral test—it's a piece of cake. What are you so worried about?"

"What about this replicating nonsense? I was leaving work the other night and could've sworn I was being followed by some monstrous creature. I had nightmares all night. I told my wife, and now she's afraid to go out."

"You're frightening your wife for no reason, Drake. There are no monstrous creatures lurking about. I'll have Jenna stop by and talk to Ambray tomorrow to put her mind at ease."

So, it has begun, Sierra thought. *I wonder when my family is scheduled for testing.*

"We'd better get back," Drake said.

"Will I see you at the club tonight?" Zen asked.

"I'm not sure," Drake replied.

Sierra stretched her cramping legs and accidentally kicked a chair.

"What was that?" Zen asked.

"I heard it, too," Drake replied.

"No one can get in here without the code," Zen whispered. "It's probably just a rat. They're as big as tomcats."

"But we need to be certain no one overheard our conversation," Drake insisted.

Zen shone his flashlight around the room, but he didn't spot Sierra, who was crouched under a desk.

"There's no one here," Zen said. "Now, let's get out of here before we're missed."

Sierra let out a long, slow breath as the men retreated into the corridor. She quickly deactivated the remaining cards and disappeared out the back door.

Malakh ended his meeting at eleven, and he hoped his little spy had completed her assignment. He was on his way to the Off-Limits area when he heard a young man in the corridor talking with the head of security. He was telling of an encounter he had had with a suspicious young lady in blue whom he had dropped off at the Hall earlier.

Malakh hid and listened intently.

"I don't know why, sir, but she seemed suspicious, and she could still be in the building," Lamar reported.

Malakh quickly pressed the red button on his watch.

"Have you seen her?" Lamar asked his superior.

"No, but I did get a call from Ms. Brandon, who also said she spotted a young woman in blue lurking in the Off-Limits corridor. That's why I came up. I'll notify Security to be on the lookout."

Sierra felt the vibration from her watch and knew it signified trouble. She heard Malakh on her Lassier Faire tell her to get out…and fast.

The elevators would be quicker, but they were heavily guarded. She moved swiftly toward the stairwell and signaled Janu's Lassier Faire. He immediately responded.

"Hello," he said.

"It's me," Sierra said, trying to keep the panic out of her voice.

"How's everything?" Janu asked.

"Fine," she calmly replied. "I picked up the outfit and I'm heading home now, but I may need a little assistance." Janu knew that meant she needed help getting out of the building.

"Rest assured I'll do everything I can. Do you understand?"

"I do. See you later."

Sierra glanced at her watch; it was eleven twenty-five. She was supposed to be out of the building by eleven o'clock, but the employee rendezvous in the forbidden room put her behind schedule.

Jordan was waiting for her at the northeast corner of the building. She had to hurry or he might come under suspicion, as well.

She took off her heels and quickly tiptoed down the stairwell to the main floor. She donned her shoes, pushed open the door, and peeked out into the lobby.

She was heading toward the exit when she spotted Lamar looking around frantically and speaking into a two-way radio. He had checked out Alaina's clearance, and everything appeared in order. But she was a little too edgy and unsure for his liking. Not to mention, he knew just about every employee and would've remembered that pretty face. He had decided to follow his instincts and notify his superior.

Presently, it was too late for Sierra to retreat. Lamar spotted and intercepted her as she headed for the northeast exit. "Hello again," he said.

"Hello yourself," she said confidently.

"Meeting over?" he asked.

"Yes, it was over not too long ago."

"In a hurry?" he asked.

"I'm on my way to meet a client, and I'm running late."

"You always seem to be running late. Too bad I don't have my cart this time to take you where you need to go."

"Is there something I can do for you?" she asked rather abruptly.

"Just thought I might be able to assist you… *again*," he said sarcastically.

Sierra was annoyed. "Well, as I said, I'm in a hurry. You have a nice day, and maybe I'll see you around."

"Oh, I'm sure you will. By the way, did you find everything you needed in your purse?"

Knowing the contraband she was carrying, she wanted to flee. Instead, she replied, "I sure did, and thanks for asking. Now I must run."

It was lunchtime, the lobby was crowded, and security officers were everywhere, moving throughout the people, no doubt searching for her.

Malakh was leaning over the second-floor railing searching for Sierra when he spotted her and Lamar standing by the fountain in the lobby. He knew the young man was trying to detain her.

He communicated by Lassier Faire to Janu that he should quickly get to the northeast lobby, hold an elevator for Sierra, and not let anyone else enter.

Malakh, hiding behind a column, called Lamar on his mobile and told him to report to security *stat*.

Janu reached the lobby and held the elevator door open with a brick. Grabbing Sierra from behind, he pulled her inside, then quickly placed his hand over her mouth.

"Your mother sent a change of clothes, her black wig, and a purse with a hidden compartment," Janu said.

"Dad, you scared me to death," Sierra said when he released her.

"We're going to the sub-basement, where you can change your clothes and transfer the device," he announced.

Meanwhile, an Enforcer shouted for Jordan to move his vehicle. "You've been sitting in a fifteen-minute parking zone for thirty minutes."

"Just need five more minutes, sir. My rider's running late, but she'll be here any minute," Jordan pleaded.

"I don't care what time she's coming," the Enforcer replied, "she's not here now, and I want this thing moved immediately, or I'll have it towed away, with you in it."

Now was not the time to get arrested, but he couldn't leave Sierra. Malakh had just warned him that she might be in trouble, and he was her only way of escape.

He slowly pulled away from the curb, looking back, hoping Sierra would come through the doors. When the Enforcer walked to the end of the block in the opposite direction, Jordan pulled under a clump of trees and parked. He got out of the vehicle, hid behind the tree, and waited.

Sierra, meanwhile, was changing her clothes behind a large column in the basement while Janu stood guard. She quickly ditched the suit and stepped into a black dress. She donned the dark wig, changed her shoes, transferred the contraband to the hidden compartment, and put on dark sunglasses. In seconds, her appearance was completely changed. Janu put her spy outfit in a bag, kissed her on the forehead, and watched as she got back into the elevator.

"Please be careful," he said. "And, Precious…"

"Yes, Daddy…"

"Good job."

"Thanks, and don't worry," she whispered as the door closed.

She pushed the lobby button, and the elevator rose slowly, stopping at the basement level. The doors began to close again, and she breathed a sigh of relief, until a large hand reached in and held them open.

She thought she'd faint when a large security officer entered and glared at her. When the elevator reached the main floor, she lowered her head and quickly exited, bumping into waiting passengers.

Lamar had since found out he was not wanted in Security, and he was again in search of her. She walked right past him and the other officers and headed for the northeast exit. She mingled with the other employees who were leaving the building, and she did not look back.

"This espionage business is too rich for my blood," she grumbled as she stepped outside.

Jordan spotted her, but she didn't see him. He popped out from behind the tree and whistled. She had started toward him, when suddenly the Enforcer who had chased Jordan appeared again.

"Young lady," he called, running toward her.

"Hurry, Sierra," Jordan shouted.

"Stop," the Enforcer bellowed again. "I want to talk to you."

Sierra removed her shoes and sprinted toward the vehicle. The Enforcer, slightly overweight, was no match. Jordan opened the door on the passenger's side. "A little faster," he called as he jumped into the driver's seat and started the engine.

"I'm going as fast as I can," Sierra panted.

She had barely closed the door when Jordan stepped on the gas. She almost fell into his lap as they careened around a corner.

"Fasten your seat belt," he said. "We have company." The Enforcer was chasing them.

"What if he gets the license plate number?" Sierra cried.

"He can't trace it back to me. Uncle M took care of that."

"Where are we going?" she asked.

"Just hang on."

Jordan drove at breakneck speed for ten blocks, trying to lose the red and black following them, but he couldn't. Finally, the pursuer was held up by a little old lady crossing the street, and Jordan made a quick left. He sped down an alley, parked behind a dumpster, and waited for the Enforcer to pass.

Suddenly, a black car turned in at the opposite end of the alley and blocked their exit.

"What *now*?" Sierra cried.

The vehicle slowly moved toward them and stopped. Monica stepped out and stared at her terrified friends.

"How about you guys get the lead out of your butts, so we can go," she said.

"Am I glad to see you!" Sierra cried.

"I know—I'm great, wonderful, and all that, and it's true, but now we have to go," she replied.

"What will we do with your vehicle?" Sierra asked Jordan.

"They'll find it and tow it away," he replied. He pulled several rags out of the trunk. "We don't want to leave any fingerprints behind."

"Isn't the vehicle registered in your name?" Monica asked.

"No. Now, hurry."

"I think you should ride in the trunk," Monica informed him. "If the Enforcer should catch us, he'll recognize you.

"I'm not getting in there," he replied.

"You'll be able to breathe," she said. "Now, climb in."

"Not so hard," he yelled, as Monica slammed the trunk shut.

Monica jumped behind the wheel and quickly headed toward the bridge that would take them to the river. "We'll hold up there until the heat is off," she said.

"You sound like somebody in a cops-and-robbers movie," Sierra told her. Her watch suddenly vibrated, and she pressed the green button.

"Sierra, are you there?" Malakh asked.

"We're all here," Sierra replied.

"Is everyone okay?"

"Yes. We're headed for the river now. Tell my dad I'm okay and thanks for everything. We'll see him and Mom later tonight, when it's safe."

"Go to Freelance Court," Malakh instructed. "There's a map in the glove compartment that will direct you there."

"When were you in my vehicle?" Monica asked.

"Never mind," Malakh replied. "Listen. You'll see an abandoned-looking house hidden by a grove of trees. It's my safe place. Don't worry about being followed—there's a non-tracking device under Monica's vehicle."

"And you painted it black?" she said. "I've always liked black."

"Once inside the house, use your flashlights," he continued. "You don't want to light up the place. And do not move until you hear from me. If you're hungry, there's food and snacks in the fridge and cupboard. Jordan has the key."

"I'm glad," Monica said, "because this espionage stuff has me starving."

"Sierra, you really stirred up a hornets' nest here at the CCA," he said. "The good ol' boys are running around like chickens with their heads cut off, trying to figure out who was the suspicious lady in blue, and how you got past Security. You did good, sweetheart."

"Thanks," Sierra said, smiling.

"Now, be careful," he continued, "and wait for my call. By the way, where's Jordan?"

"He's in the trunk," Monica replied.

"Well, get him out of there, or he'll suffocate."

Monica drove about a mile on Chanel Street before spotting an Enforcer following in the distance. She drove cautiously, not wanting to be pulled over for a traffic violation. She turned slowly down a side street, and the car turned in behind her. *Yep*, she thought, *we're being followed.*

"What's the matter?" Sierra asked.

"We've got a tail. I'm going to pull over and see what he wants."

"Are you nuts?" Sierra cried. "If they search us, we're doomed. I have a device in my possession that I shouldn't have. Remember?"

Monica eased the vehicle to the side of the road and stopped. Sierra stared at her friend. *Did they get to her, too?* she wondered. *Is she now one of them?* Sierra didn't know who to trust anymore.

She thought about leaping from the car, then slowly removed her hand from the door handle. She couldn't leave Jordan to face this alone. He was now yelling about his cramped quarters, and, oh yes, something about possibly suffocating.

"Put a lid on it, Jordan," Monica yelled. "The Enforcer's pulling me over."

"Hello, miss," the officer said. "Is this your vehicle?"

"Hello to you, too, sir, and yes, it is. Did I do something wrong?"

"May I please see your ID and registration?"

The Enforcer ran her information, walked back to the car, and handed back her papers.

"You can go, miss."

"I'm not even supposed to be stopped," Monica whispered as she drove off. "My plates have my dad's governor's seal on them."

"I never knew that," Sierra said.

"The Enforcer probably just wanted to make sure my vehicle wasn't stolen."

"Let me out of here," Jordan shouted.

CHAPTER 25

The Unveiling

Thomas, the elevator maintenance and repair man, was humming his favorite tune as he climbed on top of elevator number two for its monthly inspection. He hated rodents and hoped he didn't spot any scurrying about like before; they were huge and gave him the creeps. Not to mention the trouble they could cause if they gnawed on the cables. He shined his flashlight around. Something was lying in the left-hand corner. He sighed disgustedly. *I'm not a young man anymore*, he thought, as he crawled toward the mysterious object, causing further pain to his already-aching spine.

He had grown to hate his job and was looking forward to retirement in six months. "In a little while, it'll all be over," he sang. He poked the bloody thing, and after much uneasiness, picked the object up with his gloved hand.

"Well, I'll be. A bloody bootie," the old man said. He crammed it into a plastic trash bag, which he planned to turn in to Protocol.

Meanwhile, Ariana's doorbell rang. "Mrs. Calder?" the young man said. "Sign here."

"What is it?"

"I have no idea, ma'am, just sign at the bottom."

The package was from the Establishment. She tore open the large manila envelope and read the cover letter: *Be advised that the Calder family is to report to the Ares Medical Center on Wednesday July 22nd at nine o'clock in the morning for testing. Do not eat any food and be on time. This is mandatory, and no excuses will be accepted.*

Ariana glanced over the numerous documents to be filled out for each family member and immediately called Janu. "Honey, what are we going to do?" she asked. "They want our blood, and they want it prior to our leaving this crazy place."

"Don't worry," Janu replied, "we'll be long gone before they can replicate us."

"Don't make jokes, honey."

"Stop fretting, Ariana. I'll look over everything when I get home."

A week later, the Calders were sitting in the waiting room at the Ares Medical Center. They were taken separately to different rooms, where they were tested academically, then hauled like cattle to a lab where they received a complete physical and a blood draw. They were poked and prodded everywhere.

Sierra was nervous and wouldn't look the technicians in the eye for fear they would suspect she was planning to escape. Eventually all but Izaiah returned to the waiting room.

"He's been in there a long time," Sierra commented.

"Janu, maybe you should go and check on him," Ariana said.

"I'm sure he's fine," he replied.

"Young man, is your name Izaiah James Calder?" the technician asked.

"Yes."

"What is your age?"

"I'm fifteen."

"Do you live with your parents?"

"Yes."

The technician confirmed his address, then entered something into the computer. She stared at the screen for several minutes. "Wait here," she said. She was gone twenty minutes before returning with a doctor and an Enforcer.

"Young man, please stand up," the Enforcer instructed.

"Is there a problem?" Izaiah asked.

"We need you to come with us," the doctor said.

"Why, what's this about?"

"Just do as you're told," the technician replied.

"My parents are in the waiting room, and if there's a problem, they need to know."

"They're not in charge here," the doctor said. "And the sooner you cooperate, the sooner you can join them."

Izaiah was somewhat apprehensive, but he went along quietly.

Thirty minutes had passed, and now Janu was getting worried. "Why are they keeping him so long?" he asked.

"I told you to go check on him," Ariana replied, annoyed.

"Maybe he's back there revealing our secrets," Sierra whispered. "Who knows what he's capable of anymore."

"Don't say things like that, even in jest," Ariana scolded.

"Who's jesting?" Sierra replied.

"Sierra's right, honey, we don't know our son anymore, and I'm worried, too." Janu approached the receptionist's desk and asked to speak to his son.

She made a call. "He's not available right now, but he should be out any minute."

"We all took the same tests," he told Ariana. "Why should *his* take so much longer?"

An hour later, Izaiah walked through the double doors.

"What took you so long, Z?" Sierra asked. "We've been waiting forever!"

"Don't start with the third degree," Izaiah replied. "I have a headache, and I want to go."

Janu had questions, too, but Ariana shook her head and took Izaiah by the arm. "Come," she told them, "let's go home."

Ariana sat in the back seat with Izaiah, holding his unusually cold hand. He sat quietly with his head down, looking pale, as if all the blood had been drained out of him. *What have they done to you?* she wondered.

He didn't stop by the kitchen for his usual snack, but he went straight to his room. He fell across his bed, too weak to pull up the covers, and tried to recall what had happened in the lab. He remembered being tied down on a cold table and given a shot—of what, he had no clue. Someone in a white coat had said, "*It has to be him; his DNA proves it.*" Izaiah had tried to speak, but no words came out. Before blacking out, he wondered if they were going to kill him.

Presently, his mobile rang. "Hello," he said groggily. "Yes, I'll be ready at six." He needed to shower and dress before Jackson arrived, so he set his alarm before drifting off to sleep. He was dreaming of voices and lights and monsters, and he was running as fast as he could from Jackson's elongated arms. The alarm went off and startled him.

Jackson blew the horn promptly at six. "What's up?" Izaiah asked as he crawled into the vehicle.

"What's up with you? You look like crap," Jackson replied. "Did you bring your attire?" he asked.

"Yes, it's in my case. I didn't want my parents to see it."

Izaiah wasn't himself, and Jackson didn't feel much like small talk. He liked Izaiah and wasn't happy with the assignment he had inherited from the general.

The PsyOp meeting began with dinner and its usual pomp and circumstance. Then it took a different turn. Not only did Prince Diablo's head show up, but it was attached to his body.

Everyone stood, and the applause was thunderous as the Prince stepped up to the podium. He purposely waved his arms back and forth as if to emphasize the crimson robe he was wearing.

The scarlet tassels on his black velvet beret flew into his eyes as he perpetually bowed his head to acknowledge the riotous praise. After ten minutes of glass-shattering noise, with one wave of his hand, the yelps, applause, and foot stomping ceased.

Suddenly, currents of electricity encircled him as he spoke, and Izaiah wondered if he would catch fire.

"My fellow compatriots," the prince bellowed, "as you can see, I brought all of me tonight." The crowd roared with laughter. "This meeting is called to encourage you in person regarding my Great Commission, for which we've long awaited. This epic event will be implemented shortly, and all of you will play a strategic role in its success."

"You've remained loyal to me and my Establishment," he bellowed, "even when you wondered if what I was doing would benefit you and your families. Because of your devotion to me, my Establishment, and my Cause, you will receive the incalculable reward of ruling and reigning with me in Fa'i."

The Prince had successfully worked the crowd into a frenzy, and Izaiah watched the general's chest rise with pride. "It is imperative that you complete your physical exams and aptitude tests as soon as possible," Diablo continued, "so we can determine who is suitable for what positions in our new world." The members began to murmur.

"I only ask for your continued faith in me and in your Establishment. Believe that we have your best interests at heart. We're doing everything in our power to make certain that you and your family members who remain loyal to me prosper."

Once again, the applause was deafening, and Izaiah, in his robe and cap, was convinced that this was where he belonged. He was sorry his family didn't understand, but he had to live his life as he saw fit.

The meeting adjourned, and the usual meet and greet took place. Members stood in line for two hours jockeying for position to speak to or shake hands with the Prince. A raucous jostling even broke out between two women who thought they should be ahead of each other in line. Finally, Izaiah and Jackson left.

"Wow," Izaiah said. "What an honor to meet the Prince face-to-face."

"It was," Jackson replied. After a brief silence, Jackson said, "Izaiah, the Establishment has reason to believe your family is not loyal to the Establishment. It's also rumored that they are planning a political coup d'état. Can you confirm or deny this?"

"My family is planning something, but I'm not sure what," he lied. "And ever since they found out I'm a PsyOp, they stop talking when I come near. They're suspicious of me, so whatever they're planning, they're keeping it hidden."

"Can you handle being an outsider in your own family?" Jackson asked.

"I was feeling bad, but after seeing the Prince in person and listening to his message, I'm more determined than ever to be a part of his Great Commission, no matter what my parents think."

"Can you get us the information we need—you know, about what your parents are planning?"

Izaiah was still not ready to turn his parents in. Once he did, the Prince wouldn't hesitate to destroy them, and deep down, he didn't want them to be hurt.

"I might have something in a couple of days," Izaiah replied. "I'll let you know if I find out anything."

In the interim, he would try and find a way to stop his family's exodus and keep them from ruining their lives and his.

Unbeknownst to him, after the discovery of his DNA on the bloody bootie, he was more of a suspected traitor than his parents.

"So, my boy, what did you find out from the lad?" the general asked the moment Jackson walked through the door.

"Nothing much," Jackson replied. "But he said he would have something for me in a couple of days."

"He doesn't have anything because he's one of them," the general roared.

"I don't believe Izaiah's a traitor," Jackson replied. "I know how much he loves this nation and the Establishment, and he worships the Prince. He was just telling me tonight how honored he is to be a part of the Great Commission, no matter what his parents' political views are."

"And you believe him? Look, son, you've always been a little too soft for my liking, plus you're fond of the boy. Why, I don't know. But maybe his so-called commitment is part of his cover up. Maybe he's a PsyOp inside the PsyOps. Now, wouldn't that be a hoot?"

"But the worst part," he continued, "is that we sponsored him. And if he is leading a revolt against the Establishment, my head and yours will roll. Anyway, you can't deny the bloody bootie. If he wasn't there in the flesh, how did his DNA get there?"

"Someone could've planted it."

"For what purpose, and how did they get it? Protocol reported to me that there were strange goings-on at the facility center the night you took Sierra there, something you should never have done without consulting me first."

"Maybe the boy discovered who the package was and helped her escape," the general continued. "Worse yet, what if they discovered the lab, and the vault, and what we've been up to? They could ruin everything if they start blabbing to the populace about their impending plight."

"I never thought of that," Jackson muttered.

"That's because you don't think, son. If you don't have something on the Calders soon, I will give the assignment to Jason. Fix this, Jackson, and I mean yesterday."

"May I remind you, Father, it was Jason who let Sierra escape in the first place," Jackson replied.

"You'd better find some answers soon, son, or we can both kiss our futures, and maybe our lives, goodbye."

Meanwhile, Janu and Malakh were at the safe house going over the final details before the great escape. This would be their last meeting, and there could be no loose ends, or all of their hard work would be in vain.

Janu scratched his head, amazed at all they had accomplished in such a short time, things he never could have done on his own. He was grateful for Malakh's help and wisdom.

"Malakh."

"Yes, Janu?"

"Thanks."

"You've thanked me a hundred times. Maybe you should hold the applause until the mission is accomplished and you and your family are safe in Fa'i. But I do appreciate your gratitude. Are you nervous?"

"Petrified."

"To be expected," Malakh said, slapping his friend on the back. "I have an errand to run, so I'll see you later." He had worked hard to regain Janu's trust, and now that he had it, he could proceed with his own plan.

He had been summoned to report to the facility center tonight. He tried getting out of it, but no excuses were accepted. He arrived promptly at eight and was greeted by Galtero, the powerful warrior who had been Prince Diablo's bodyguard as far back as Malakh could remember.

A large, dark, hairy man with a body of steel, Galtero stood about seven feet tall, spoke in a deep, gravelly voice, and could take down the best of them.

He quickly escorted Malakh to the lab and gave him a white suit and mask to don. The Prince, the general, and the twelve governors were standing around a large vat all dressed in like manner, awaiting his arrival. Malakh wondered why he had been summoned to the meeting.

"There you are, my boy," the Prince said. "Now we can begin." Diablo pointed to a group of large metal containers.

"Gentlemen," he said, "these vats are filled with vials of the tested blood cells of most of our citizens. The containers are labeled with the date of testing, the donor's full name and address, ID number, and date of birth. Subsequent tests will be forthcoming shortly."

"However, in order to stay within our strict timelines, our team of illustrious scientists and doctors has begun mutating some of the populace to determine if they can be of use to us in our Great Commission, if they should be eliminated, or if they should be *re*-created.

"The genetic makeup tells us if the person is healthy, what diseases he or she is predisposed to, if any, and why, *and* if they have any mental disorders—yes, we can even determine that."

The Prince raised his arms in the air. "Comrades, you're looking at the future of our new and perfect world. Can these cells live?" he bellowed. "Yes, they can." As expected, everyone applauded.

Malakh tried to hide his emotions, but his pulse was racing. "Excuse me," he said, "what happens to the people who are…shall we say…discards?"

The Prince, annoyed by that question, stared at Malakh. "Please hold all questions until after the presentation," he announced.

"Take a seat, gentlemen," Galtero boomed. Most governors scrambled for seats closest to the screen, but several didn't know what to make of it all.

One governor whispered, "I hope my wife fails the exams—maybe she'll go in the discard pile." The men chuckled.

The general requested that the lights be dimmed, and you could hear a pin fall on cotton as all eyes were glued to the screen, including Malakh's. Dr. Darius stepped up with a remote, and the screen suddenly separated into six different compartments.

"Gentlemen," he said in a broken dialect, "as you can see, the first box contains a twenty-five-year-old female, who we'll call Susan. The second box tells us that she is obese. Box number three depicts her unhealthy diet. And box number four portrays that she will most likely develop osteoarthritis. Box number five discloses that she has genetic diabetes, and that she is a prospect for heart disease. Finally, box number six reveals that she will most likely develop Alzheimer's, if she lives long enough."

"Now, gentlemen, these are just a few quick diagnoses for your benefit, and a minute amount of the data we're researching. A complete analysis will be done when the cells are taken to the Ares Regional Medical Center. There, our advanced technology will confirm or deny our findings."

"Through stem cell reformation," Diablo interjected, "we've already replicated some of the misfits and have successfully incorporated into them the genetic structure necessary for our purposes." Not certain of the fundamental procedures himself, he stated, "It is a lengthy and complicated process, so we won't bore you with the details."

Dr. Darius pressed the remote and continued, "You've seen the 'before' pictures of Susan—now look at her after the stem cell restructuring. She is one hundred pounds lighter, her IQ is off the charts, and she is no longer diabetic. How's that for success?"

"When can we see a live specimen?" Monica's dad asked.

Beaming like a new father, Diablo proudly announced, "Tonight, gentlemen. We're also displaying a crossbreed that will astound you. In the meantime, eat a little something, then follow me to the vault where the species are housed."

Malakh had skipped dinner and was famished. Galtero handed him a glass of punch, and the waiter shoved a tray of mini sandwiches at him. After gulping down the sandwiches and drinking the punch, he immediately felt faint.

Prince Diablo led the governors to the vault, where a Biometric Iris Scanner x-rayed his eyes. A purple beam of light flashed, and the lock made a loud clunking sound.

The large round handle automatically turned counterclockwise, creaking as if it needed a lube job. The huge door slowly opened, and Diablo, overcome with excitement, waved his arms in the air.

"Hit the lights," he ordered. Everyone gasped as the room was illuminated. "Gather 'round, gentlemen. This is a once-in-a-lifetime experience, and you don't want to miss it."

Some governors began pushing and shoving, wanting to be the first to witness...what, they didn't know. But most hung back, not sure what to expect.

"Oh...my...goodness," one man cried out, holding his head. "Can this be?" another gentleman asked. In awe, Monica's dad shouted, "Look at that one!"

Malakh was growing weaker, and he garbled his words. "What was in that punch?" Galtero grabbed Malakh's elbow, but he didn't answer.

"My Prince, what are your plans for these re-created crossbreeds? "one skeptic asked. "And does your plan include women and children?"

"Yes," the Prince replied. "Every man, woman, and child will be re-created with the genetic makeup of a warrior and the ability to fight and not be defeated."

"There is one who illegally occupies *my* throne in Fa'i, as you know," Diablo continued. "And he has great power. Thus, I'm creating indestructible beings to cross the river and assist me in dethroning that imposter."

Everyone murmured simultaneously. "Also included in their genetic makeup will be mature, antibody-secreting plasma cells, which will cause wounds or scars to rapidly heal. This will allow our soldiers to stay on the battlefield, where they're most needed, rather than in sickbay, where they would be of no use to me whatsoever."

"These re-created beings will also have the ability to become invisible when necessary," he continued, "an added guarantee of our success in battle. This specially formulated plasma is currently working in most of our cross-breeds."

Diablo nodded to Galtero, and the giant took a stumbling Malakh to a small room down the hall and strapped him to a table.

"What are you doing?" Malakh mumbled before blacking out.

CHAPTER 26

Distrust

Meanwhile, Janu was in his study reviewing the details of the plan. The time for their departure was fast approaching, and if things didn't go exactly as designed, his family would be destroyed.

"Hey, Dad," Izaiah said as he entered the room.

"Hey, son. What's up?"

"Mom and Sierra are packing. Are we leaving soon?"

Janu stared at the floor.

"I'm sorry you don't trust me," Izaiah said, "but I don't agree with what you and Mom are doing."

Janu observed his son with a mixture of disappointment and love. He was sad that he could no longer trust the son he was once so close to, but there was no way he was telling him the date and time of their departure.

Janu had tried so hard to keep this nation's philosophy and creed from infiltrating his children, yet his only son had been seduced by its wicked values and Janu was now at a loss as to what to do.

"We're not quite sure when we're leaving," Janu finally replied. "But we'll let you know."

"I thought it was settled at the meeting in the basement."

"Originally, it was. But if you had stayed long enough, you would already know that the date wasn't finalized."

"But how can I be ready if I don't know when we're leaving?"

"Put a few things that mean the most to you in your backpack," Janu replied. "Then you'll be ready whenever we decide to leave."

"Is that all I can take?" Izaiah asked incredulously.

"If everyone took what they wanted, there wouldn't be room enough for *us* in the vehicle," Janu replied, "nor would we be able to carry it on foot. Whatever you leave behind, you can purchase in Fa'i."

"Dad, I don't mean to sound selfish, but this is the only home I have ever known. If we get to this place and I don't like it, I'll never be able to return home again. And if Keres is so evil, why aren't we taking our friends with us?"

"Because right now this family is my first priority," Janu replied. "But if things go as planned, we won't be separated from our friends for very long."

Izaiah went to his room, convinced his parents would never call off their stupid flight. *I just want my life back*, he thought as he stared at the light across the river. *To save them, they'll have to be caught in the act.*

Izaiah had a migraine from all this escaping business. And ever since his trip to the Ares Medical Center, his ribs had been extremely sore. The medication they had given him for the pain had made him drowsy. He dozed off mumbling, "Why won't they listen to me?" Thirty minutes later, his mobile rang.

"Hey, Jackson. What's up?" he slurred.

"Meet me at the Diner in an hour. I have another assignment for you that will put you in good standing with PsyOps."

Izaiah remembered his last assignment: *Kidnapping my own sister.*

"What's the assignment?" Izaiah asked, slurring his words again.

"You feeling okay?" Jackson asked. "You sound out of it."

"I'm okay. What do you want me to do?"

"I'll explain when I see you, and don't be late."

Izaiah took a seat in the booth at the diner and ordered a malt. Five minutes later, he spotted Jackson in the rear, motioning for him.

"Where're we going?" Izaiah asked. "Should I bring my bike?"

"Is it locked?"

"Yes."

"It'll keep until we get back."

They were in the back of the parking lot when Izaiah was grabbed from behind and a hood was placed over his head. He could feel himself sinking into nothingness as he was shoved into the back of a SUV.

Everything went black, and when he awoke, he was once again tied to a table in a freezing cold lab. He heard familiar voices and lifted his head. Staring at him was Morpheus, that horrible creature he had seen at the facility center, and two Jacksons standing side by side. He wondered if he was in the place of the living dead.

He tried telling them that he didn't want to be put in a tank with the blue solution, but he couldn't speak. A horrible-smelling mask was placed over his nose and mouth, and he was out once again.

Meanwhile, Ariana was putting dinner on the table. "Sierra, please call Izaiah to dinner."

"He's not here, Mom. And come to think of it, I haven't seen him for a while."

"Neither have I," Janu commented.

"He might be late for school and chores, but he's never late for his favorite meal," Ariana said. "We'll have to start without him."

Monica rang the doorbell. School was out for the summer, and as usual, she would spend it at her home away from home.

"Just in time for dinner," Ariana said. "Wash your hands and grab a plate. By the way, have you seen Izaiah?"

"You mean he's not here for dinner?" Monica asked.

"Nobody's seen him," Sierra said.

Ariana noticed Monica's red and swollen eyes and asked, "Have you been crying?"

"I'm okay," she said, then burst into tears. "I think my dad hates me. I don't know him anymore. He acts as if Mom's disappearance is my fault."

"Did he hurt you?" Janu asked.

"Just my feelings, but I'll get over it. So, Auntie, what did you prepare to satisfy my palette tonight?" she quipped, as she dried her eyes on Ariana's apron.

"Good ol'-fashioned spaghetti and meatballs," Ariana replied. But she was worried about Monica... and her son. Where could he be?

Meanwhile, Jacque was glad to be rid of Monica for a while. She was a nuisance, always asking about his work and what the Establishment was up to.

"Dad, you're a governor," Monica had voiced before leaving home. "If anybody knows what's going on in this place, you do. Please tell me."

You tell me what the Calders are up to, he thought, *and I'll tell you what we're up to.* But he kept the thought to himself.

"Anyway, I was wondering if I received a letter about being tested or examined…or something?" she had asked.

"No," her father informed her.

"The Calders have received theirs, and they have already been tested."

"You'll probably receive yours any day," he had stated. He was annoyed that she had interrupted his work with her nagging questions.

He had peered at her with disdain. Her short black hair was cropped and gelled, and she wore heavy black makeup. A spiked dog collar was wrapped around her neck, and she had on a black leather jacket. She donned a red-and-black-plaid miniskirt, and black thigh-high socks were peeking out over the top of her black leather boots.

"I hope you clean up before your exams," he had barked. "You might not pass on your appearance alone, and I have a reputation to uphold in this community."

Monica was crushed…and angry. She ran to her room and grabbed her suitcase. "He never would have spoken to me like that if Mom was here," she mumbled.

Jacque Stoner had loved the fact that his daughter wasn't like everyone else, that she was her own person with her own sense of identity. *"You're comfortable in your own skin, kitten, and I like that,"* he would say.

"And I liked the fact that you were my hero," she had said aloud as tears rolled down her pixie-shaped face.

She had decided to tell Jacque that she was tired of his insults. She knew he missed her mom, but she missed her, too. No, she actually ached for her. But still she treated him with respect, and she deserved the same.

"She was my best friend, too," she had mumbled as she headed toward his office.

Hearing Jacque on his mobile, she had tiptoed to the slightly ajar office door. His back was to her, but she could tell he was frustrated.

"What have we on the Calders?" he had asked the other party. "Has their son come up with positive proof? We can't arrest them on assumption alone. He's a suspect? You found what? This is better than we hoped." He paused.

"Izaiah's not smart enough to engineer such a coup," he continued. "His parents are still suspect. And if they've found out the intent of the Great

Commission, they'll stop at nothing to warn Uriel and start a revolution in Keres." He paused again, as he listened to the person on the other end of the line.

"Unfortunately, I think my daughter is also involved. No, I don't have anything concrete yet, but she practically lives at their home since her mother's…you know. Yes, as soon as I know something positive, I'll let you know."

Monica was stunned. *Now they think I'm a traitor, too.* She couldn't believe her own father was willing to turn her and his best friend's family in to the Establishment.

She had left her home in tears. Sobbing like a baby, she had to pull off the road. "I don't even know my own father," she had cried between gasps.

Presently safe at the Calders, Monica smiled and said, "Please pass the spaghetti."

Izaiah walked through the door as the meal was being served. "Are you all right?" Ariana asked. "You're never late for dinner."

"I'm not really hungry, Mother. May I please be excused?"

Everyone stared at the young man who never missed his favorite meal. *And who talks like that?* Sierra wondered. "Z, are you ill?" she asked.

"In truth, I'm very tired," he replied. "May I please be excused?"

"Yes, you may," Janu replied, gawking at his son.

"I'll fix you some soup when you come back down," Ariana offered, not sure what to make of his strange behavior.

"Thank you, Mother. I'm going up to my room now."

Sierra left the table and watched as Izaiah roamed the hallway in search of his bedroom.

"Mom," Sierra whispered, "he doesn't even know where his bedroom is."

"I told you they did something to our boy," Ariana whispered. "He hasn't been the same since we took those tests. How does he not know where his own room is? Janu, maybe you should go see about him."

Janu's burner mobile rang. "It must be important if you're calling me on this line," he said when he answered.

"Is Izaiah home?" Malakh asked.

"He just walked in the door, but he's acting strangely. He pretended he didn't know where his own bedroom was, and he wasn't hungry."

"He's not pretending, Janu, because he's not Izaiah—it's his replicate… Isaac."

"How do you know this?"

"I was at the facility center when they handed him Izaiah's keys. They must've brought him to your home. The real Izaiah is here with me, and we're on the lam. Meet us at the safe house as soon as possible, and make sure you're not followed."

"What do you mean you're on the run…from whom?"

"I'll explain when you get here. And bring some food, we're starving. Leave by the alley, Janu. They're watching your home."

Janu was stunned. "Guys, come with me to the restroom…now," he whispered.

"But we haven't finished dinner yet," Sierra replied.

"Just do as I say."

Janu was sweating profusely, and his heart was racing. "As if I don't have enough to contend with, now there's this madness," he mumbled. "What is going on in this crazy town?"

They all crowded into the restroom, and Janu locked the door. "Are you going to tell us what's going on?" Ariana asked.

"That is not our son upstairs," he whispered.

"What the devil do you mean?" Ariana shouted.

"Shhhhh! He may hear you," Janu replied. "That's not Izaiah."

"Then who is he? And where is my son?"

"He's Isaac, a replicate of Izaiah. Our real son is on his way to the safe house with Malakh."

"What kind of foolishness—" Monica remarked. "When did all of this replicating take place?"

"Probably at that medical center," Sierra replied. "We don't know what they did to Z, but he's looked pale and sickly ever since."

"It's impossible to replicate anything that quickly," Janu remarked. "This madness has probably been in the works for years...maybe decades. I have to meet Malakh and Izaiah at the safe house."

"And leave us here with that...*thing*?" Ariana all but screamed. "We're going with you. I won't have you wandering these streets alone."

"You'll do no such thing," Janu replied. "I'll be okay, and so will Izaiah. But I can't worry about getting all of you and him home safely. Plus, I'm not leaving that...that charlatan alone in this house."

He handed Ariana a small pistol he'd been carrying with him since this madness began. "Don't let on that you know what he is. But if he tries anything, shoot him. I'll call when I get to the safe house. And don't go outside. They're watching the house."

"By the way, honey, you know that my coworker, Drake, has been missing for several days," Janu said. "It's as if he fell off the planet."

Sierra gasped.

"What is it?" Janu asked.

"I was hiding in the file room at Rotunda Hall when two men came in. A man named Drake told another man named Zen that he wasn't happy about the experiments the Establishment was conducting on the citizens. Zen didn't seem pleased that Drake was questioning authority. Do you think they did away with him, Dad?"

"I don't know. Now, go back to the table and try to act normal."

"Please be careful," Ariana said. "These evil people will do anything to protect Diablo and his so-called Great Commission."

"Maybe we should question the…thing," Monica suggested. "Find out what it knows."

"You'll do no such thing," Janu cautioned. "He could be dangerous." Janu exited the back alley, mumbling, "They've actually replicated my son." Then he noticed a black vehicle cautiously following in the distance.

When he stopped, the shadow stopped. Every corner he turned, the black vehicle turned. There was no way he was leading them to the safe house.

Janu came to a stoplight and pretended to wait. As soon as the *tail* stopped, Janu ran the red light, hoping no one would enter the intersection.

He drove at breakneck speed, making a sharp right turn into a backstreet and disappearing into a parking structure just as the black vehicle turned into the alley.

Janu drove to the fourth floor of the garage and parked. He peered out of an opening and saw the SUV speed by. He left the garage, then drove a route he had used many times to get to the safe house without being followed.

Monica, meanwhile, had convinced Sierra they should get a closer look at Isaac. They crept up the stairs while Ariana pretended to watch TV.

"I wonder what he's really like," Monica asked.

"Shhhh," Sierra replied, "we don't want to announce our arrival."

Meanwhile, the TV was watching Ariana as her thoughts were on her son and the creature upstairs in his bedroom. Izaiah's bedroom door was ajar, and Isaac was sitting up in bed pretending to read the encyclopedia. The girls were amazed at how much he physically resembled Izaiah.

"Shouldn't we go in and say something like, 'what's up?'" Monica asked.

"Let's ask him if he's ready to eat now, then we can question him," Sierra replied.

"Girls, where are you?" Ariana shouted.

As the replicate watched the girls retreat down the stairs, he sneered, his inky-black eyes rolling around in their sockets. *Fools*, he thought. *They didn't know I was watching them watching me.* He snickered, then closed and bolted the door.

CHAPTER 27

Narrow Escape

Morpheus had spotted Janu leaving his house. He and his fellow ogre, Benoit, immediately became invisible and took to the air, shadowing Janu to the safe house. The two trolls had been ordered by Diablo not to return without the fugitives, so, they settled in the nearby tree, prepared to wait as long as it would take. Unaware of the invisible creatures, Janu knocked on the door of the safe house.

"What could be in that rundown shack?" Benoit asked.

"Your guess is as good as mine," Morpheus replied.

Malakh opened the door. "Quick, Janu, come in. What took you so long?"

"I was being followed."

"Did you lose them?"

"Yes. Where's Izaiah?"

"He's resting, but he doesn't look good. I called a doctor I think I can trust—he's on his way."

"What happened?"

"I'm still reeling from what I witnessed," Malakh replied. "And my invitation to the meeting was a ruse. When I arrived, they tried to drug me. They bound and gagged me and left me on a cold table, planning to do who knows what to me."

"What do you mean, they tried to drug you?"

"No one else had been offered a beverage. So, I pretended to drink and pass out."

"How did you come across Izaiah?"

"I heard a noise in the next room. I freed myself and peeked in. Izaiah was out cold, lying naked on a table, and his blood was being drained into a container from a small puncture in his right side. Simultaneously, someone's, or *something's*, blood was being pumped into his left side. Unfortunately, we have no way of knowing if the blood's a match. Anyway, he urgently needs medical care."

"How did you get away?"

"I removed the boy's tubes, poured antiseptic into the wounds, and patched him up as best I could. I gave him my elixir, and when he came around, I got us out of there as fast I could."

"Why did you bring him here?"

"Because your home would've been the first place they'd look."

"Well, who…or what…is that thing in my house?" Janu asked.

"Izaiah's replicate," Malakh answered. "For years they've been experimenting, trying to create the perfect community by re-creating humans. Long ago, I was replicated for my intelligence, but it didn't go as they'd expected; I saw to that. However, they're still experimenting on my other self, trying to determine what went wrong."

"Shouldn't I have known this at the beginning of our relationship?" Janu demanded. "So, who are you really: Malakh or his replica?"

"If I was my replicate, I wouldn't have known about this safe house," Malakh replied. "Nor would I have helped Izaiah escape. Come to think of it, I've been rescuing *your* children a lot lately, and some gratitude would be in order."

"And I appreciate it," Janu stated. "But every time I think I can trust you, you shock me all over again, and quite frankly, I'm dog-tired of these surprises."

The doctor arrived, interrupting what was about to become a heated argument. "We'll finish this later," Malakh stated. "Right now, your son needs help."

"Hello," the doctor said. "Did something die in your yard? It smells awful."

Malakh peeked out to see if the medic was alone. "This is Mr. Calder," he said, "the young boy's father."

"Nice to meet you," the doctor replied. "Now, show me the boy."

The doctor took one look at Izaiah. "He should be in a hospital. I'll call the paramedics."

"Doc, you're the only person besides us who knows about this place," Malakh said, "and I'm not about to change that. Tell us where to take him and we'll meet you there."

"The facility center across the bridge," the doctor replied. "They have the modern technology to do a good job on your boy. I often practice there myself."

"Thanks, Doc, I think I know the place," Malakh said, then quickly ushered him to the door.

"Why didn't you let him call for help?" Janu asked.

"The facility center is where all this replicating is taking place—it's where we just escaped from. Why would he practice there if he's not involved in this madness? I'd stake my life he's notifying the Establishment of our whereabouts as we speak. Hurry, get Izaiah. We have to leave."

"But we can't move him," Janu said. "He's lost too much blood."

"We have to get him underground."

"You have a bunker?"

"You're not the only one who's been preparing an escape," Malakh replied.

"You never cease to amaze me," Janu remarked. "I'm not even sure you're human sometimes. The speed with which you accomplish things is incredible."

Janu gathered up Izaiah, and Malakh grabbed a few necessities. Just as they were sealed inside the chamber, the front door was kicked in.

"They didn't waste any time," Malakh said, quickly turning on the large monitor to see what was going on outside the compartment.

Benoit entered first, his hooves clip-clopping on the wooden floor. Morpheus followed, his beady eyes moving disjointedly in their sockets as he searched the room.

"What in the world are they?" Janu asked, wide-eyed.

"They are the horrors of cross-breeding, my friend."

"To what end?" Janu asked.

"To defeat Uriel and capture the throne of Fa'i. That's the short version."

"That's madness. Is that what this Great Commission is all about?" Janu asked.

"Diablo is manufacturing a supposedly indestructible force capable of fighting for days with little or no food…or rest," Malakh replied. "And women and children are included. Diablo's plan is to annihilate anyone who is not with him in his madness, including his governors."

Izaiah was suddenly coughing up blood and struggling to breathe. "We've got to help him," Janu lamented. Malakh quickly gave Izaiah another dose of elixir.

"He's not coming around," Janu remarked. "Give him some more."

"If I give him too much of the bitter liquid too soon, it'll cause a reverse effect, and he'll be worse off than if he'd never taken any at all."

"What's in that stuff, anyway?" Janu asked. Malakh didn't reply.

Two minutes later, a confused Izaiah opened his eyes. "Dad?" he said.

"It's okay, son, I've got you."

Minutes later, glass was breaking outside the chamber and Malakh ran to the monitor. The creatures were tearing the place apart.

"Where can they be?" Benoit asked.

"They can talk," Janu moaned. "That's…*nasty.*"

"Three that we know of were in here," Morpheus replied, "and one left. Two are still here somewhere."

"Well, we need to find them before backup gets here," Benoit remarked.

"Quick, grab Izaiah and I'll grab the files," Malakh said. "They won't stop until they discover this room."

"What about all this technology?" Janu asked.

"We'll have to destroy it," Malakh replied.

Janu was incredulous. It was here that he was made to believe his plan could actually be realized. It was here that Malakh had earned his trust, after working many long nights together. Yet, there were so many things about this strange man he didn't know.

Meanwhile, Benoit asked Morpheus if the fugitives had the ability to dematerialize.

"Don't be silly," Morpheus replied, as he continued to press the wall.

Malakh removed as much incriminating data as he could from the PCs and laptops, unplugged the equipment, then quickly followed Janu into the bunker.

"We'd better hurry," he said. "Morpheus is still searching around the partition. It won't be long before he finds the secret panel, and with his intelligence, decipher the code."

"You know their names?" Janu asked.

"I, uh, previously heard them referring to each other," Malakh replied. "Once we clear this upcoming threshold, I will cause the block wall to come down. When we're away from the building, I'll press the remote again and the place will implode."

"Don't tell me, you've had this planned long ago," Janu remarked, in awe of this man who had thought of every possible contingency.

"When dealing with the likes of Diablo and his Establishment, you have to be prepared for anything," Malakh said. "Here, I'll help you carry Izaiah."

Meanwhile, Morpheus informed Benoit that sometimes when humans wanted to hide something important, they placed it in a secret passageway. "Even the general has a secret chamber," he interjected.

"How do you know?" Benoit asked.

"I saw him slip behind it one day," Morpheus replied. "I guess it's a bunker of some kind for him and his family in case of an emergency. He doesn't know I know, so don't tell anyone." Morpheus was unaware that the general's plans for his emergency hideaway included neither his son *nor* his wife.

Meanwhile, backup arrived just as Morpheus discovered the paneled wall that swung inward, exposing a room that surprised the onlookers.

"Well, well, well," Morpheus said. "Some hi-tech shenanigans have been going on in this room."

"Take all the equipment back to the lab and search the hard drives," the captain instructed.

Meanwhile, the three outlaws, sweating and out of breath, had reached the opening at the end of the bunker. "Well, my friend, our magnificent chamber is about to go up in smoke," Malakh remarked.

After Izaiah was placed out of harm's way, Malakh instructed everyone to cover their ears. He pressed the remote, and several seconds later, the safe house imploded in on itself. Smoke billowed everywhere.

"Let's get out of here!" Malakh shouted.

CHAPTER 28

The Dispatch

When the Prince was notified that Malakh had escaped with Izaiah right under his nose, he had tried hard to contain his true self. But constantly disguising his inhumanity was becoming tiresome.

"Find them," he had roared, spittle collecting in the corners of his mouth. "If my plans for replication and cross-breeding are leaked to the populace, it could jeopardize my Great Commission. Don't just stand there, General. Organize something… *anything*, and bring those fugitives back."

Envisioning his position and maybe his life disappearing before his eyes, the general had scrambled about like a mad dog, barking orders at everyone. Finally, he had dispatched Morpheus and Benoit to find the renegades.

The assemblymen were begging to see a living replication. However, when Isaac was brought forth, he was met with mixed emotions. Some men were awestricken; some wept; but most stared in disbelief.

"Izaiah's not likely to return to his home," the general had whispered to Diablo. "Let's send his replicate in his place to test how feasible our plan is."

Meanwhile, back at the Calders' home, Monica suggested they stun-gun Isaac, set him afire, or bind and gag him while he slept. "Do replicates sleep?" she asked. Just then Isaac entered the room.

"What are you watching on TV?" he asked.

"What we always watch every week this time," Ariana replied. Truth be told, they were watching for him.

"May I watch with you?" he asked.

Ariana smirked. "I usually have to beg you to watch TV with us," she said.

"Maybe he's missing his mommy," Monica said.

Unable to detect cynicism, Isaac missed the remark; it went right over his head. He sat on the floor. "Mother, do you plan to participate in the Great Commission?" he asked.

The real Izaiah already knew that neither Ariana nor anyone else in the family intended to participate in the Great Commission; still they played along.

"Remember when we were kids, we'd make up our own great commission, then fight over who would be the prince?" Sierra said.

"I remember," Isaac replied. *Liar,* Sierra thought. *That never happened.*

"Now that you're a PsyOp," she continued, "tell us when the Great Commission will be initiated and how it will affect us citizens."

"I don't know all the details," he replied, "but I think it will be implemented soon."

Smiling wickedly, Ariana said, "We haven't had family time like this in a long time."

"Yeah," Sierra said. "It's a real blast."

"Peachy keen," Monica added.

Again, all the sarcasm flew over the replicate's head. "Can I get you that soup now?" Ariana asked.

"I don't have much of an appetite," he replied.

"Don't wait too long," Ariana said with a smile. "It's not good to eat late at night." *You might have Izaiah's looks,* she thought, *but they forgot to give you his appetite.* She was heading to the kitchen when her mobile rang.

"Hello," she said.

"Hey, honey, what's going on there?"

"All's well," she whispered. "I can't believe this thing is trying to pass himself off as Izaiah, as if I don't know my own child. He didn't even want my chicken soup—can you believe that?"

"No, I can't," Janu replied.

"How's Izaiah, and where are you?" she asked.

"He's much better, but I'm leaving him with Malakh overnight. He's too weak to move again. By the way, we had to destroy the safe house. I'll tell you about it when I get there. Watch the charlatan closely, and don't use the telepad. I'm sure it's bugged."

"I'd feel better if you stayed with Izaiah, Janu."

"There's no way I'm letting you and the girls sleep alone in the house with that…thing. We don't know what he's capable of. I should be there within the hour."

"Please be careful, Janu. You know who are everywhere."

"I will."

Food was something the replicates were programmed to do without. But in order to avoid suspicion, Isaac decided to eat anyway. He stood and waited in the kitchen door until Ariana finished her conversation.

"Mother, I think I'll take that soup now," he said.

"Geez, Izaiah, you scared the bajeebers out of me. How long have you been standing there?"

"Not long," he replied.

Long enough to eavesdrop on my conversation, she thought. "Would you like crackers or corn bread?"

"Crackers, please," Isaac replied.

Gotcha again, Ariana thought. *My Izaiah always has corn bread with his soup.*

Janu was racing home when he spotted blinking lights behind him. In a flash, the Enforcer was upon him.

"Registration and ID card," he bellowed. While the Enforcer called in Janu's tags, Janu quickly called home.

"Ariana," he whispered, "I've been stopped by an Enforcer. No, I don't have any penalties." He had a sudden foreboding. "But if I don't make it home, call Malakh and tell him what happened. Get rid of the twin any way you can. I mean that literally."

"You'll make it home," Ariana insisted. "Oh, and I drugged the imposter. He's asleep with his head in his soup. He'll be out for a long time."

"Good girl. Remember to contact Malakh and proceed with the plan—you know it as well as me. I'll meet you at the cemetery. I have to go, he's coming back."

The Enforcer handed Janu his identification. "Please step out of the car, sir."

"What's the problem?" Janu asked.

"You were speeding," the Enforcer stated.

"I have an emergency at home," Janu replied. The Enforcer wrote out a penalty and handed it to Janu.

"Pop the trunk," the Enforcer said, "and then you're free to go." But his mobile rang, and after his conversation he instructed Janu to follow him.

"But I'm in a bit of a hurry," Janu stammered.

"Follow me," the Enforcer reiterated. Aware that he and his family were wanted by the Establishment, Janu reluctantly followed the Enforcer.

Meanwhile, Sierra went into the kitchen and found Isaac's head literally in his soup. "Mom, did you kill him?"

"No," Ariana replied, "he's just heavily sedated. I'm buying time until we figure out what to do with him. Hopefully, your dad will be here soon."

"He looks dead to me," Monica said, wandering in on the tail end of the conversation.

"I gave him a little something to help him sleep," Ariana muttered.

"To *make* him sleep, is more like it," Monica replied.

"Are we going to leave his head in the bowl?" Sierra asked; he could drown.

"His head is turned sideways," Ariana replied.

Sierra stared at the replica. "They did a great job," she said. "If I didn't know better, I'd think he was Z."

"Well, he's not," Ariana said, annoyed that this thing was in a warm, comfortable home, while Izaiah was goodness knows where.

"I wonder if he has real blood," Monica said.

"I would think so," Ariana replied.

"Let's cut him and see," Monica remarked.

"Is his skin real?" Sierra asked, moving in closer. "It could be synthetic."

"Let's light him up and see if he melts," Monica said. "That'd be one way of getting rid of him."

"We're not cutting or setting fire to anyone," Ariana said. "He's still a person… I think."

"Where is everyone?" Janu called from the hallway.

"In the kitchen," Ariana replied.

Janu followed the voices. "So, you're in here."

"I said we were in the kitchen," Ariana replied.

"Who's this guy, and what happened to him?" he asked.

"Honey, you know who this is," Ariana replied, "and you sound nasally. Are you all right?"

"I'm just tired."

Janu was staring at everyone with a blank look on his face. "Come sit down, Dad," Sierra said. "I'll get you some water."

But Monica wondered how Janu, who, according to Ariana, had been lucid just moments earlier on the telephone, had suddenly contracted amnesia. She placed some ice cubes in a dish towel and pressed it to his brow before peering into his dark cold eyes.

"Hold this on your head," she said. "You'll feel better. Auntie, Sierra, a word in the living room... now."

"What is it?" Ariana asked. "We need to see about your uncle."

"I don't think that *is* Uncle J," she whispered.

"Of course it is," Ariana replied.

"I think he's another replicate," Monica insisted.

"If you'd been through what he's been through tonight, with Izaiah fighting for his life and the safe house being destroyed, you'd behave oddly, too."

"The safe house is gone?" Sierra asked in disbelief.

"Your father said he'd tell us about it when he got home."

"Then, if that's Uncle J in our kitchen, he should be able to tell us what happened," Monica replied.

"I don't want to bother him with that right now," Ariana said. "He's not himself."

"My point exactly," Monica insisted.

"And, anyway, they only recently took our blood," Ariana said. "They can't replicate a person in a matter of weeks."

"I agree with Dad," Sierra said. "I think this business has been going on longer than we care to believe. How else could Izaiah's twin just suddenly show up? They didn't pick him off the rack. I believe we've all been replicated."

"But how could they do that without our knowledge?" Ariana asked.

"By taking our blood and tissues every time we visited our physicians."

"I have a confession," Monica said. "Before I left home tonight, I overheard my dad telling someone that your family is plotting to overthrow Diablo's Great Commission, and that I might be involved."

"Why didn't you say something?" Sierra asked.

"I was ashamed that my own father hated me and your parents so much that he would put a mark out on us."

"That's why they've been watching our house, and why they kidnapped Z," Sierra remarked.

"Slow down," Ariana said. "Let's think about this."

"Mom, I bet they know we're planning to escape," Sierra said, "and the lookalikes in the kitchen are probably spies. Why else would they be here, and what do they plan to do to us?"

"Sierra, call Malakh and fill him in," Ariana said. "Maybe he can come over."

"What do we do with those two until he gets here?" Monica asked.

"I have no idea," Ariana replied.

Sierra's mobile rang. "Hello," she said hurriedly.

"Sierra, this is Malakh."

"I was just about to call you," she said. "We've got a ginormous problem. Z's replicate is in our kitchen, drugged, and Monica thinks Dad is a replicate, too. And we're not sure what other replicates might show up before the night is over. It's like a horror movie, and we're the cast. What should we do?"

"I knew about Z's replicate, but why do you think your dad's a replicate?"

"He called Mom earlier and said he'd been pulled over by an Enforcer. He expected foul play because he told her if he didn't make it home soon, we should proceed with the plan and he'd meet us at the cemetery. Then he suddenly showed up acting weird. Can you come over?"

"I can't leave Izaiah right now, but I'll send Jordan over to stay the night. Lock the doors and windows and set the alarm. Go into the bunker until he arrives."

CHAPTER 29

The Twins

Meanwhile, Diablo was on his tiny throne, unconsciously running his tongue over his lips. He imagined tasting the powerful waters of Fa'i and envisioned himself as the city's eternal light.

A knock on the door interrupted his fantasy. "Come in," he said, annoyed. It was the general. He neither liked nor trusted this man, but he needed him.

"What can I do for you, General? It's late."

"It seems that Morpheus and Benoit followed the young fugitive's father to a shed in the woods, where they believed Izaiah and Malakh were hiding. But the creatures and several Enforcers were killed by a terrible implosion while inside the shack, and their remains have yet to be found. Izaiah's father, however, was picked up tonight for speeding and is currently being held at the facility."

Do I care about two freaks and a team of worthless Enforcers? Diablo thought. *Yes, Morpheus was my masterpiece, a formidable foe and a brilliant ally, but such is life...and death.*

"Thank you, General," he said. "I can always count on you to keep me informed." The general bowed low, having no clue that the Prince loathed him as much as he loathed the Prince.

"Idiot," Diablo murmured as the door closed. His focus turned immediately to the upcoming National Day of Celebration on Friday. And although it was a time of jubilation for the nation, his officials, replicates, and cross-breeds would be receiving their final orders regarding the implementation of the Great Commission.

Meanwhile, Jordan rang the Calders' bell, and the door flew open. "Come in quickly," Sierra whispered. "We're being watched. Did you check the trees for creatures?"

"The streets and the trees," he whispered. "Where's everybody?"

"They're in the kitchen trying to determine if my dad is really my dad. But Mom has my real dad's gun." Jordan frowned.

"Good evening," he said as he entered the kitchen. "And what happened to him?" he asked, peering at the back of Isaac's head as his face lay in the soup bowl.

"He's tired, is all," Ariana replied, trying to cover up her evil deed.

Jordan lifted Isaac's head and gasped. The resemblance was uncanny. But he knew the real Izaiah was at his house recovering. *This is some serious stuff*, he thought.

"It's late," he said. "I'll get the boy up to his room. You ladies should turn in as well."

Ariana had no intention of sleeping with her fake husband. She gave Jordan keys to lock her and Izaiah's bedroom doors from the outside.

Jordan settled Izaiah's replicate in bed and locked the door. The other fraudster was searching for the master bedroom, further confirming that he was not Janu. Once the man was inside, Jordan locked that door, as well.

Meanwhile, Janu was being brutally tortured at the facility center. Suddenly, a creature threw cold water in his face.

"I knew seventeen years ago when you were released from the conformation camp that I would again have the pleasure of arresting you," the general said.

"You and your wife only pretended to conform to the ways of Keres to obtain your freedom, only to later try and escape. Well, you should have fled sooner."

Janu's left eye was closed shut, and he could barely see out of the right. Blood was streaming from his nose and mouth. But he didn't care—by now his family was on their way to the river.

"I'm not an unreasonable man," the general continued. "Tell me your plans and maybe I'll spare your life. Or I'll simply arrest your wife and children. And when I'm finished with them, they will talk."

Knowing the general would make good on his threat, Janu struggled against his restraints. Before leaving the room, the general instructed Dugbhan to watch Janu closely. "We wouldn't want him escaping, too."

The sentry's dark, hairy face resembled an eagle's, but he walked upright like a man. His arms and legs were covered with feathers, and a tail hung from a hole in the seat of his trousers. The creature reeked with the same sickening smell Janu had encountered at the safe house, and he wanted to puke.

"How long have I been here?" Janu garbled.

"Don't talk," the creature replied.

"You speak with an accent," Janu said, amazed. "Listen, whatever you are, unless you want to clean up a puddle of urine, you'll get me to the restroom… now."

"I'll see if you can go," the creature replied.

"I'm going whether you *see* to it or not," Janu muddled.

The creature left the room and came back with two more ogres as disgusting as himself. *How gross*, Janu thought.

"They'll escort you to the restroom," Dugbhan said.

"I'm capable of going by myself, if you get my drift."

"I do," Dugbhan replied, "and that's why you'll be accompanied."

Janu had never heard an accent like that before, and he could only imagine what other beings the Establishment had manufactured.

"I'm going to remove your handcuffs," Dugbhan said, "but if you try anything, I will drug you."

The other two creatures untied his feet and stood him up. "Let's go," they said, shoving him toward the door.

Janu was herded to the restroom like a steer, his photographic memory embracing every escape route in the stark-white corridor. Admittedly, he was afraid.

Jordan, meanwhile, was on his second pot of coffee as he stood watch over the ladies. He heard a loud thump upstairs and took out his stun gun. As he crept up the stairs, he heard a loud crash.

Ariana leaped out of Sierra's bed and grabbed her gun. Sierra was on her heels with a bat and a can of wasp spray, while Monica, who had announced that she would not sleep alone with two replicates in the house, followed with a can of Mace. When they saw Jordan in the dimly lit hall, they screamed.

"Shhhhh," he said, then tiptoed to Ariana's bedroom. He peeked through the keyhole, quickly covered his mouth, and then leaned against the wall gasping.

"What is it?" Sierra whispered.

"You don't want to know," Jordan replied.

"I do," Monica stated, and ran to the end of the hallway, followed by Ariana and Sierra. They peeked through the keyhole and wanted to be sick.

"What's that in my bed?" Ariana whispered.

"It's certainly not Uncle J," Monica replied.

"Whatever it is, it's going through some kind of metamorphosis," Jordan whispered. "I've never seen anything so disgusting. Let's check on the other one."

He unlocked Izaiah's bedroom door and peered inside. Isaac was not changing—he had already changed. He was leaning against the headboard, exhausted from his transformation. Sweat was running down his monkey-like face; his former hands were now talons, and his feet were webbed.

"Everyone dressed and downstairs," Jordan ordered, relocking the door. "Bring your packed bags—I have Izaiah's. We'll leave from the bunker."

Ariana and the girls were bumping into each other as they quickly dressed. "Sierra," Ariana said in a panic, "we don't have time to brush our teeth, we have to go."

Ariana led out first, with Sierra and Monica close behind. They were tiptoeing past Izaiah's room when they heard a sickening growl. Sierra's quick hand stifled Monica's yelp. As they approached the stairs, a loud *thump* made the walls vibrate. Monica slid down the banister, and Ariana and Sierra jetted down the stairs two at a time, almost knocking Jordan to the floor.

After much effort, they moved the table away from the trapdoor. Jordan opened the hatch, and they followed him down into the bunker. "The trapdoor is exposed," Ariana whispered.

"I'll go up, recover it, and meet you at the exit," Jordan replied. "I'm driving a red and black Establishment vehicle."

"I'll go up with you," Sierra said. "You'll need help with the table."

"Be careful," Ariana whispered.

Once they were topside again, Jordan closed the hatch. They put the rugs back, but it would take three or four people to replace the table properly.

"We'll walk it back and forth until it covers most of the rug," Sierra whispered. "It won't be perfect, but it'll hide the trapdoor."

Suddenly, the creatures were breaking down the bedroom doors. "We can't leave the hatch exposed," Sierra whispered. But a gut-wrenching growl sent the two tearing out the back door.

"Nothing's going as planned," Sierra said, sadly, as Jordan gunned his vehicle and raced out of the alley. "And we don't know where my dad is."

"It may seem as if everything has gone awry," Jordan replied, "but I promise, all will be okay."

"How can you promise that?" Sierra asked.

"I know somebody who knows somebody," he replied.

"It's unusually dark tonight," Sierra said, changing the subject, "and I don't see Mom or Monica."

"There they are," Jordan replied. The ladies threw their bags in the trunk and literally dove into the back seat.

Meanwhile, Janu had made it to the restroom. "Use the urinal," the smaller creature said.

"What I have to do calls for a stall…if you get my drift, which you will, if you keep standing there." The creature stared at him. "In other words, you might want to wait in the hall."

"We'll be right outside," the taller creature announced. "Don't try anything, or you won't live to regret it."

The beautiful accents coming out of their ugly faces were appalling. Janu retrieved his Lassier Faire from the undershorts into which Ariana had the forethought to stitch a small pocket. He placed the tiny earplug in his right ear and switched on the communicator.

"Malakh," Janu said, "I need your help."

"Time is up," Dubghan shouted from the hallway.

"Where are you?" Malakh asked. "Your family's going nuts."

"I'm in a place that has a lab and the ugliest creatures I've ever seen," he whispered.

"You're at the facility center," Malakh said. "I'm coming for you."

"Aren't you finished yet?" Dubghan yelled through the bathroom door.

"I'll be out in a minute," Janu replied.

"I've got to go, Malakh, but come and get me before they replicate me…or worse."

"They already have," Malakh replied, "but I'll explain later. Whatever you do, keep your communicator on so I can track you, but don't let them find it."

"Just get me out of here," Janu whispered.

He was escorted back to the room and strapped into a chair again. But Janu had accomplished his mission. Malakh knew where he was, and if anybody could rescue him, Malakh could.

"I've located Janu," Malakh reported to the rest of the family on their communicators.

"Where is he?" Jordan asked.

"At the facility center. I'm on my way there now. Unfortunately, I have to take Izaiah with me."

"You think that's a good idea since they're looking for him, too?"

"I can't leave him behind. They might locate the house while I'm gone. How are the ladies? Are you still at Janu's? Are the replicates still behaving?"

"Okay. No, and no way. The replicates have metamorphosed into hideous monsters. We literally had to run from the house. We're on our way to the cemetery now."

"Go to the safe house instead. Use your communicator to let me know when you get there."

"I thought the safe house was destroyed," Ariana stated.

"Uncle always prepares for the 'what-ifs'," Jordan replied.

Ariana suggested they use her pistol to raid the facility center and free Janu. Sierra, while chewing her nails, blurted out something about blowing up the place. And dear, dear Monica. Jordan thought she had the wackiest idea of all.

"Let's hack the general's computer again while he's at the facility," she said. "There has to be some new info we can use. From his computer, we can hack into Diablo's. Between the two, we may discover what other wickedness they're planning."

"Good idea," Ariana agreed, shocking everyone. "Maybe we'll discover something that might help protect the lives of the unsuspecting citizens."

Jordan smiled. He was dealing with a bunch of vigilantes.

"I'll need help with this one," Monica stated.

"What kind of help?" Jordan asked.

"A hacker extraordinaire," Monica replied. "Someone smarter than me, who can get out of the house this time of night."

"Where can you find one of those?" Ariana asked innocently.

"I know just the person," Monica replied.

Sierra glared at Monica. "You're not talking about who I think you're talking about...are you?"

"Sure am," Monica said and pulled out her mobile. "Hey, it's me. Can you get out? I know it's late, but I need your help. I wouldn't ask if it wasn't deathly important, and I mean that literally. I'll be there in twenty-five in a black and red."

"Who was that?" Ariana asked.

"One of the smartest people on the planet," Monica replied. "She's even smarter than me, and I'm not bragging. If we want to hack into Diablo's stuff, this is the girl for the job."

"She's talking about brainiac Leila," Sierra interjected. "Tell the truth, Monica. She is crazy, isn't she?"

"Like a fox," Monica replied.

"She's like weird brilliant," Sierra added. "She knows everything. Ask her about anything in the world, and she'll give you a whole thesis on the subject. Boy, is she a pain."

"Jealousy is a terrible monster," Monica teased.

"Sounds like the right woman for the job," Jordan remarked.

"She dresses kind of strange," Monica warned, "but don't hold it against her." The others laughed, considering Monica's mode of dress. "And sometimes she speaks in a geek language even I don't understand."

"What are you talking about?" Ariana asked.

"Sometimes she talks in equations, numeric stuff. It's hard to explain. You'll have to hear it for yourself. Just don't laugh, okay? Oh, and sometimes when she's working, she's so locked in she won't speak at all or know what's going on around her. She calls it her out-of-mind experience."

"Sounds right to me," Jordan chuckled.

"She sounds weird," Monica stated, "but she's brilliant. I admire her, guys, so please don't make her feel bad...okay?"

"We would never do that," Jordan said, winking at Sierra. They all snickered, glad they had something to laugh about.

Leila was sitting on her stoop with her chin in her hands when she spotted the black and red. She jumped up and waved at the quartet.

"What is she wearing?" Ariana asked.

"Auntie, please don't say anything to hurt her feelings," Monica begged. "We really need her."

"Okay. But...*what is she wearing*?" Sierra and Jordan were rolling.

Leila was a replica of Monica in style, except she was tall and thin. Her thick black hair resembled two pom-poms on either side of her head, and she wore a brown leather bomber jacket with a cream faux-fur collar. The sides of her ears were pierced and covered with small gold earrings. A long, gray feathered tassel hung from her left lobe down to her shoulders, and her lips and eyelids were painted black. Brown, yellow, and blue striped leotards peeked out from beneath her yellow plaid miniskirt, and her feet were shod with thigh-high brown leather boots. She flung a large gold satchel over her shoulder and headed down the steps, bumping a suitcase behind her.

"Where does she think she's going, and how long does she plan to stay?" Sierra asked, choking with laughter.

"She carries all her nerd stuff in there," Monica replied in her defense, "and she takes it everywhere."

"Sounds like somebody I know," Sierra said, smiling at Monica.

Jordan stifled his giggles and got out of the car to help his newest passenger. "Hi, I'm Jordan."

"I'm Leila, nice to meet ya," she replied faster than a locomotive.

"What you got there?" he asked.

"My carryall, get it? I carry all my stuff in here."

"Well, jump in the back," he replied, and she literally did.

"Good to see you," Monica said, quickly moving over.

"You, too," Leila replied and hugged her friend. Introductions were made, and Ariana wondered if she was as brilliant as Monica attested.

Wasting no time, Leila asked, "Is what you want me to do something that will try my little gray cells to the utmost, or are we simply blowing things up again?"

"This will truly try your little gray cells," Monica mimicked. "And no, we're not blowing up anything…this time."

"You've blown things up before?" a stunned Ariana asked. "Never mind, I don't want to know. Dear, are your parents okay with you coming out this time of night?" she asked, as any concerned mother would.

"As long as I'm with Monica, it's okay," she said at the speed of lightning. "My dad and Monica's dad are good friends. They belong to the same club, or something. He thinks Monica and I have a lot in common."

"He's right about that," Sierra mumbled.

"I haven't been out of the house since school recess, and my parents are worried that I spend too much time on my computer. So—she giggled—"I told them Monica had called and wanted me to spend a couple of days with her. They quickly helped me pack."

"I can see why," Ariana whispered.

Jordan, trying not to choke from laughter, was interrupted on his communicator.

"Uncle M here. I'm trying to get into the facility center, but the creatures *and* the guards are out in droves tonight.

"Be careful," Jordan said. "Do we have any extra communicators at the safe house?"

"Yeah. Why?"

"We've got another ally who is willing to help us."

"Bringing someone else on board could be dangerous, son. We're not sure who can be trusted. They could be a replicate. But I trust your judgment. The Lassier Faires are in the safe."

Jordan turned and stared at Leila, wondering if she, too, would transform right there in the back seat. Instead, she asked, "Is someone going to tell me what wonderful mischief we're up to?"

Meanwhile, a frustrated general was getting nowhere with Janu, who kept reciting the same answers over and over. The general wanted him dead, but being able to uncover the traitors' plans was more important to the mission.

Meanwhile, Malakh was behind the facility donning a blue uniform and mask retrieved from his trunk. He slipped down the dark alley alongside the building, climbed through the basement window, and snuck into the storage room.

"I have all night," Malakh heard the general say on his communicator. "And unless you want your family brutalized, confess your treasonous plans to escape Keres and warn Uriel of our Great Commission. Tell the truth and you might be pardoned." Lies.

The general got in Janu's face. "I've wasted enough time on you," he barked. "Your family will beg for mercy, and one of you will talk tonight."

Meanwhile, Leila asked again, "Why am I here?"

"We're going to break into General Armon's home and hack into his and Prince Diablo's computers. Can you do that?" They waited anxiously for her reply.

Leila chuckled. "Of course, I *can* do it. The question should be, *will* I do it?"

"Will you...*please*?" Monica begged.

"Yes," she replied suddenly, clapping her hands like a kid in a candy store.

"She's really strange," Ariana muttered.

"When do we start?" Leila asked.

"Now. We can break in again while the general's at the facility," Sierra suggested.

"You mean you've done this before?" Leila asked, intensely overjoyed.

"That's a long story," Monica said, "but it'll have to wait."

"Watch out!" Ariana shouted. Jordan slammed on the brakes. "That looks like Ambray crossing the street. Pull over, she may be in trouble."

"Who is she?" Sierra asked.

"Remember your father's coworker, Drake, who went missing? It's his wife. I called several times to see if there was anything we could do to help her find him, but no one answered, which I thought was odd."

It started to rain suddenly, and Ariana quickly jumped from the vehicle. "Ambray," she shouted, waving her arms. But the woman kept walking. When she caught up with her, Ariana asked, "Didn't you hear me calling you?"

Suddenly, two small creatures were snatching at Ariana's hair. The trolls were flapping their ugly wings and shrieking loudly. Ariana quickly pulled her friend into the storefront doorway.

"What do you want?" the woman asked.

As Ariana peered into her friend's inky, expressionless eyes, eyes she had recently seen at her own kitchen table, Ambray began to convulse. Her mouth was twitching, and foam was oozing out of its corners. The muscles in her jaw began to elongate. She was transforming right in front of Ariana.

Ambray threw her head back and let out an earsplitting yelp. Her arms were jerking back and forth as if they weren't attached to her body, and a shocked Ariana backed away. Talons began protruding from the woman's wrists, and Sierra leapt from the vehicle.

"Mommy," she yelled, "that is not Ms. Ambray." Sierra quickly grabbed her mother and led her, shaken and soaking wet, back to the vehicle.

"Let's roll," Sierra told Jordan after shoving her mother into the back seat. Ariana turned and, with tears rolling down her cheeks, watched the creature completely transform.

"I can't believe what just happened," she cried. Monica held her as Ariana had held Monica many times since her mother's disappearance.

"Uh…people, did I just see what I thought I didn't see?" Leila asked, her eyes big as saucers.

"This is why we need you," a terrified Monica replied.

"Wow," Leila said, "even I couldn't make this stuff up." There was no clapping for joy this time.

Meanwhile, Malakh shone his flashlight around the storage room of the facility center in search of anything that would aid him in Janu's rescue. He spotted a blue stained uniform hanging on a rack that might do, and he could use the laundry basket on wheels to hide Janu in.

As he searched for a mask and booties, someone entered the room. He quickly slipped into the elfin closet. He cracked the door and gasped in disbelief. It was Morpheus.

How did he survive the blast? Malakh wondered, as the creature waddled over to a drafting table with a file folder from the safe house. Malakh then realized that the Establishment knew of Janu's plan to escape, thus his abduction.

CHAPTER 30

On the Lam

There were any number of Enforcers the general could've assigned to abduct Janu's family. But only one would not be put off because it involved a woman and her children.

Aengus, whose name meant "exceptionally strong," was Commander in Chief of the Enforcers. He had held the rank longer than anyone could remember, because no one dared to challenge him for the position.

His six-feet, seven-inch frame carried three hundred and four pounds of muscle. His comrades called him the Rock because his physique resembled chiseled stone. No one seemed to know his age, as his long silver hair had no correlation to his youthful looks.

He sometimes roared like a lion before striking his victims, paralyzing them with fear. Many times, he had challenged three of his best men to take him on at one time, and each time they would all end up on the ground bleeding and in pain. So, when he was told to take four officers to Janu's home to arrest a woman and her two children, he was insulted.

However, he and his team arrived at Janu's home in combat gear with weapons drawn. He ordered two of his men to follow him, and then he sent the other two round back before he himself slithered up the front porch like a snake. He peered through the windowpane but saw no one.

"The element of surprise is our best weapon," he advised his men. He kicked the door in with his size-sixteen boot, splintering it down the middle.

"What is that funky smell?" he roared, as he crossed the threshold. "Get the gas masks." But the two young officers had already fled the property and were heaving their guts onto the grass.

Aengus stepped inside. "Smells like pigs lived and died in here," he declared. Adorjan, recovering from the nausea, joined Aengus inside, followed by rookie Enforcer Elek, who was still green around the gills.

Suddenly, a noise from the kitchen caused Adorjan to draw his weapon. Aengus eased the door open, and the young officers all but maimed themselves running from the house.

"What was that?" Adorjan asked when safely outside. "I've never seen anything so disgusting. Are they eating the family?"

The creatures were devouring one another, and Aengus wondered if the family had already been part of their feast. "Don't be silly," he replied, sucking in air. "Appears they're eating raw meat…or something," he lied.

"But what are they?" Adorjan asked.

"Whatever they are and whatever they were eating, it was *disgusting*," a trembling Elek replied. "And the *way* they were eating it?" He then emptied the rest of his stomach on Rock's boots.

"*Clean my boots*," Aengus barked, sending Elek scurrying to the Jeep for a rag.

"Sir, I love my job, and I mean no disrespect, but I'm not going back in there," Adorjan stated. Aengus tried to appear stoic, but he, too, was shaken.

"We'll report we found no humans at this site," he replied. "And if you say otherwise, you'll have me to deal with."

"What about our men?" Elek exclaimed.

They ran to the side of the house and entered the basement. The other two officers were staring in disbelief. "Rock," one Enforcer said, "it's a literal fortress down here. Whatever these people were up to, it was major."

"Elek, use your mobile and get a picture of this for the general," Aengus whispered, almost in reverence of what he beheld.

Meanwhile, Malakh was still in the cramped closet, terrified Janu would spill his guts to save his family. He watched Morpheus gnaw on a piece of raw meat while thumbing through a red file folder, and he wondered how he and the file both could've escaped the implosion.

Morpheus' mobile buzzed, and he scurried off. "A creature with a mobile," Malakh muttered. "I've seen it all." He snatched the documents from the table, then searched the room. He found a crumpled mask, but no booties.

Each floor had an emergency room with an alarm system. He hurried over to it and read the directions. *Once the lever's pulled, you have twenty-eight minutes to vacate the building. Subsequently, a sticky white acid chemical, designed to burn through anything but the uniforms, will be released.* Malakh would only have minutes to locate Janu, get him into the uniform and a mask, and escort him out of the building before they were destroyed. He now knew that the unusual uniforms were designed to keep the facility staff from being annihilated, if ever the chemical was accidentally discharged.

Janu felt the Lassier Faire vibrating on his right hip and knew that Malakh was trying to locate him.

"Where am I?" he asked his keepers loudly enough for Malakh to hear.

"It wouldn't benefit you if you knew," Centaurus replied.

"If we're near the duplication lab, maybe I could get a peek at a replicate," Janu persisted.

"We're nowhere near that lab, and it would take too long to get there," Centaurus replied. "Now, be quiet or I'll gag you."

"I'll try every floor until I find you, my friend," Malakh whispered. He reached inside his uniform, retrieved a mini GPS-like gizmo from his trouser pocket, and headed for the upper levels.

Meanwhile, Jordan was parked across the street from the general's mansion under a tree. Sierra had offered to connect Leila's miniscule, spiderlike meter to the general's computer, giving Leila access to his files from outside the home.

A long silence ensued as the danger of her mission was on everyone's mind, especially Ariana's. "Look," Sierra said, "Jackson's not home, and the general's at the facility center. Mrs. Armon walks around like a zombie, and she might well be, and Barnard is too old to do anything about anything. And I know where to hide if I have to."

"How will you get in?" Ariana asked.

"Barnard sometimes forgets to lock the window in the general's office," Sierra said. "Let's hope tonight is one of those nights."

"The last time I visited," Monica interjected, "I found a way to unlatch the window from the outside...just in case...you know."

"Really?" Sierra replied, impressed.

"That's why I'm going with you," Monica stated.

"I want to go," Leila cried.

"You're staying here," Ariana ordered. "Worrying about those two is enough. Not to mention, your parents have no idea what we're up to, and I don't want to be held responsible if something goes wrong in there."

"A little encouragement would help," Sierra remarked.

"I'm sorry," Ariana replied. "But what you're about to do is seriously dangerous."

Meanwhile, Malakh had located Janu in Ward X, a heavily guarded maximum-security area on the fifth floor. He quickly identified the nearest exit, then cautiously headed to the emergency room. He searched frantically and found a mallet behind the alarm's encasement. He broke the glass, pulled the lever, grabbed Janu's uniform and mask, and rushed into the corridor. The alarm was deafening. Sudden pandemonium broke out. He now had twenty-eight minutes before the deadly chemical would be released throughout the building.

Izaiah was camped in Malakh's car when he heard the alarm. Creatures were screeching at the top of their vocals, while people were screaming and scurrying like rats inside the facility.

The elevators were on lockdown, and the associates were stampeding, pushing and shoving their way into the stairwells. One woman was being trampled, but Malakh couldn't stop to help. Seven minutes had passed.

Workers, resembling a sea of blue jays, were sprinting from the building, still clad in their uniforms. Chaos was everywhere.

As Malakh pushed and shoved his way through the chaos, the green light on his gizmo was flashing rapidly. He trotted toward the north wing.

Parked in the corridor were two creatures, one on either side of a door. Their gross faces were almost too much for Malakh's stomach. He looked down at his gizmo, and the green light was all but jumping out of its case.

He wondered why the creatures hadn't left. "Attention!" he shouted, cautiously moving toward the ogres. They jumped to their webbed feet.

"Evacuate at once," he ordered. The creatures did not move. "I have orders from the general to safely remove the prisoner from the building. He'll be of no use to the general if he is fried alive."

"Our original orders have not been rescinded," Dugbhan stated with an air of superiority. Malakh was aghast. Such an ugly creature producing such elegant speech...and with an accent, no less.

"Well, I have my orders, too," Malakh replied. "If we don't leave now, we're all going to die."

Malakh felt a cold chill move through his body as he rushed past the creatures into the room.

"What do you think, Dugbhan?" Centaurus asked.

"Makes sense," he replied, and they moseyed off.

Malakh was fortunate the creatures didn't contact the general to verify his bogus orders. He unbound Janu and stood him up. He wasn't in the best condition, but he could have been worse.

"Glad to see you," Janu whispered. "What took you so long?"

"Never mind that," Malakh replied. "I've got to get you out of this building in ten minutes, or we're both going to die...then Ariana will kill us both."

Janu's eyes were shut and bleeding, his lips were swollen, and his face was frightfully bruised. Malakh removed his shoes. "I couldn't find booties," he said, "but your white socks will do." Janu tried to keep standing but couldn't.

Meanwhile, the general was humiliated and furious that this debacle would happen on his watch, knowing the Prince would blame him. He was crazed as he ran from floor to floor trying to restore order and keep his prisoner from escaping. He repeatedly shouted on a bullhorn, "Where is my prisoner?"

Malakh quickly placed the blue jacket and mask on Janu, and all but carried him out the side door and down the back stairs. They were soon lost in a crowd of people running for their lives.

Meanwhile, Sierra and Monica were on the side of the general's manor, trying to open his locked window. Monica pulled out a thin wire from her backpack, twisted the end into a loop, and handed Sierra a large knife.

"When I tell you, slip the knife between the frame and the sill," she said, "and push down as hard as you can. I'll slip the wire in and jimmy the lock."

"What if we trigger the alarm?" Sierra asked.

"Leila's already taken care of that," Monica replied.

"You guys are geniuses," Sierra stated.

"You're just saying that because it's true," Monica quipped. Sierra heard rustling and quickly pulled Monica to the ground.

"Did you guys hear that?" Jordan whispered into their Lassier Faires.

"I'm going in after them," Ariana cried.

"You'll only make matters worse," Jordan said. "They've been in tighter situations."

The crunching noise was getting closer. Monica wanted to run, but Sierra held her down. They closed their eyes and waited for the inevitable. Something cold and wet licked Sierra in the face. She screamed and jumped to her feet.

"Are you guys okay?" Jordan yelled into the communicator.

"It was only a *cat*," Sierra whispered.

"Hurry up," Jordan replied.

"We're waiting to be sure no one heard my scream," Sierra said.

The girls forced the window open, and Sierra crawled inside. She shone her flashlight around and quickly moved to the general's desk.

Her hands were shaking as she affixed the spider to the general's computer. She turned to leave then spotted a brown leather folder just begging to be read. It appeared to be phase two of the planned Great Commission. She held the flashlight between her teeth, pulled out her mobile, and photographed the material. Someone was coming. She quickly closed the folder, turned off her flashlight, and moved behind the heavy drapes. But there was no way to warn Monica, who was standing just outside the window.

Barnard was making his rounds. "I thought I just closed these windows," he said aloud. "I guess I'd better see Doc Austin about my memory after all," he mumbled. He closed and locked the window, then shuffled to the door, switching off the light as he left the room.

Sierra let out a long-held breath and climbed back out of the window. "Sorry I couldn't warn you, Monica, but he took me by surprise."

"I saw the light come on and hid in the shadows," Monica whispered. "Now, can we go?"

The girls dashed from the side of the house and were standing near the curb when they heard Jackson's music blasting. They ducked behind the tree just as he pulled into the driveway. He checked his rearview mirror before exiting his vehicle and could've sworn he spotted the girls scurrying across the street.

"Thank goodness," Ariana cried when the girls climbed into the car.

"How did you do?" Jordan asked.

"Better than expected," Sierra replied. "Not only is the spi'meter in place, but phase two of the Great Commission was just lying on the desk. My mobile just happened to leap from my pocket and photograph the contents."

"Imagine that," Ariana mumbled, not at all impressed with Sierra's heroics. "Now, can we go anywhere but here? Just knowing what goes on inside that house gives me the creeps."

They rode in silence, Jordan on the lookout for Enforcers, Sierra trying to slow down her adrenaline, and Monica more charged up than ever. Leila was busy typing away on her laptop, and Ariana, weary of all the espionage, laid her head back and sighed. She wanted to go home, but then she realized...*she had no home.* Tears warmed her cheeks.

By the time Malakh reached Main Street, the light drizzle had become a deluge. The heavy rains pelted the car, and the downpour made visibility almost impossible. Janu screamed in pain every time Malakh swerved to avoid a water-filled pothole, indicating to Malakh that Janu's ribs were broken. Izaiah was trying to comfort his dad, but with little success.

"Izaiah, get the Elixir out of my bag and give your dad two drops," Malakh said. "That should dull the pain until I can take a closer look at him."

Meanwhile, the general was at the facility barking at Centaurus. "They escaped on your watch. Find them and don't return without them, dead or alive."

The creature immediately set out in pursuit of the humans. With his powers of invisibility, he hovered high above the traffic, employing his supernatural eyesight to espy the renegades.

Jordan and the women, meanwhile, had reached the safe house without incident. "Are you guys hungry?" he asked.

"I can't eat anything until I know Janu's safe," Ariana replied. "When do you think Malakh will call?"

"I'm sure it won't be long," Jordan replied reassuringly.

"Well, I'm starving," Leila remarked. "What you got?"

"Uncle M stocked the fridge yesterday," Jordan replied. "Check it out."

As Monica went on tour, she spotted a closed door halfway down the hallway and opened it. She stood staring at the most sophisticated hi-tech equipment she had ever seen.

She approached a black console resembling a large kitchen island sitting in the middle of the floor. She gently rubbed her hands over the shiny glass as if she had just discovered gold, and suddenly, the console came alive.

"This is awesome," she whispered reverently.

The black top disappeared as the table beeped, pinged, and hummed. Suddenly, a bright, multicolored screen emerged, displaying all sorts of grids and graphs with names and addresses. Jordan watched as the friend he had come to admire played with the computer like a child in a toy store. He was impressed that she was impressed.

"Will this do the job?" he asked.

"You bet," Monica replied respectfully. "Where's Leila? She's gonna freak when she sees this. We can hack into the moon with this setup."

Leila entered the room with a sandwich and a glass of lemonade. "Whoa," she said. "What do we have here? This is like finding a million dollars when your pockets are empty."

"What's going on?" Sierra asked, placing several chips between her teeth. "Wow and double wow!" she blurted out while the girls played with the console. "I have never seen a monitor that covers an entire wall."

"This screen can be transformed into multiple smaller screens," Jordan said, "allowing us to view more than one venue at a time."

"Come and take a look at this computer," Monica said breathlessly.

"Where did you get all of this?" Sierra asked.

"Uncle M is a genius," Jordan replied proudly. "He's been setting this up for some time. The original safe house was temporary—that's why destroying it was not a big deal."

"We'd better get started," Monica said, as Ariana came to see what all the excitement was about.

"Wow," Ariana commented softly, "it all looks impressive, although I have no idea what all it does."

"Where do we start?" Leila asked, rubbing her hands together.

"With the general," Sierra said. "I'm sure there's more we can discover from his files."

"You mean you guys have done this before?" an energized Leila asked.

"I think you're right, Sierra," Jordan said, ignoring Leila's remark. "Diablo's files will most likely be harder to access."

"Then let's have at it," Leila remarked. "I can't wait to see what they've planned for the good ol' citizens of Keres."

"Pull up a chair, everybody," Monica said.

Leila sat at the main console while Monica pulled out her laptop. Both were finally online. Leila went through her usual routine of stretching, cracking her back and neck, and flexing her fingers before she began.

But Monica sat quietly, taking in the enormity of it all. They already knew, in part, what Diablo and the Establishment had planned for the unsuspecting citizens of Keres.

Finally, she said, "I'm not so sure I want to know more of what's going on in this crazy place."

"Monica," Sierra said softly, "maybe the files will give us some clue as to what really happened to your mom. She could still be alive, along with the others, like Mr. Drake, who seemed to drop off the planet. I know Auntie Liz would want us to know the truth."

"You're right," Monica said, choking back tears. "It's not just about me anymore."

"That's my girl," Sierra whispered, and hugged her friend.

Meanwhile, Malakh continued on the rough road to the safe house, and Janu continued to scream in pain. But it was the best road to avoid detection.

"I can't stand it," Janu said between gasps.

"Dad, I'm sorry," Izaiah said tearfully. "I didn't want to believe they were after our family."

"It's…okay…son," Janu replied.

Malakh, spotting the tunnel ahead, heard the unsettling flapping and screeching of a creature, but he couldn't see the obnoxious thing. Whatever happens, he couldn't lead it to the hideaway. As Malakh sped toward the tunnel, the invisible Centaurus swooped down alongside the car and peered in. The vulture tried to overtake Malakh before he reached the entrance to the tunnel, but it was unsuccessful. Its speed caused it to fly headlong into the concrete overhead. Malakh heard a loud *thump*, a horrible screech, and then silence, as he sped through the underpass like lightning.

"What was that?" Izaiah asked.

"A creature," Malakh replied. "But they're invisible, so there could be more. Keep your heads down. I'm taking the Berksham route—it's shorter."

When Malakh reached the edge of the woods, he turned off his engine and laid his head on the steering wheel. He breathed deeply, knowing how close they had all just come to losing their lives. Unable to take the car deeper into the forest, Malakh and Izaiah carried Janu's deadweight body through the woods. Malakh's lungs burned with every breath, and his cramped arms were locked in pain. Izaiah was also suffering, but he dared not complain—this was partially his fault.

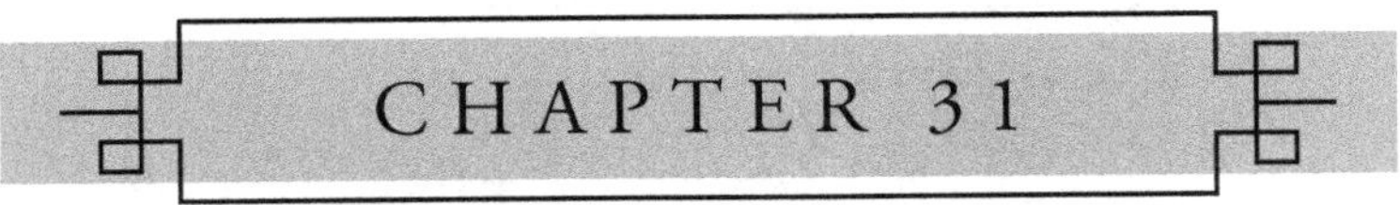

CHAPTER 31

Hacked

Meanwhile, Leila tried desperately to open the locked files using Malakh's technological state-of-the-art equipment. Suddenly she paused, cracked her neck and knuckles, then moved her head from side to side before kicking the console.

"That is one weird child," Ariana whispered to Sierra.

"It's a geek thing," Sierra whispered back.

"Where do we start?" Monica asked Leila.

"Right now, I'm trying to connect with my spider in the general's office."

"I remember the general's password," Monica said, trying to be helpful.

"I'm sure it's been changed since you last breached it," Leila replied. "Just give me a moment."

They all watched as Leila worked her magic, banging against the console when the computer wouldn't give her what she wanted.

Finally, she said, "I'm in."

"Shhh," Ariana whispered, "someone's at the back door."

Jordan tiptoed to the window and moved the curtain slightly to one side.

"It's me," Malakh whispered.

Meanwhile, a cemetery appeared on the console's monitor and headstones rolled back. Graves opened, and adults and children alike emerged wearing black robes. They had unknown names written across their foreheads and were surrounded by fire. A huge white scroll appeared, and the names listed in black had blood dripping from the bottom of each letter.

"I recognize some of those names," Leila cried.

"Can you put it up on the big screen?" Sierra asked.

"Keep scrolling," Ariana said, shocked that she, too, recognized the names of friends and neighbors.

"Your family's names are listed here," Leila cried, "as well as my aunt's and uncle's, and my neighbors' across the street."

"We have a skull next to our names," Sierra exclaimed, "and Jordan has two next to his."

Jordan suddenly interrupted. "Guys, we have company."

Everyone except Leila screamed in unison; her eyes never left the screen. Sierra wept for joy and hugged Janu long and hard.

"Not too tight," Malakh said. "His ribs might be broken. Let's lay him on the sofa."

Ariana fell to her knees, tenderly kissing Janu's bloody and swollen face. She gently laid her head on his chest, remembering that fateful day when she'd found his lifeless body at the bottom of the gorge.

Sierra hugged Izaiah gently. "Z," she whispered, "I've been so worried about you. You look like the devil. Are you okay?"

"I'm fine, but I'm worried about Dad."

"He'll be fine, too," Sierra said. "What matters is that we're all together again."

Ariana then squeezed Izaiah gently, in case he, too, had something broken. Her tears washed away the fear of Janu and Izaiah being gone forever.

Monica also wept, relieved that the only family she'd known since the disappearance of her mom and the abandonment of her dad were safe.

Ariana hugged Malakh. "Thank you," was all she could muster.

"Not necessary," he replied, then clapped his hands. "Now that we're all fugitives, it'll be more difficult to escape Keres. But it can be done, if we work together."

Leila turned quickly. "Fugitives…escape Keres? Escape to where?" she asked.

"And who is this?" Malakh asked.

"Monica's friend, Leila," Jordan replied. "She's the tech genius who's helping us retrieve data from the general's and Diablo's impenetrable files."

"Leila," Malakh replied, "if I told you where we're going, it would endanger the lives of you and your family. We'd appreciate your help, but if you refuse, you must leave immediately."

"Leila, please help us," Monica begged. "I don't know anyone else we can trust who has your capabilities."

"You're my best and only friend," Leila chuckled. "I'll help, if I can. One thing I ask, Mr. Malakh. Wherever you're going, please come back for me and my parents."

"I promise," he answered. "Now, show us your stuff."

"I've already connected to the spi'meter we placed in the general's office," Leila said.

"How did you get into the general's office?" Malakh asked.

"Sierra broke into his house," Leila replied, as a matter of fact.

"She did what?" Malakh shouted, staring at Sierra. That was the first time anyone had witnessed Malakh lose his cool.

"But she didn't get caught," Ariana quickly stated, trying to calm him.

"Did anyone see you?" he asked.

"We saw Jackson pull into the driveway, but it was dark, and I don't think he saw us," Sierra replied.

"You don't think. Do any of you understand the force of evil we're dealing with here, not to mention the creatures they've dispatched to destroy us?"

Sierra quickly connected her camera to the console. "Malakh, come look at what I found," she said, trying to refocus his attention. "I copied part two of the strategic plan for the Great Commission," she continued, "and they're holding a council meeting tomorrow regarding the timelines."

Malakh stared at Sierra. "If you were my child, I'd discipline you good," he said. "Since you're not… *good job*. Now, let's see what these demons are up to."

While the general paced back and forth at his home waiting for news of the fugitives' capture, Diablo was in his office studying the strategy for the upcoming annihilation of Uriel and the people of Fa'i. His assistant buzzed him.

"I told you I didn't want to be disturbed."

"They said it was urgent, sir. And it's late. I'd like to go home."

"Yes, yes, all right, but be here early tomorrow morning."

"I'm always here early, sir."

Cecilia had a master's degree in business administration, but she was only allowed to perform menial tasks. She'd been Diablo's assistant since she could remember and had not grown within the organization. It was unsettling, but after recent events, she had been afraid to push the issue.

Last month, she had been preparing to clock out when she'd heard a loud noise coming from Diablo's suite of offices. She rushed in, but he wasn't at his desk.

The noise coming from his bathroom sounded like the howl of an animal. Thinking the Prince might be in danger, she peeked through the slightly ajar door. The reflection in the mirror depicted a horrendous beast wearing the Prince's clothes.

After recovering from temporary paralysis, she quietly closed the door and rushed back to her desk. If she reported the incident to the authorities, they would think her crazy. She was quickly clearing her desk when the disheveled Prince emerged from his office. One of his ruby-red eyes was still enlarged. He noticed the stunned look on her face and eyed her suspiciously.

"I thought you were gone," he had panted hoarsely.

"I'm leaving now, sir," she had stammered and grabbed her purse, vowing never to return. However, the next morning, still shaken, confused, and with a splitting headache, she found herself back at her desk.

Presently, Diablo's telepad rang, and he berated himself for allowing Cecilia to leave. "Yes, this is Diablo, may I help you?"

"This is Governor Jacque, sir. I was calling to confirm the time of tomorrow's meeting."

"Eight o'clock, as always," Diablo replied, annoyed with such incompetence. "We've a lot to accomplish, so be on time."

"Yes, sir. I'll be there, on time… I will."

Jacque must have a cold, Diablo thought. *He sounds peculiar. And why is he disturbing me with such trivia?*

"I've got it," Leila announced when she disconnected from the Prince. "Once I call the general, I'll have access to both his and Diablo's conversations."

"How did you do that?" Sierra asked, impressed.

"If I tell you, I'd have to hurt you, and you're beginning to grow on me," Leila replied, jokingly. "Quiet," she told everyone. "General Armon, please," she said.

"Who may I say is calling?" Barnard asked.

"Governor Jacque. I only need a moment of his time."

"I'll see if he's available."

"Hello, Governor," the general said. "How may I help you?"

"My apologies, General, but I received word anonymously that tomorrow's meeting might be canceled. And since you're second in command, I thought I'd get it straight from the horse's mouth. Not that you're a horse, mind you."

The general loved being deemed important, and he decided not to hold the governor accountable for comparing him to a horse, or for disturbing him at this late hour.

"By the way, Governor, you sound a little hoarse yourself." The general chuckled.

"Fighting a cold, sir, but I'll be fine."

"Good. And no, the meeting has not been canceled. Please be on time."

Leila disconnected her voice control gadget and winked at the onlookers, who were fast becoming great admirers of her genius.

"I think we've got it," she said. "Now, if we can decipher their strategy, maybe we can try to save our unsuspecting citizens from annihilation."

"Wow," Malakh said. "You *are* good."

Sierra was amazed. Even Monica was impressed.

Meanwhile, an invisible Centaurus came to on a grassy knoll near the tunnel. Blood oozed from his right eye and beak, and his tongue was swollen.

His neck hurt terribly, and he was afraid to move his aching head, lest it roll down the embankment. He was seeing waves of colored lights when he suddenly remembered bashing his head into the overpass.

Suddenly, an invisible Keleos, the flaming avenger, created a fiery rainbow in the night sky before coming to rest beside Centaurus.

"What happened?" he asked his friend. "I've been looking all over for you."

Ashamed, Centaurus told how the fugitives had escaped...again. "The worst part is, I have no idea where they could be," he mumbled.

"No worries," Keleos replied. "I'll find them. But first I'm taking you back to the facility for a checkup."

"I dare not return without those rebels," Centaurus replied emphatically.

Meanwhile, during Leila's much-deserved break, Monica opened several files. Nothing of interest appeared until a file buried within a file caught her attention. It was entitled: *CAPTIVES*. The file contained a list of people currently being held in captivity, and the date each of them had been removed from their homes. Her heart raced as she searched for one name and found it... Elisabeth Stoner, along with the date of her abduction. Monica went limp, and the tears that wanted to fall, wouldn't. She called to the others and pointed to the screen.

Malakh read the file and was not surprised. He had believed all along that the people who had suddenly disappeared were being used for Diablo's Great Commission. He just didn't know how or where they were being held.

"There's Drake's name, Janu's former coworker," Ariana cried, "and Anna's daughter. Malakh, should we temporarily abandon our plan and help these people?"

"Only Janu can answer that," Malakh replied. "After all, it's his plan. Just remember, you're closer to returning to Fa'i than ever before. But whatever you guys decide, I'll support you."

Sierra was consoling Monica, who was now weeping tears of joy that her mother was still alive. "Whoever's in that tank is not my mother," Monica moaned.

Ariana hugged her adopted daughter and knew she could not sail off to paradise and leave her best friend behind. "Don't worry, little one," she said, "we'll find her."

Meanwhile, Centaurus told Keleos that while hovering above Malakh's vehicle, he had heard mention of a safe house in the woods.

"We'll fly over all the wooded areas and see if we can spot it," he said.

"You're going back to the facility," Keleos stated. "I'll search."

"I can't go back emptyhanded," Centaurus replied.

"The general has left for the night, but the lab is still open," Keleos said. "I won't be responsible if something else happens to you." Keleos bent low, Centaurus climbed aboard, and they flew away.

Diablo, meanwhile, was propped up in bed. After administering the drug that helped him maintain his humanity, he was soon asleep and standing before Uriel.

"Prince Cass, your name means Vain Glory," Uriel announced. *"But because you embody all things evil, your name is now changed to Diablo, meaning Cast Apart. You are now separated from all things good."* Lightning flashed and thunder roared, and Diablo trembled in his sleep.

"You have instigated division among my people and have sought to set up your kingdom in my home. Whatever possessed you to think you could be greater than me?" Uriel shouted.

"Henceforth, you and your followers are exiled to a place I have prepared for you across the river. This decree can never be revoked and will stand throughout eternity."

"I deserve to rule my own domain," Prince Cass hissed.

"You will rule... by deception and coercion," King Uriel replied. *"You and your followers will long for the paradise of Fa'i again, but never experience it."*

"Freedom of choice will be nonexistent in your realm, and your subjects will live in bondage to your made-up rules, following you because you will give them no other option."

"It's these people who are in bondage to laws they cannot abide," Prince Cass raged, waving his arms at the crowd of witnesses.

"There's but one law here," Uriel countered, *"of which you know nothing...the law of love. That law is willingly adhered to because we love all that is good."*

The Prince started to speak.

"Silence," Uriel roared. *"You have slithered throughout my kingdom long enough, spreading your evil. Now your beauty is no more. You will share your body with a hideous serpent so vile no living soul will want to behold it. Now, depart from me. I never knew you."*

Diablo awoke screaming, aware that the perpetual nightmare of that awful day was, indeed, part of his torment. His head ached, and he felt as if he'd been dropped in boiling oil. He swore revenge, as he longed for the paradise of Fa'i, where nothing ugly could exist, and the River of Life, which could reverse his curse forever.

He swallowed twice the usual dosage of his medication, hoping to keep the monster inside at bay. But the effects of the medication had diminished over time, and he was once again succumbing to his obnoxious self. As powerful as he proclaimed to be, he would never get used to his transformation. The pain, agony, and stress were taking a toll on his mind, body, and emotions, and he blamed Uriel.

He raised his fist as maggots crawled under his skin. "I'm coming back, Uriel. And I promise, you and your subjects will serve and worship me."

Meanwhile, the refugees were preparing to shut down for the night, but no one wanted to sleep alone. Janu was in a bedroom with Ariana. Sierra, Monica, and Leila shared the larger bedroom, and Izaiah was in a room with Jordan. Malakh's bedroom was near the computer room and equipped with several cameras and detectors to alert him to uninvited guests.

Unable to sleep, he opened the *CAPTIVE* file again and pulled it up on the big screen. While perusing it, he came upon a hidden file containing the names and email addresses of the citizens of Keres. He emailed a letter to the Keresians in all twelve districts, hoping most would read it before the council meeting the next morning.

Dear citizens, he wrote, *it is with urgency and a heavy heart that I must be the bearer of dire and devastating news. But you have a right to know what fate awaits you and your families, especially when that fate is being orchestrated by the most evil and diabolical of all creatures.*

There is no personal gain from my exposing this information, only the satisfaction that I have been true to myself. If I and my family were about to face what you're about to face, I would want to know how I could escape the terrible things to come.

You've been brainwashed by Diablo to believe that no other place exists outside of Keres. However, there is a paradise across the river called Fa'i. You've witnessed the inextinguishable light that shines day and night. It emanates from the ruler himself, King Uriel, the God of Light.

The Prince has deceived your governors into believing he can take Uriel's throne. But the truth is, he was exiled from that paradise many years ago because of his treasonous plots against the king, and he can never return.

Because of circumstances too unbelievable to discuss at this time, all I can tell you is that Diablo is not who he appears to be. He's a liar and a deceiver.

Along with General Armon and your governors, who've sworn to serve and protect you, they are currently using your DNA to replicate you for the purpose of creating an army to try to defeat Uriel and destroy the innocent people of Fa'i.

They're currently cross-breeding your DNA with that of animals and fowl, and any other creatures they deem fit, to serve their quest.

My question is this: What are they planning to do with you once they've created their monster army from your DNA? Will they hold you in captivity, like some of your friends and relatives, or will they simply destroy you altogether? Scary thought, isn't it?

Some of your family members, friends, and neighbors have mysteriously disappeared. You've held memorials in their honor. But the truth is, they're alive and being held captive against their wills—and I can prove it.

You must rise up and demand to know the whereabouts of your loved ones. Let Diablo and his Establishment know that for the sake of all that is good and right, you will NOT stand by and allow this travesty to continue.

Rise up and fight for your lives and the lives of your children, families, and friends. There's a meeting tomorrow at eight o'clock at Prince Hall, located at One Prince Drive, Royalty Lane.

I apologize that this is so last minute, but it's imperative that you show up and protest what Diablo and the Establishment have planned for you and your children. ***You can stop this madness.*** *You and your children's lives depend on it.*

If you know anyone who's away from their computer, call them on their mobile and let them know about this important meeting. Unite, fellow citizens.

For my safety, I've encrypted my email address. I will, however, report any additional information I receive regarding this gross injustice when I have further details.

So long for now, and I hope to see you there.

Someone who cares.

Malakh drew a deep breath and shut down the computer. He knew smart-aleck geeks would try to trace his email address. He turned off the lights and went to bed.

At eight o'clock the next morning, there was quite a ruckus outside Prince Hall. Some residents had stayed up all night making banners and flyers. Some had come with bullhorns to announce their disapproval of the Prince and his Establishment. Some didn't know *why* they were there, but they simply followed the crowd.

Malakh and Leila sat in the car watching the scene develop as they hoped it would. Leila's palms were sweaty as she continually rehearsed her lines. She wasn't sure she was up to the task.

"You're on, Leila," Malakh said.

"Mister Malakh…"

"Just call me Malakh."

"I don't know if I can do this."

"You'll be fine, Leila. Just stick to the script and keep your earpiece in at all times. If you have any trouble, simply say, '*the shrimp are great today*'."

Leila ran her hands over her hair and straightened her short-waisted red jacket and black pants, the customary maître d' uniform for Prince Hall. She was trembling all over, her knees literally knocking together as she slowly emerged from the vehicle.

"If my parents knew I was about to die, they'd kill me," she muttered.

Her feet, which were normally flat on the ground, were already aching from her high-heeled black pumps. She had, however, tucked a pair of black flats in her purse in case she needed to make a quick exit, stage left.

Malakh spoke into his Lassier Faire as Leila climbed the steps to Prince Hall. "How're you holding up?"

"So far so good, but I'm still not sure I should be the one doing this. Can you speak a little louder?"

"Just push your earpiece in a little further. And, Leila, you're the only face we have that's not recognizable. Look around you. These innocent people may soon be dead or in captivity in a week or two. Children as we know them will no longer exist, but they could become monstrous creatures devouring everything in their path. Sweetheart, we cannot let that happen."

"Now, focus," he continued. "I'll be on the inside as one of the guards, and I'll be with you every step of the way. Just make sure your earpiece is snug inside your ear so you can hear me clearly. And if you need me, say the code phrase. Now, become the maître d' as we rehearsed."

Leila exited the elevator on the third floor and checked in at the front desk.

"Hello, my name is Leila, and I've been sent over by the Servers Union to work the big party today."

"Nice to meet you," the coordinator in charge replied. "My name is Abir, and this is not a party,—it's a Governor's Gala, a very important, high-level meeting, a summit, if you will. May I see your résumé?"

Abir grabbed Leila's papers, and Leila thought the woman was wound a little too tight. "You must be sharp and alert and on your toes at all times," Abir stated rapidly. "Have you served dignitaries before?" she asked.

"Yes, ma'am," Leila lied. She had never served dignitaries or anyone else. But she had watched her parents host large dinner parties and was sure she could handle it. Suddenly, she was rubbing her sweaty palms together as she envisioned spilling the food and drinks on the guests.

"Will I be serving the head table?" Leila asked.

"We have a head server coming in, but she's running late. If she doesn't show soon, you can take her place. Your résumé says you have head server experience."

"We're about to begin," Abir continued. "Go inside the hall and check every table to make sure each glass has one lemon wedge on the rim, the place settings are neatly and correctly placed, and a chilled bottle of Tempeste water is sitting in front of each place setting…unopened. Check the Prince's water, especially. He will not drink anything that has been previously opened or poured."

"Is there a place I can store my things before I get started?" Leila asked.

"The lockers are down the hall to the left," Abir said. "Now, hurry."

Leila removed the key from an empty locker and put her purse and backpack inside. "Did you hear that, Mister Malakh?" she asked. "They're expecting a head server. If she shows up, I'll be assigned to one of the lesser tables and won't have access to the Prince."

"I'll see if I can intercept her," Malakh replied. "Do you have her name?"

"No. You'll have to hang around the lobby and ask the women entering in waiter's uniforms if they're the head server."

"Now you're giving me orders?" Malakh said, smiling.

Leila quickly found her way to the Hall and checked each place setting. She moseyed her to way to the head table and stood behind the red chair. *Only the Prince would sit in something this large and ostentatious*, she thought.

She checked for detection devices on the podium, then attached a miniature microphone under Diablo's chair. While pretending to straighten the drapes directly behind the podium, she placed a small ocular spi'cam on the wall between a slit in the curtains before quickly leaving the platform.

Circling the entire room, she placed additional cameras in strategic places, giving the guys back home a bird's-eye view of this grand mini ballroom and its distinguished guests.

"Abir, I've checked the tables, the water glasses, and the bottled Tempeste, and all is well," she reported. "Has the head server arrived yet?"

"No, and she hasn't called to say she's not coming. This is the last time I'll be using her."

"What's her name?" Leila asked. "I'll check to see if she's in the building."

"Her name is Dorian, and if she doesn't show in fifteen, you're on."

Leila walked into the hallway. "Did you get that, Mister Malakh?"

"You'd make a good detective, and you can drop the 'mister'." A heavyset woman is running in, and she's out of breath. She looks as if she's about to have a coronary. I'll intercept her, and if she's Dorian, try to assist her. I'll keep you posted."

Malakh stepped in front of the out-of-breath woman and blocked her way. "Miss, are you Dorian?"

"Yes," the woman wheezed.

He took her by the arm and led her to a bench. She plopped down, and Malakh sat down beside her.

"I'm sorry, but you're too late," he said. "The summit is about to begin, and everyone's in place. I'm giving you a day's wages for your time and trouble." He didn't know how much a day's wages were, but he was certain he was overcompensating.

"I was held up in traffic, but I still have five minutes to get upstairs," Dorian replied. "I've worked these galas before, and Abir is going to need all the experienced help she can get."

"I'm sorry," he said, "but all the positions are filled." He handed her three hundred dollars. "Abir will be in touch. Thank you for your time."

While Dorian sat still catching her breath, Malakh hurried to the third floor. "Package intercepted and sent home," he said into his Lassier Faire. "Now, do your thing. I'm right here if you need me. Leila?"

"Yes, sir."

"Do you even know *how* to serve?"

"I'm not sure."

"Neither am I. Just watch the others."

"Thanks for your expertise," she chuckled.

CHAPTER 32

Prince Hall

Leila's devices allowed Monica and Sierra to witness the Gala. "Have you ever seen such opulence?" Monica asked.

"Never," Sierra replied.

The general called the meeting to order, his tone and mannerisms reminding his audience of his superiority. "Let us receive our Lord and Prince," he announced.

The governors and council members stood in reverence, and the serving staff ceased moving. Diablo entered the stage and the applause was thunderous. He strolled across the dais, then smiled and waved at his audience, hoping the beast inside would behave. His aide pulled his cumbersome chair out, and he sat down.

"They do love and revere me," he whispered, proud to prove Uriel wrong.

"Remain standing as we beseech our Lord and Master," the general resounded.

"Guys," Monica yelled, "you have *got* to see this."

"Our most reverent Lord Diablo," the general began, "we beseech you this day because you alone are all knowledge and all-powerful. Grant us your wisdom and the courage to assist you in your Great Commission, that of seating you on the throne of Fa'i."

"Help us open our minds to the new and unfamiliar, and to be in tune with and obey your perfect will. We pray in your name alone."

The room was filled with a chorus of amens as they each took their seats. Malakh had heard the prayer through the hidden microphones and wanted to puke. Meanwhile, the growing crowd outside was raucous and demanding.

"Are they really duplicating us?" one man shouted to the Enforcers.

Aengus was angry as he stood on the steps of Prince Hall shoulder to shoulder with his subordinates. It was way too early for this stuff.

He could take them all at once. Instead, he ignored their protests, their ridiculous signs ordering the Big E to "*Free Our Friends and Relatives*". *Free them from what?* he wondered.

Meanwhile, Malakh knew that when the Prince wanted to make a good impression on the citizens, he would occasionally air his meetings so they could hear his bogus concern for their welfare. Malakh thought today was a good day for such an airing.

"Leila, is the Prince happy with the food and the service?" Abir asked.

"Yes, ma'am," she replied, but she really didn't have a clue.

"The Prince stays extremely hot," Abir added, "so keep him supplied with plenty of ice-cold Tempeste. If you see him fanning himself, lower the temperature on the air-conditioning unit."

"Yes, ma'am."

"You can call me Abir."

"Yes, ma'am."

"You're doing good," Malakh whispered. "It's a lot to digest, but you'll get through it."

"Thanks," she replied.

"Hurry back to your post. Time is running out, and we need that passcode," he reminded her.

When the general left the dais, Leila immediately approached the Prince, flashing a wide smile. "Lord Diablo, my name is Leila. Is there anything I can get for you?"

"Another cold bottle of Tempeste would be nice, if it's not too much trouble."

"No trouble at all," Leila replied.

"Are you new?" he asked.

"Yes, and may I say it's an honor to serve such a praiseworthy person as your Lordship?"

"I'm honored that you're honored," the Prince replied.

"Your Lordship, I know this is an important occasion, but could you spare a minute or two after your meeting? I would love to interview you for my school project."

"Me?" the Prince asked, touching his heart and displaying the most despicable sense of false modesty Leila had ever witnessed.

"I'm doing a paper for my entrance exam into University, and I know my interview with you would aid in my acceptance. I want to show how studying and applying your reason and logic helped me acquire the most important interview I'll ever obtain...your Prince-ship."

"I wish more students would see the benefit of making my reason and logic their way of life," Diablo replied.

"Personally, I sometimes feel you're taken for granted and misunderstood," Leila whispered. "I believe you have a lot to say, and I'd like to help you say it."

"Well, since you put it that way... I'd be honored," he replied. "There are a few things I'd like to clear up. In ten minutes, then? I eat very little at these functions."

"There's a meeting room down the hall that would give us privacy," Leila replied. While placing his napkin in his lap, she attached a tiny magnetic bug under his lapel, then slowly walked away, sweating profusely.

Malakh was impressed. "Where did all that come from?" he whispered.

"I don't know," Leila whispered back. "I also have his fingerprints on an empty bottle of Tempeste, which will simplify getting past the biometric scanner outside his office. I'm taking it to my locker now."

"Are you sure you haven't done this before?" Malakh asked.

"I'm just winging it, sir."

"And you know about the scanner how?"

"I took a little detour earlier," she replied.

"Be careful," Malakh replied. "His bodyguards are watching everyone's every move."

"Are you coming with me to the meeting?" she asked.

"I'm on Diablo's most-wanted list, Leila. Not to mention, my mole would give me away."

"Put on your sunglasses, sir. I'm scared to death, and if you're not there, I don't think I can do it."

"She's crazy," Monica barked, and Sierra agreed.

Meanwhile, Keleos was flying over the wooded area near the safe house but didn't see anything. He pointed his beak downward and mumbled, "I know something's down there."

He was unaware that the plasma energy surrounding the house rendered it invisible. And that anyone coming within twenty feet of the property would be electrocuted while simultaneously setting off the silent alarm. As long as the fugitives stayed indoors, they could not be detected.

Meanwhile, Abir spotted Leila leaving the area.

Frustrated, she asked, "Where are you going?"

"I have an appointment with the Prince."

"No one speaks with him privately."

"Then I'll be the first. I'll be back after my break."

Malakh had arranged two chairs facing each other and had turned up the air-conditioning in the room, hoping the Prince would be comfortable enough to stay until Leila could obtain his passcode.

"Monica, are you with me?" he asked.

"I think Leila's lost her senses," she replied, envious for being excluded from the excitement.

"Maybe," he replied, "but it's too late to back out now. Jordan, put the ballroom on screen two and keep an eye on the general. Stay alert, everyone, in case we run into trouble. Quiet, the Prince is coming."

Diablo appeared with an entourage in tow, and Leila was right behind with her tablet, appearing every bit the reporter. Malakh stood on the wall nearest the door and lowered his head, adjusting his sunglasses to hide his ghastly mole.

Four bodyguards came in and lined the four walls. The Prince was not happy with his chair. But for the sake of the Great Commission, and to try and calm the people, he lowered his standards and sat down.

"Shall we begin? I don't have much time," the Prince announced.

"Thank you again for your time," Leila began. "I don't know if I'll ever experience such a cherished moment…"

"Young man," the Prince interrupted, "what's your name?"

"Dillon, sir," Malakh replied, disguising his voice and lowering his head.

"My apologies. You look familiar."

Malakh nodded to Leila, then flipped the speaker switch so the interview could be heard by the citizens outside Prince Hall.

"Prince Diablo," she began, "are you Lord of all?"

"That is true," the Prince replied, grinning from ear to ear.

"How long have you governed this great nation?"

"Since time began."

"And you care for the citizens of Keres?"

"My people mean everything to me," he replied.

"Is that why you're launching the Great Commission...for the sake of the people?"

"Absolutely," he replied.

"What exactly is the Great Commission, and what effect will it have on the citizens?"

"I'm not at liberty to disclose the entire mission at this time. But soon my people will realize that everything I'm doing is for their benefit. I'm just asking for their continued patience. Although my enemies are trying to impede my progress with lies, rumors, and innuendos, the Great Commission is on schedule and will soon be launched."

As Leila leaned in closer, the miniscule camera, barely protruding through the eye of her jacket lapel, took a flash-less picture of Diablo's badge and sent it directly to the safe house to be decrypted by Monica.

"Your Lordship," Leila continued, "rumors are that you're using the citizens' DNA to cross-breed and create genetically modified creatures for this Great Commission of yours. If that's true, what will be done with the current citizens? They have a right to know."

She quickly continued, "It's also rumored that our citizens who have suddenly disappeared are not dead but are being held captive for use in this Commission of yours."

Beads of sweat suddenly formed on Diablo's brow. "Rumors, rumors!" he shouted. He could feel the demon lizard stirring inside. "Has anyone seen these so-called replicates? Better yet, has anyone seen his or her other self?"

"Sir, my sources say…"

"Excuse me," he replied. "I've guests waiting." He rushed from the room and ordered his bodyguards, "Find out who she really is."

While Diablo's attendants escorted him back to the Gala, Malakh instructed Leila to quickly gather her things and meet him near the back entrance.

Meanwhile, the riotous crowd outside had grown to almost two hundred. The noise was deafening and could be heard in the ballroom.

"Liar!" one man shouted, as he waved his placard. Then a chorus of "liars " rang out.

"Where are you holding my husband?" a woman cried.

"And what have you done with my son?" an elderly man shouted.

The general suggested a twenty-minute recess, and a shaken prince left the dais.

Meanwhile, Leila emerged from the ladies' room wearing a streaked wig, jeans, and a T-shirt, her feet comfortably shod in tennis shoes.

She wanted to do as she was told, but her gut said the process for replicating the citizens, as well as the whereabouts of the captives, were in Diablo's vault file that couldn't be opened at the safe house. She headed up the stairwell.

"Malakh," she said, "I'm making a pit stop. Wait for me in the parking lot."

"Leila, they're searching for you as we speak. Get out…now."

"I'll be out in fifteen."

"You don't have fifteen. Get out now."

She switched off her communicator, climbed to the sixth floor, and peeked into the hallway. It was empty. At the end of the corridor was an ornate double door with stained glass and no inscription. Leila guessed it was Diablo's quarters.

She listened intently at the door, then donned rubber gloves. She removed Diablo's empty bottle of Tempeste and a clear plastic strip from her bag. She pressed the strip down over Diablo's fingerprints, then placed the strip onto the biometric scanner. She heard a *click*, then she quickly slipped inside, bolting the door behind her. Edging her way past Cecilia's desk, she found Diablo's private office and inserted a metal gadget into the door lock. Once inside, she noticed the fiery red Mac-Daddy of all computers, designed and built especially for Diablo, sitting on his desk. A strange foreboding came over her as she eased herself into his chair and turned on the laptop. She pulled her firewall password decoder from her bag, jammed it into the portal, and waited anxiously. "This is taking way too long," she muttered.

Just as she was about to give up, the vault suddenly opened and the files appeared onscreen. She copied the files, shut down the system, and switched on her communicator in time to hear Malakh shouting.

"Leila, where are you?"

"I've just copied the vault files from Diablo's computer," she whispered.

"You are going to give me a coronary," Malakh roared. "Get out of there."

As she removed the flash drive, she heard voices. "Mister Malakh, someone's coming," she whispered. "What should I do?"

"Get out of there."

"I don't think I can."

"I'm coming in."

"You'll draw too much attention," she said. "I'll find a way out."

"Hurry, Leila!" the fugitives were screaming.

"Please be quiet, everyone. I'm petrified, and I can't think."

Sierra was biting her nails, Janu was rubbing his head, and Ariana was pacing the floor, mumbling to herself.

"She'll get out," Jordan said confidently.

"How can you be sure?" Sierra asked. "Those monsters will kill her."

"Monica, I've sent you the copied files from Diablo's computer in case I don't make it out," Leila whispered.

"You *have* to make it out," Monica cried. "Now, use that brain of yours and get out of there."

"I'm working on it," Leila replied, "I just need a few more minutes."

"You don't have a few more minutes," Malakh shouted.

"No more talking," Leila whispered.

"I told you she was strange," Ariana mumbled.

Diablo entered his office with three of his bodyguards. He suddenly stopped and stared at his desk. "Someone's been in here!" he shouted.

"No one's been in here, sir," a bodyguard assured him.

The Prince was a stickler for detail, and he knew exactly how he had left his desk. He sat down in his chair and touched his computer.

"Then why are my chair and my laptop warm?" he whispered, drool seeping out of the corners of his twisted mouth.

"I don't know, sir."

"Why are you standing *here?* Find the intruder, and don't come back without him. Or her," he added.

The guards were tripping over one another as they headed for the door. They had previously experienced Diablo's wrath and knew there was something bloodcurdling about the man.

Diablo, meanwhile, was trying to keep his emotions in check. He couldn't deal with Hagop's emergence right now.

"Leila, it's been more than fifteen and I'm coming in," Malakh yelled into his Lassier Faire.

Leila was stretched like a spider's web at the top of the coat closet, her legs throbbing. "I'll be out in a minute," she whispered, silently thanking her mom for her athletic genes.

Suddenly, the Prince let out several gut-wrenching screeches. Leila quickly peeled herself from the ceiling and peeked out the door. Things were strewn everywhere. She watched as Diablo stumbled toward the bathroom. *How can a god be sick?* she wondered.

Suddenly she heard glass breaking. She tiptoed to the bathroom door and peeked in. The Prince was mutating into a two-legged lizard with hair, scales, and a tail.

She had never seen anything so disgusting in her life, and quickly covered her mouth to stifle her screams. *Nobody will ever believe this*, she thought, then she nervously videoed the horrific scene with her mobile.

Diablo's jaw lengthened, and fangs hung over what used to be lips. His back humped, and his outfit shrank twenty sizes as it ripped and tore against the pressure of his transformation.

Thick, foamy saliva oozed from his nasty mouth, and short flashes of fire flared from his nostrils. His bulging scarlet eyes resembled cue balls, and one by one, his fingers were replaced by talons that protruded from his shrunken, hairy arms.

As he watched his metamorphosis in the mirror, he let out a mournful cry. So sad was the cry, Leila almost felt sorry for him—but not sorry enough to stay.

"Mister Malakh, I'm coming out, and I'm going to need your help," she whispered, knocking a photograph of Fa'i from Diablo's desk as she headed for the door.

The Prince quickly turned and spotted someone fleeing his office. His fear of someone witnessing his grotesque makeover had been realized, and he cursed Uriel. The intruder had to be stopped, but he was in no condition to give chase. If word spread about his condition, the council might conspire to destroy him.

Leila ran quickly to the elevator and pounded the down button. Suddenly, a beastly sound exploded throughout the corridor, and she took the stairs instead. She reached the lobby out of breath, then quickly donned her shades and headed for the back exit.

"Stop!" someone yelled.

This is it, she thought. *They'll take me back and feed me to the monster, an arm and a leg at a time. My dad is going to kill me.*

"Stop, young lady," the man insisted, "or I'll arrest you."

Sweat seeped from Leila's pores as she waited nervously to be apprehended. She felt a hand on her shoulder and turned to stare at an angry Malakh.

"When I tell you to do something, you do it. Do you hear me?" he whispered loudly.

"Yes, Mister Malakh," she said, then fell into his arms and wept. "I'm so glad to see you."

"It's all right," he said soothingly, patting her gently.

"Can we go now?" she asked.

They drove in silence until he finally asked, "What happened back there?"

Choking back tears, Leila explained in detail how she had witnessed the Prince transform into a monstrous ogre. "I'll have nightmares for the rest of my life," she cried.

Malakh phoned Jordan on the secure line. "Yes, Uncle?"

"We're about two minutes out."

Meanwhile, just as Keleos caught glimpse of the dark blue sedan moving between the trees, it vanished. He signaled for Centaurus, who had recovered, and he was there in record time.

"Are you sure you just didn't lose track of them?" Centaurus asked after hearing Keleos' explanation.

"I'm sure," Keleos insisted.

"Cars don't just disappear into thin air," Centaurus persisted.

"I don't know what I saw or didn't see, but something odd is going on down there."

"We'll comb the forest," Centaurus replied. "If they're down there, we'll find them." Keleos then let out a gut-curdling howl.

CHAPTER 33

Kidnapping

Leila trembled as she displayed Diablo's disgusting transformation on the big screen. Sierra puked in the wastebasket while Ariana dashed to the toilet. Monica just stared in amazement.

"Ugh," Sierra said. "Is he man or monster?"

"Both," Malakh replied.

"We're not equipped to fight demons," Janu exclaimed. "What if there are more like him? We don't know who they are, or how many. It'll be hard enough getting us out, let alone the captives."

"We can't leave them behind," Malakh argued.

Back at Prince Hall, the general was at his wits' end. The Prince was nowhere to be found, and he had run out of things to say and slides to show to the congregation.

He was about to end the meeting when suddenly Diablo beckoned from the shadows. "Excuse me, but we have an emergency," the general announced. "More drinks for everyone."

"Come see this, guys," Monica said. "Diablo looks as if he's been run over by a tractor."

The Prince appeared to be human again, but he was growing weaker with each transformation. His hair was rumpled, and the whites of his eyes were a deep crimson. Globs of spittle resembling cottage cheese were caked around his mouth, and his shirt was in tatters. His trousers looked as if they had had a run-in with a shredding machine. And although his jacket was torn, the hidden mike was still intact, allowing the fugitives to eavesdrop.

The general couldn't believe his eyes. "My Lord," he whispered with a raised eyebrow, "you look a frightful mess."

"You should have seen him earlier," Leila quipped.

"We've been searching everywhere for you," the annoyed general persisted. Then he considered the angry mob. "Are you hurt? Should we take a break? Your subordinates shouldn't see—or smell—you in this condition." The fugitives roared with laughter.

The Prince was in no mood for criticism. "There's no time," he barked. "My enemies are in the building. Announce me now."

The general handed him a handkerchief. "At least remove the…the…goop from your mouth."

Diablo knew he should have checked his appearance in the mirror. But the mirror had become his enemy, and how he looked was his least worry right now. There were spies in the camp that had to be flushed out and destroyed.

"My fellow comrades, I apologize for the delay," he began, rubbing his hands over what was left of his clothes. "But unbeknownst to me, our enemies infiltrated our sacred meeting and served me food and drink, *right under our very noses.* I tried to apprehend them, but I failed," he lied. "However, my Enforcers are in pursuit, and they will be caught."

The delegates were shocked that someone who was always so meticulous in his appearance now looked and smelled as if he'd slept with…pigs.

"We must implement my Great Commission sooner than planned," he announced. "Help me give you and your families the lives you deserve." He raised his glass. "To Fa'i, the City of Eternal Light."

Suddenly, Malakh announced that Leila and her family would have to accompany them to Fa'i.

"This convoy is growing out of control," Janu complained.

"They probably have Leila's DNA," Malakh argued. "And if we take her and leave her family behind; they'll destroy them."

"I agree," Sierra said.

"As do I," Ariana added. "Honey, I know this is not what you planned, but it is the right thing to do."

"And don't forget about Mom," Monica added.

"*All right*," Janu cried.

Malakh left immediately with Leila and Monica to retrieve Leila's parents, hoping they would come peacefully. He reactivated the energy surrounding the house and the sedan, backed out of the garage, and drove through the forest undetected. He turned onto Magnus Street in time to see Aengus and Adorjan approach Leila's porch.

"We're too late," Leila cried.

"Is there a back entrance?" Malakh asked.

"Yes."

"Go in and get your parents out of the house."

Malakh parked around the corner, opened the trunk, and retrieved an Enforcer jacket. He donned his sunglasses to hide his mole, then walked to the front of the house.

"Can I help you?" Aengus asked.

"I have orders to bring this family in," Malakh replied.

"As do I," Aengus retorted.

"Must be a breakdown in communication," Malakh replied, trying to detain the Enforcers.

Meanwhile, Leila entered the kitchen. "Hi, sweetheart," Mrs. Gersham said. "Are you having fun?"

"Yes," Leila replied.

"I must thank Monica for getting you out of the house."

"Mom, Dad, she's outside and needs your help."

"Is she hurt?" they asked in unison.

"Yes. Please come."

"Why didn't you take her to the emergency room?" Mr. Gersham asked.

"Leila, you're pulling my arm out of socket," Mrs. Gersham complained as she was quickly dragged from her home.

Aengus ignored Malakh and told Adorjan to search the premises. Leila, meanwhile, was having a hard time convincing her parents to get into the sedan. Finally, Monica shouted, "Get in, or we're all going to die."

"What's going on?" Mrs. Gersham asked.

"I'll explain later," Leila replied.

Malakh leaped into the driver's seat just as Aengus and Adorjan came around the corner. They were aghast when the sedan suddenly disappeared.

"What just happened?" Adorjan asked.

"Can't say," Aengus replied.

"Leila, I demand to know what's going on," Mr. Gersham shouted, as the vehicle suddenly became visible again.

"Sir, please sit back and relax," Malakh said. "I'll answer your questions shortly."

"We've been abducted by our daughter and a man I don't even know, and you're telling me to relax? I want answers now," Mr. Gersham demanded.

"I left my purse," Mrs. Gersham cried.

"I have it, Mom," Leila replied. "Now, I need you guys to trust Mister Malakh." Furious, Mr. Gersham rode the rest of the way in silence.

"Jordan, we're here," Malakh said into his communicator. "But don't deactivate the energy—creatures are still circling overhead."

Malakh drove the invisible vehicle into the invisible garage, the energy field causing their bodies to vibrate and tingle. Mrs. Gersham was screaming.

"What was that?" Mr. Gersham shouted.

"Relax," Leila said. "It only lasts a short time."

"Don't tell me to relax, young lady," Mr. Gersham said. "I'll never encourage you to leave the house again, because you're grounded for life."

Aengus, meanwhile, wasn't sure what had happened. One minute a vehicle was parked by the curb; the next it was gone. The two bewildered Enforcers returned to the Gersham house, searched it from top to bottom, then left.

"You understand there's nothing here to report," Aengus told Adorjan. "And I do mean nothing."

It was raining, and the safe house had become cold and damp. Turning on the heat would have negatively affected the plasma energy and exposed their whereabouts. So, the fugitives huddled together, trying to stay warm.

"We're here," Malakh announced, followed by his entourage.

Ariana went to greet them. Mrs. Gersham was sobbing bitterly, pulling at her hair and clothes, and squealing like a pig. Ariana thought, *Now I know where Leila gets her peculiarities.*

She wanted to slap the woman silent; instead she said in a soft voice, "Mr. and Mrs. Gersham, my name is Ariana." As she began introducing the others, she was abruptly interrupted.

"What's this about?" Mr. Gersham demanded. "And what have you gotten my family involved in? What is this place that cannot be seen from the outside, and how are vehicles disappearing into thin air?"

"We know you're confused," Ariana calmly replied. "Have a seat, and we'll explain everything. Can I offer you a beverage?"

"A glass of water, please," a trembling Mrs. Gersham replied.

"All I want are answers," Mr. Gersham shouted.

"Sierra, would you bring Mrs. Gersham a cold glass of water?"

"Why were we brought here against our wills?" Mr. Gersham persisted.

"And when can we go home?" Mrs. Gersham wailed.

"Never," a teary-eyed Leila replied.

"What do you mean, 'never'?" Mr. Gersham screamed.

"Please calm down and I'll explain everything," Malakh replied.

He explained the Great Commission and what awaited the citizens of Keres, but Mr. Gersham didn't believe him. Sierra, tired of bringing Mrs. Gersham one tissue after another, finally handed her the whole box.

Meanwhile, Diablo was on a conference call with the general and several of his advisors. "Have we any information about my enemies' whereabouts?"

"No," the general replied, exhausted from having been up all night. Diablo, who rarely slept, if he slept at all, could work nonstop for days at a time.

"Well, do something," Diablo screamed. "I want those heathens caught…tonight."

Meanwhile, Mr. Gersham was trying hard to make sense of creatures and genetic replication. "These topics were never discussed at our meetings," he said.

"What meetings are you referring to?" Janu asked.

"My *PsyOp* meetings," he proudly announced. "I'm part of an elite organization working closely with the Establishment to better our great nation. And since we've vowed to report anyone we deem to be anti-Establishment, I'll be reporting all of you."

Janu ignored that last remark. "We know all about PsyOps," he replied. "Sad to say, my son is one of you."

Jordan led Mr. Gersham to a chair in front of the big screen. "If you don't believe us, read what Diablo has planned for your family and the entire nation," he said.

"According to this, we'll all be enslaved, and our replicates will be utilized to fulfill the Great Commission," Mr. Gersham said. "This is hard to believe."

"Just so you know, our replicates already exist," Malakh interjected. "This plan was developed in Diablo's mind the day he was exiled."

"Exiled…from *where*?" Mr. Gersham asked.

"Fa'i," Ariana said excitedly. "The most beautiful paradise in existence, the one Diablo has plans to overthrow."

"She's right," Janu added. "As he's indicated in his files, he's only taking the replicates with him because they've been programmed to obey his commands. Since he has no use for a free-thinking society, he will either kill the citizens or enslave them to do his bidding and keep him happy in his new world."

"Dad, watch this," Leila interrupted. She displayed the horrific transformation, and Mrs. Gersham screamed and swooned. Ariana thought about letting her hit the floor, but instead she eased her into a chair and gave her more water.

"Mr. Gersham, we plan to escape to Fa'i, and we need every able body to help us," Janu said.

"You're kidding," Mr. Gersham replied.

Malakh stepped away from the window and announced, "The creatures are still trying to locate us. Remember, if we stay inside, we can't be detected."

"How does this invisibility stuff work?" Mr. Gersham asked.

"It's a plasma energy developed by the Establishment. I borrowed their technology and equipped this house and three of the sedans with the same force."

"Once the energy is activated, the house and the vehicles are invisible to the natural eye. This is one of the weapons Diablo intends to use against Uriel. You can't defend what you can't see. By the way, no one is to go out without permission."

"I must admit, I thought you were crazy driving into an invisible garage," Mr. Gersham commented.

"Cool, isn't it?" Leila remarked.

"I also duplicated their eyewear," Malakh replied, "and there's enough for everybody. They're not easy on the eyes at first, so wear them occasionally to get used to them. We're going to need them."

"You've been a very busy man," Janu said, slapping Malakh on the back.

"I also borrowed several plasma suits, along with the remotes that activate the energy, only to be used as needed," Malakh continued.

"When are you leaving?" Mr. Gersham asked.

"Within the week," Janu replied.

"And where is this paradise?" he asked cynically.

"Across the river, where the light shines continually," Ariana replied. The thunder clapped. "And where there's no foul weather."

Unexpectedly, she began to portray Fa'i's beauty. She explained that Uriel was pure love and that he was the embodiment of the brilliance they all could see across the river.

She tried keeping her emotions in check as she explained how she had been beguiled by the *Whisperer*, and the shame she'd had to endure. But her tears fell as she confessed that it was her disobedience that had caused her family to be trapped in this awful world.

She mentioned crossing the treacherous River of Woe with Sierra in her womb, and sobbed, "Sweetheart, that's why you're so afraid of water. You experienced my fears. Your father taught you and Izaiah to swim at an early age because he knew we were going to cross that river again to go home, and that day has finally come."

She begged her family's forgiveness for the mess she had made of their lives, and there wasn't a dry eye in the house—even Mr. Gersham's eyes were dewy.

Sierra hugged her mother, and Janu joined them. Izaiah unemotionally moved in for the group hug. "Mom, we've all made mistakes," Sierra said, "and you've punished yourself enough."

Ariana gently squeezed Sierra's cheeks. "I can't wait for you to meet my King," she said. "You're going to love him because he *is* love." She laughed. "And he has the most marvelous sense of humor."

"I've never heard of this place…or this so-called King," Mr. Gersham interrupted.

"Then you must meet him," Janu interjected.

Izaiah was now watching from the back of the room. His head ached and his body tingled, and the voices in his head were getting louder.

Although Izaiah had read the general's files and seen the transformation, yet, suddenly, he didn't believe any of it. Somehow he would reconnect with PsyOps and explain that after all, it wasn't his fault that he had been born into this crazy family and forced to go along with their maniacal schemes. He would prove his allegiance to Diablo by not leaving the only home he knew.

Malakh had been watching Izaiah. There was something cold and insincere about his reaction as Ariana poured her heart out.

"I'll need all of our mobiles," he suddenly announced, and Izaiah wondered if he had read his mind.

Later that night, Jackson's telepad rang. "This had better be good," he moaned to the caller.

"Can you see my ID?" the caller whispered.

Jackson leaped out of bed and ran to the general's bedroom.

"Where are you?" he asked, waking his dad and putting the caller on speaker. "Give me your location, and we'll come get you."

"I don't know my location," the caller whispered. "I'm being held against my will in some out-of-the-way backwoods. I'm calling from my throwaway."

"The rescue won't be easy," the caller continued. "I'm in a safe house surrounded by a plasma energy that renders the house invisible. This guy says he stole the protocol from the Establishment."

"The Establishment knows of no such protocol," Jackson replied. But the general knew better.

"Look," the caller whispered, "if I give you the rebels, I expect leniency."

The general nodded. "Deal," Jackson said. "How soon will you call again?"

"When the plasma's been disabled," the caller replied. "Then you'll be able to locate me, and I can get my life back."

"That you shall have," Jackson agreed before disconnecting.

"Who is he to give us ultimatums?" The general laughed. "We'll capture them all and be handsomely rewarded." Suddenly, he was giddy.

"By the way," the general continued, "the idea for the mobile throwaways for the PsyOps was brilliant." Jackson was stunned. He had never before received one compliment from his father for anything. But what the general was really thinking was, *There's hope for you yet.*

Meanwhile, Malakh spotted Izaiah in the hallway. "Where have you been?" he asked.

"In the bathroom," Izaiah replied. "Why, do you want to tuck me in?"

"The rest of the family's in bed, it's time you were, too," Malakh retorted.

Izaiah sneered and closed his bedroom door. Malakh knew the boy was up to something. *What's it going to take?* he wondered. *He almost lost his life, he knows what his family's up against, yet he continues to resist.* But Malakh knew that Izaiah was under Diablo's evil powers of persuasion, and that on his own, he would never combat the wickedness controlling him.

He rechecked the alarms and the energy, then went to his own room, prepared to do whatever was necessary to protect the families in the safe house. With the energy remote tightly in his hand, he turned out the light and went to sleep.

Suddenly, he awoke to find Izaiah searching his room. He watched as the boy opened one drawer after another, then he tiptoed to his bed, where he eyed the remote. Malakh pretended to snore, and Izaiah quietly left the room.

The next morning, Leila sat on the side of her bed, regretting involving her parents in such a mess. Except for Monica, she knew nothing about these people. Now she wasn't sure about Monica, either.

Meanwhile, Ariana was preparing blueberry pancakes with warm maple syrup, sausage, bacon, eggs, and black coffee. One by one the starving fugitives followed the aroma to the kitchen.

"Come and get it," Ariana yelled, "and Leila, wake your parents."

Malakh had already eaten and was in the computer room monitoring the general's home. The others grabbed plates, piled them high, and were seated around the dining room table.

Suddenly, Leila cried, "My parents aren't in their room."

"What do you mean?" Janu asked, a piece of pancake hanging from his mouth.

"I've searched the entire house, and they're nowhere to be found," she replied.

"But how did they get out?" Sierra asked.

Janu rushed to the computer room with the others in tow. "Malakh, have you seen the Gershams?"

"They're on the back porch," Malakh replied. "Finish your breakfast—everything's under control."

The others retreated to the kitchen to salvage what was left of their repast while Janu stayed behind.

"What's going on, Malakh? Why did you let them out?"

"I found out this morning that the Establishment has discovered Leila's identity, and they're assuming that her missing parents are part of our conspiracy. In addition, when I checked the system this morning, I found that someone had made a late-night call to the general's home."

"Are you sure?" Janu asked.

"When I told the Gershams they were now fugitives, too, Mrs. Gersham sobbed uncontrollably about the life she no longer had. But Mr. Gersham reassured her that he had taken care of everything and that their lives would soon be back to normal."

"They are trying to digest a lot in a short period of time," Janu said.

"I know that. But we're in a life-and-death situation here, and I have to know what they're capable of. I can best determine that if they think they're not being watched. We'll keep an eye on them and hope they don't try to escape. Lock the door—I want you to see this."

Malakh pressed *play*, and the two men watched Jackson stumble out of bed and race to his father's bedroom. They listened to the entire conversation between Jackson and the caller, whose voice was cleverly disguised.

"Long after everyone had gone to bed, I caught Izaiah sneaking out of the community bathroom," Malakh said. "I think he didn't use the bathroom in his own bedroom because there was something he didn't want Jordan to overhear."

"But you confiscated all the mobiles last night," Janu said.

"But I didn't search everyone's belongings. I just assumed they turned them all in."

"Does my son hate us that much that he'd betray us again?" Janu asked.

"He's young, impressionable, and brainwashed by the Establishment," Malakh stated. "Diablo's doctrines have caused many people to make unwise choices. It's the absence of absolutes and boundaries in his life that has led him to be deceived."

"But I've taught him absolutes," Janu replied. "He's chosen to ignore them."

"You're a good father, Janu. But he's lost, as are many of his peers and most of the adults in this crazy society. Diablo is the father of lies, who has even convinced his council members that he's taking them and their families back to Fa'i, even though they know they've been banished forever. He's promised them prestige and prosperity in the new world, and because of their greed, they believe him. But they're being used like everyone else."

"So, what do we do about Izaiah?" Janu asked.

"We find out what he's up to," Malakh replied. "He's in over his head, but we must keep him from drowning."

"Thanks, Malakh, not just for this safe haven that I never could have afforded, but you've saved our lives and thought of things I never would have. The plan was mine, but you've done most of the heavy lifting. We couldn't have gotten this far without you."

"Ain't that the truth," Malakh replied, blushing. They both laughed.

Janu stared at his friend. "Malakh, do I know you? Many times, I've felt that we've met before, but I can't remember where…or when."

"Maybe you'll figure it out," Malakh replied. "Until then, we've got work to do."

Janu turned away, missing the uneasy look on Malakh's face.

CHAPTER 35

Discovered

Darkness fell, and Malakh couldn't stay awake. Having had minimal sleep two nights in a row was taking its toll, and doubt was challenging his commitment. He was tired, and yet they had so far to go. "I need your help," he whispered, then drifted off to sleep.

The next morning, he awoke to a feeling of dread. The remote was still on the nightstand, but he berated himself for leaving it out in plain sight. Scrambling out of bed, he walked briskly to the kitchen. No one was talking—unusual for this bunch.

"What's happened?" Malakh asked.

"The Gershams have left," Janu replied softly, "and they've taken Leila and one of the unprotected cars with them."

"I thought someone was in my room last night, but I was too exhausted to investigate," Malakh exclaimed. "Why didn't someone wake me?"

"Sierra just discovered them gone," Janu replied. "But we immediately reactivated the energy force."

"It may be too late," Malakh said woefully.

"What now?" Janu asked.

"They'll come for us at sundown," Malakh replied. "Are we ready?"

"Yes," Janu said. "We've been rehearsing the plan."

"Eat something, Malakh," Ariana said. "You must keep up your strength."

"I have strength you know not of," he replied, and Ariana gave him a sideways glance.

"Anyway," she continued, "we've packed food and water in case you do get hungry."

"It's time to go *home*," Malakh said. "Where's Izaiah?"

"He's with Jordan, making sure we leave nothing behind that could jeopardize our escape."

It was late the previous night when Mr. Gersham awoke with an eerie feeling. As if in a trance, he found himself unexpectedly standing in Malakh's bedroom. He grabbed the remote from the nightstand and disengaged the plasma force. He awakened his wife, gagged Leila, and carried her, kicking and squirming, to the garage.

He chose a car without the protective shield. And, taking no thought for the unsuspecting occupants, he left the house exposed. Keleos and Centaurus were flying over the wooded area when Keleos spotted the Gershams leaving the compound.

"Did you see that?" he had asked.

"See what?" Centaurus replied.

"Headlights moving through the trees," Keleos answered giddily. "And I think that's the hideaway on our left." He told Centaurus to keep an eye on the cabin while he notified the general.

While Keleos had resembled a hot bolt of lightning speeding toward the facility center, Leila was screaming for her dad to turn back. "The plasma force is down," she had cried, "and our friends are sitting ducks."

"They're *your* friends, not *ours*," her mom replied.

"Are you two under that spell Malakh talked about, or just plain crazy?" she had asked.

"Don't talk to us like that, little girl," Mr. Gersham scolded. "I'll set you out on the side of the road, and then where will you be?"

"Probably better off," she murmured.

"They are not our concern," Mr. Gersham had insisted. "I had no idea you were involved with these renegades. Do you understand the danger we're now in? The Establishment doesn't take kindly to traitors. Now, sit back and use fewer words." That was a phrase he often applied when telling his daughter to shut up.

Presently, this morning, Diablo was battling his metamorphosis, once again. His nemesis was showing up more frequently and growing stronger with each visit, while leaving him weaker after each departure. He *had* to invade Fa'i soon, or the beast within would take over completely.

He quickly hung up from the general after hearing that the traitors had been found. The pain was unbearable as his twisted mouth foamed and the writhing monster within tried to surface. Groping for his medicine bottle, he growled at the demon in the mirror.

"When I get to the River of Life, you will be no more," he roared. But the beast within continued to materialize.

Meanwhile, the general summoned Aengus, his strongest and most capable Enforcer, five deputies, and Keleos and Centaurus to the basement of his home.

"Keleos and Centaurus have located our enemies," the general began. "At sundown, the rest of you will go with them and bring the traitors out."

"It won't be easy," Centaurus said. "They've surely reactivated the energy force by now, making it almost impossible to find them." He had no idea how much his proper accent and mannerisms irritated the general. *What an ugly thing*, he thought.

"Keleos' body heat will help you locate the area," the general replied. "Dead or alive—do not return without them."

"These rebels are sophisticated beyond imagining," he continued, as he passed around their photos. "And their leader is one of the most brilliant minds on the planet. So, I need you to devise a foolproof plan."

"And, if one of you has to lay down his life for these people to be brought to justice, do it," he continued coldly. "Now, get to work."

While the Enforcers waited for darkness to implement their plan, Malakh was rechecking the energy force, the locks, and the alarm system. He felt bad for Leila; she had been instrumental in helping them. Not to mention the fate that awaited her and her family, if they were captured.

His mobile vibrated. "Hello," he said, disguising his voice.

"It's me, Mister Malakh," Leila whispered. "Can you come get me? I think my dad's under that spell you mentioned. He still thinks everything is as it was. I tried to explain, but he won't listen."

"Leila, it's getting dark. You shouldn't be out alone."

"That's why I'm calling, Mister Malakh. I'm going to Fa'i with you. I don't want to die or be a slave. I saw the monster that Diablo really is, and I'm terrified. Please come and get me."

"If I do that, I'll jeopardize the others. The enemy is coming tonight, and the guys need me here."

"Are you sure they're coming tonight?" Leila asked.

"Yes. And when they come, we'll have to move quickly. Where are your parents?"

"We're charging the car at the station, and they're in the restrooms."

"Can you really leave your parents behind?" Malakh asked.

"Yes, Mister Malakh. If what Miss Ariana says about Uriel is true, he'll come back and save them."

"You have great faith, little one. Give me your location."

Shortly afterward, Leila's parents were handcuffed in front of the station. "You need me," Mr. Gersham cried. "I can give you the real fugitives' whereabouts and their plan of escape."

"Where's your daughter?" the Enforcer barked.

"We don't know," Mrs. Gersham cried. "She left the car while we were in the restrooms."

"Take me to the general," Mr. Gersham demanded. "I'm a PsyOp, not the enemy."

"You'll see the general, but it'll be from behind bars."

"Then take me and let my wife go," Mr. Gersham cried.

Leila was hiding behind a tree, weeping like a baby. *It's my fault they were arrested*, she thought. "Please hurry, Mister Malakh," she whimpered.

Malakh took Sierra with him because of her level head and calm spirit. After reactivating the energy field, he drove into the night.

"Can we find her in time?" Sierra asked, knowing they were jeopardizing their own lives.

"We have to," Malakh said quietly.

They were five miles from the house when a bolt of lightning traveling east lit up the night sky; it was Keleos. Enforcers were following in cars, and Malakh knew they were headed for the safe house.

"We should be coming up on the rendezvous spot in about five minutes," he told Sierra. "Take these binocs and see if you can locate her."

"What if she's not there?"

"She'll be there," he replied.

Malakh had returned everyone's mobiles because of their dire situation, and he rang Janu. "Hello."

"The enemy's headed your way," Malakh said. "Take everyone into the computer room and stay calm. The plasma force is activated—draw the drapes and turn off the lights. We'll be back as soon as we can."

"There she is," Sierra shouted, "behind that tree and wearing my shirt."

"Signal three times with the flashlight."

Leila recognized the signal, quickly ran to the car, and fell into the back seat.

"What took you so long?" she cried.

"You're welcome," Sierra said, annoyed that she didn't appreciate the danger they had put themselves in to rescue her.

"I'm sorry," Leila sobbed. "But my parents were handcuffed, gagged, and hauled off to goodness knows where. What am I going to do, Mister Malakh?"

"You're going to Fa'i with us," he replied. "Your parents are PsyOps—they'll probably go easy on them. Right now, we have to figure out how to reenter the safe house undetected."

"What about the energy force?" Leila asked.

"The force displays a spark of light that can be seen at night when the barrier's crossed. It will expose us," he replied.

Meanwhile, Mr. Gersham was behind bars when the general arrived to interrogate him. "Well, Brett, my brother, how did you land in a place like this? I understand they're holding your wife, and your daughter has been extremely naughty, as well."

The general laughed cynically, and Mr. Gersham was no longer certain about his future. "I was trying to tell the idiots who arrested us that we are PsyOps," Mr. Gersham stated firmly, "but they held us anyway."

"A true PsyOp would have immediately reported this treason," the general replied indifferently. "Anyway, all the traitors will be arrested tonight, including your daughter, if she's found."

"General," Mr. Gersham pleaded, "you *know* I'm trustworthy. I've been a PsyOp since its inception, both me *and* Charla. We just want to go home and for things to be as they were."

"My dear Brett, you're leaving here, but you're not going home. You two will spend the rest of your days where your services can be best utilized."

The cell door opened, and a burly Enforcer held Mr. Gersham while another forced a huge needle into his arm. Suddenly, the prisoner was laughing while fighting an urge to tell all. However, the psychoactive medication prevailed.

"So, General," Mr. Gersham slurred, "you people have been lying to us all along. But I'm not fooled anymore. I've seen things, and this Fa'i place is real—isn't it? Diablo wants this paradise for himself, and he's using little ol' us to help him get it."

Ignoring the outburst, the general prodded, "Tell me about the revolt."

"He never intended to take us to the so-called Promised Land, did he?" Mr. Gersham ranted. "Just another ruse to get us all to do what he wants us to do."

"And if you think Diablo's taking *you* with him, General, you're sadly mistaken. I've seen his personal diary, and he's using you and the governors as pawns."

Mr. Gersham continued raving like a drunkard, spittle flying from his mouth. He ended his blather with a description of the Prince's transformation, his own daughter's involvement in the escape plan, and the invisible plasma force. Unaware he wouldn't remember a thing he'd said, he fell back onto the filthy cot.

The general stared at Mr. Gersham long after he had passed out, wondering if Diablo was really intending to leave him behind. But his pride quickly assured him that he wasn't like the others.

Meanwhile, Malakh spotted Keleos and Centaurus in the big oak tree near the safe house, and Aengus with his mini army was combing the forest on foot.

"Sierra, take the wheel," Malakh ordered. "I'll distract them while you drive into the garage."

"They'll kill you," she argued.

"Just do as I say." He rang Janu.

"We're outside surrounded by Enforcers and the big, ugly birds in the trees. I'll distract them long enough for the girls to get inside. If I'm not back shortly, leave without me. I'll catch up with you later. Peace and blessings to you and your family."

Malakh slipped from the car and was headed deeper into the woods when Centaurus spotted him.

"Over there," the creature shouted.

Sierra drove as fast as she could through the force field, but Centaurus' eagle eye caught the spark of light and swiftly flew back toward the safe house. He landed on the tree he had previously occupied, and crouched, his sharp eyes searching for any sign of life.

Once inside, Leila fell into Ariana's arms and sobbed like a baby. "Monica, please bring her some water," Ariana said.

Meanwhile, every attempt Janu and Jordan made to break through Diablo's and the general's firewalls failed.

"I'm not surprised, after all that's happened," Janu admitted. "They'd be crazy not to change their access codes."

"We need to know what they're up to, Mr. C, and we're running out of time."

"Maybe Leila can help us when she's a little calmer," Janu replied.

It started to drizzle as Malakh scurried through the woods. He could hear his pursuers crunching through the slightly damp leaves on the ground.

"Over there to the right," the creature shouted.

The man-bird flew directly over Malakh, dislodging limbs with his huge, strong wings. A large branch fell in Malakh's path, and he tripped. Adorjan grabbed him, but a light as bright as the sun blinded him, and Malakh was gone.

"Did you see that?" Adorjan asked. "He vanished right in front of me."

"I've seen more disappearing acts than I'd care to," Aengus mumbled.

"What do you mean, sir?" a subordinate asked.

"Never mind, keep searching the area, he's here somewhere," Aengus replied. But he didn't believe his own words. He'd seen and heard enough strange things lately to last him a lifetime.

Meanwhile, Centaurus leapt from his perch, tucked in his huge wings, and combed the nearby woods on foot. Rotating his ugly head back and forth, he sniffed the damp air for the fugitives' scents.

Back on the other side of town, Brett and Charla Gersham were found guilty of treason without a trial. They were blindfolded, handcuffed, shackled, shoved into the back of an armored car, and whisked away under heavy guard.

Mr. Gersham knew they were headed for Skull Mountain, the place of the living dead, and he was terrified. Not for himself, but for his fragile wife. He had begged the general to let her go, but he said she was as much a threat as he was.

He had previously testified against friends and relatives who were exiled to the Skull for nonconformance. But he'd never envisioned himself spending one day in those awful tombs. Now, he and Charla were the victims, and no one would listen. He held his wife close as she sobbed uncontrollably.

They rode for hours before reaching their destination. A large gate opened, and they were shoved up a long walkway, clutching each other's hands. A heavy door squealed as it opened, and the couple was thrust inside.

Their blindfolds and shackles were removed. The place reeked of stale urine and feces, and Brett fought the urge to vomit. Prisoners were moaning and groaning, as if in torment.

Frequently, an inmate would cry out, sending chills up Mrs. Gersham's spine. She grabbed her husband but was pried loose from his waist and dragged away.

"We've done nothing wrong," she screamed. "We are PsyOps."

Tears rolled down Mr. Gersham's face as he shouted, "Don't be afraid, honey. We'll be cleared soon." But he didn't believe that any more than he believed their arrest and imprisonment.

"I love you," he yelled, her screams ringing in his ears. His only consolation was that Leila would have no part in this.

Meanwhile, Malakh contacted Janu. "It's time, my friend. Is everything ready?"

"Yes, we're in our suits but a bit nervous. You sound so far away."

"I'm not so far that I can't help you."

"But they're upon us now. I hear yelling, shouting, and dogs barking."

"Stick to the plan and don't be afraid, Janu. You have more help than you know. Leila's parents have been exiled to Skull Mountain, which is where I believe all the citizens who mysteriously disappeared are being held, including Monica's mom. But don't tell the family—they need to focus on their assignments."

"Where are you?" Janu asked again.

"Not far. I'll meet you at the Acheron River and further instruct you there. This time, you won't have to cross it—you'll go around it. Peace, my friend, and be safe."

Meanwhile, Keleos met the others on the way back from their rendezvous with Malakh. They looked stunned and befuddled.

"Well, where is he?" Keleos asked.

"He disappeared," Aengus whispered.

"I had him," Adorjan interjected, "but the next minute…poof. Nowhere. That's the second time I've witnessed…"

Aengus gave Adorjan the evil eye. His superiors would not be happy to learn that he had not reported the previous disappearance.

"What do you mean 'he disappeared'?" Keleos questioned.

"He simply vanished," Aengus replied.

Meanwhile, Mr. Gersham was changing into his prison uniform when a frail and disheveled man approached him. The pitiful-looking man smelled so bad that Mr. Gersham wanted to stop breathing.

"My name is Jacque. What's yours?" the man asked.

"Brett, Brett Gersham." The two men shook hands, after which Brett wanted to wash his.

"You're just coming in from the outside?" Jacque inquired.

"My wife and I have been imprisoned, and I'm not sure why."

"They don't need a reason," Jacque replied, scratching his crusted beard. "My wife and I have been here seemingly for ages," he chuckled.

"They took me first," he continued. "Told my wife and daughter I left town on business, then later placed my replicate in my own home. Did you know we've all been replicated? Then they brought my wife to this disgusting place. And for what, I'm still not sure. It's bad enough *my* being here, but to bring my sweet Elisabeth to a place like this is almost too much for me to bear."

"My wife is here, too," Mr. Gersham stated. "But she's very fragile and probably won't last long in this hellhole."

"She'll survive," Jacque replied. "I didn't think my Elisabeth would last, either, but her anger has helped her. Now, each time I see her, she's stronger than the time before, and your wife will be, too."

"A heads-up," Jacque continued. "There are no mirrors. Part of the torment is seeing how horrid we all look to each other. When you see your wife over time, don't appear shocked."

"How do you keep going?" Mr. Gersham asked.

Jacque chuckled. "We're determined to see our daughter, Monica, again. We talk about taking her to our home."

"And where *is* your home?"

"Why, Fa'i, of course." Brett looked stunned. "Do you have children, Mr. Gersham?"

"Yes. A daughter. She's beautiful, intelligent, and her name is Leila."

Meanwhile, Aengus, determined not to blow this assignment, shouted to his men, "Spread out and comb the woods again. I'll call in the hounds."

"My nose is keener than any hound's," Keleos replied, but Aengus made the call anyway.

It was midnight when three additional Enforcers showed up with ferocious animals. The beasts leapt from the cars, sniffing the damp air and drooling on the forest floor. They were horrible-looking hybrids, with the body of a hyena, half the neck of a giraffe, and the face of a wolf with blood red eyes. Their long ears resembled a hound's, and their dark coats were as thick as lamb's wool.

It was all their handlers could do to restrain them as they yelped and snarled at everything, literally dragging the officers through the woods.

Meanwhile, Leila was once again eavesdropping on the general and Diablo. "Guys, you need to see this," she shouted, and split the monitor on the wall into two.

The general was in his study while Diablo sat on the side of his bed recovering from one of his out-of-body experiences. He was annoyed at being disturbed before he was himself again.

"According to the most recent report," the general told Diablo, "the fugitives are holding up in a safe house somewhere in the north woods. Yes," the general said, "I have a team combing the area as we speak. I called in the best-trained hybrid hounds to hunt these fugitives like the dogs they are. Also, the house might be invisible."

"What do you mean by 'invisible'?" Diablo replied.

"The word is that one of the traitors—and I think you know who—duplicated our formula and is using it to keep the fugitives from detection. They said he himself disappeared, a phenomenon witnessed by the whole team."

"What you're saying, General, is they're using our own weapons against us? They must be stopped. How much longer should I put up with such incompetence?" Yellow sweat oozed from his pores, and foam trickled down the sides of his mouth.

"General Armon, those people cannot be allowed to escape and reveal my Commission to Uriel," Diablo hissed. "If your team comes back emptyhanded, your head will be on the chopping block."

"They're closing in on them as we speak," the general assured him.

Meanwhile, the fugitives could hear the hounds barking and the Enforcers running through the woods shouting orders at one another.

"Over here," an Enforcer yelled. "I think we've found them."

Keleos, jealous that the hounds had reached the safe house before he did, bellowed, "I don't see anything."

"The lieutenant is right," Aengus remarked. "There is something here—we just can't see it."

"How's that possible?" Centaurus asked.

"I don't know," Aengus replied, "it just is." He called the general. "I think we've found the safe house," he remarked with vigor.

"Are the fugitives inside?"

"We're still trying to find a way in, sir."

"I'm sending someone over," the general stated. "He'll be there in thirty minutes. Surround the house and stay close. If the traitors are wearing what I think they're wearing, they'll be invisible too. Tell your men to stay alert for any sound or movement, no matter how insignificant."

"Yes, sir," Aengus replied. He ordered Keleos and Centaurus to position themselves in the trees. "From your height advantage," he said, "you'll be able to see what we can't. Stay alert, everyone. I know they're here."

Meanwhile, Janu ordered the ladies to go quickly underground and to ensure that their bodies were completely covered by the body suits, masks, and booties.

"Any exposed clothing or body parts will give us away," he reminded them. "Jordan and Izaiah, destroy everything in the computer room, including the files."

Leila and Monica watched in horror as the magnificent and costly computer system, along with all the files and flash drives, was destroyed. But this was no time for sentiment.

"Downstairs, ladies," Janu shouted again.

The women rushed to the basement, huddling together as they listened to footsteps and yelping hounds. The noise from upstairs was deafening, as every piece of computer equipment, including the big-screen monitor, was destroyed. They were all terrified, wondering if they could survive prison for the rest of their lives…or worse.

Ariana knew the girls were afraid. She began singing a lullaby from Fa'i that her mother had sung to her when she was frightened as a little girl.

"Hush my child,
"Rest your head,
"On Mother's bosom, sleeping.
"And when you wake,
"The Light will dawn,
"A brand-new day; no weeping."

She sounded like an angel. Suddenly, the girls were no longer afraid, but more determined than ever to reach Fa'i.

"Jordan, drive the van out of the garage and bring it around back—and hurry," Janu instructed. "Be sure the plasma forces on the house and car are activated. Izaiah and I will take the gear underground."

The hounds could smell Jordan as he entered the garage. They were squealing as if their throats were being cut; ramming their heads into the side of a house that no one could see.

"Now what?" Izaiah asked as they entered the basement.

"We wait," Janu replied.

They all knew the task ahead would not be easy. But in order to return to Janu's and Ariana's beloved Fa'i, they would have to first overcome the evil obstacles lurking outside their door.

CPSIA information can be obtained
at www.ICGtesting.com
Printed in the USA
LVHW080910110620
657583LV00010B/117